Reasonableness of
The Law

The Reasonableness of The Law

The Adaptability of Legal Sanctions to the Needs of Society

By

Charles W. Bacon

Member of New York Bar;
Author of " The American Plan of Government "

and
Franklyn S. Morse

Instructor in History in the
Collegiate School of New York City

With An Introduction
by
James A. Woodburn
Professor of American History
at Indiana University

BeardBooks
Washington, D.C.

AUTHORS' PREFACE

The thesis of this book is stated in its title. The law in the United States of today, as in the England of Sir Edward Coke, is the "perfection of reason." Now, as then, the law is the application of reason to the problems of social control. The rules of the law are founded upon principles of right and justice that never change. The application of these rules varies with changes in social and economic conditions and in conceptions of right and justice.

As the problems of social control have grown more and more complex with the progress of civilization, the rules of the law have been so extended as reasonably to satisfy the needs and the hopes of the human beings who look to them for protection and welfare. In these pages, an effort is made to show how reason has directed that extension.

CHARLES W. BACON
FRANKLYN S. MORSE

New York, February, 1924.

INTRODUCTION

THIS volume has its basis in history, which gives it a firm foundation. Human experience has given us our law. There is a wide-spread conviction that the best text book in Political Science is History. It is so with Law. The causes and forms of law are found in the experience of mankind. Law is an experimental science, since it has grown out of the customs as well as out of the reason of men. In the history of Anglo-Saxon law and governments, reforms and changes have come about to meet specific and concrete needs. Laws and institutions are not created out of hand for all future possible needs; they have not originated in an *a priori* fashion from the contemplative inner consciousness of men; but new requirements in government and new provisions in the statutes and new decisions in the common law, have all come from new needs and situations as they have arisen. When the law has been changed there has always been a reason. The immediate practical results, not a distant ideal goal, has been the end in view.

Thus we find that our free government and our legal code have been an evolution. We must, perforce, go to history to see how our law has come to be, and as its evolution is traced from age to age we are led to see how very natural and reasonable it all is. There have been exceptions, but laws that have not been founded on reason and experience have been excrescences and have proved untenable and transient.

The authors of this volume have abundantly shown the value of history for the student of law. Their volume is full of citations from the great judges who, as is here so well shown, have based their historic decisions on the laws, precedents, and constitutions of the past. The student who is interested in the history of government and its origin in America can find in these decisions of State and Federal Courts information and enlightenment as to how our early government came to be, where sovereignty resided, and how the laws became established. Here the reader may find both the law and its history. The authors trace the origin of colonial law and the establishment of the United States Government, basing their exposition on court decisions. The law is their authority, and this authority is set forth by the reasoning and conclusions of the highest courts.

The volume is not only a study of State and local law as seen in its history, but it offers a valuable study of the Constitution of the United States as set forth by sufficient excerpts from outstanding decisions of our highest courts. Here we find the Constitution as it has been judicially interpreted. This, again, leads us to the history and development of our supreme law.

The origins of the Union; the relation of the Federal Government to the States; the government of Territories; the limitation of powers as between State and Nation; the growth of national functions; the beginnings and admissions of new States; the division of governmental powers; the content and amendment of State constitutions; the guarantees of the Constitution; the law of contracts and their inviolability; the police powers, and the taxing powers; prohibition, common carriers, the regulation of commerce, sanitary regulations; all these vital subjects and many others of equal importance are developed with fullness of authority in judicial citations.   Here is a study in social legislation and case law, in all these fields of our legal system.   In each case, the authorities seem conclusive, and together they involve a vast deal of legal history which lead to an understanding of the reason of the law.   We are led to see, also, the *progress* of the law, and that guarantees of liberty and property are to be construed in the light of the social and economic conditions that existed when laws are passed and not in the light of such conditions as they existed when the guarantees were made.   The guarantees were intended to promote the welfare of society and, therefore, new social conditions require new social laws.

Not only public and constitutional law is given treatment here which brings out matters of importance in the history of government, but the common law, private law, criminal law, the law of torts and of equity, are all considered and they are generally brought to the attention of the student on the lines of their growth and evolution.   The law is seen to be an unfolding process.   In such a volume the law is made both an historical and a social study.

The English origin of equity and the later development of courts of equity in America are traced, and reasons are shown why equity courts were not called into frequent use in our early colonial days.   The cases that did arise were decided by governor and council instead of by judges and juries.   "The Americans of that day were a nation of farmers.   Land was cheap and easily obtainable.   There was very little commerce and almost no manufacturing. Hence few cases arose in which the interference of a court of equity was at all needed." Thus, for instance, the historical condition explains the existence and operation of the law.

The authors explain not only the history of the law in its origins but the *principles* of the law in its reasonableness. For instance, "equity delights to do justice," and he who "comes for equity must do so with clean hands," and equity is "for the vigilant and not for those who sleep on their rights," and that equity follows the law so far as the law goes in securing the rights of the parties to a suit, and no farther; and when the law stops short of securing this object equity goes on with a remedy till justice is done. "In other words, equity is the perfection of the law and is always open to those who have just rights to enforce where the law is inadequate." Such is the language from an Indiana case, one of a multitude in this volume used to prove the righteousness and reasonableness of the law in all departments of legal adjudication and jurisprudence.

In the field of public law the volume traces the beginnings of international relations in ancient days and deals with the salient features of modern international law, including the law of the seas, the law of treaties, neutrality and belligerency, the equal rights of nations, the right of self-defense, and the public law for the protection of nationals holding property or being domiciled in other lands than their own. All conclusions are fortified by cases and decisions. The law of discovery and occupation as giving sovereign title to the soil; of Indian relations in early American history; of the Monroe Doctrine in relation to international relations; of fugitives from justice and of a state's obligations in relation thereto; international usages in diplomacy and arbitrations,—all these topics of special interests to the legal mind and to students of international law and diplomacy, come within the purview of the author's attention.

Another important division of the work covers the whole field of statute law, which deals with legislatures, their methods and their powers, the nature and scope of statute law, and the relation thereto of the executive veto and of the large and controverted field of judicial control over legislation, and of the power of constitutional amendment. The giant powers of construction and interpretation are indicated as they have been applied in our constitutional development.

I have thus attempted a brief review and summary of this work. What I have said is inadequate for giving a full appreciation or understanding of the content and value of the volume. From these indications, however, it will be seen that the volume is a comprehensive treatment on all phases of the law. While it is a good text book for law students to whom it will seem invaluable, it is more than a law book. It is an interesting treatise for the historical student and for the ordinarily intelligent reader. When I had read the manuscript I was convinced that here was a volume which would be not only heartily welcomed by all teachers and students of law but that all students of political and constitutional history would find it of great use in their work. The book deserves a large and appreciative clientele which should prove encouraging and gratifying to its authors.

JAMES ALBERT WOODBURN.

INDIANA UNIVERSITY,
BLOOMINGTON, IND.,
February, 1924.

CONTENTS

PART I

The Legal Basis of American Governments

CHAPTER I

Evolution of American Governments.

The first English colonies in North America were business enterprises. At the beginning of the seventeenth century the forests of England had been depleted through the expansion of agriculture and the increasing use of wood for fuel, for shipbuilding, and for the construction of houses. Great and increasing quantities of wood were needed

for three all-important industries, the industries upon which the prosperity and wealth of the nation were largely dependent—shipbuilding, for which were needed timber, masts, pitch, tar, resin; the manufacture of woolens, calling for a large supply of potash; smelting of all kinds, since three hundred years ago wood and not coal was the fuel used in the furnaces.[1]

Ship timber and potash were imported by the Muscovy Company from Germany, Poland, Russia, and Sweden, where the forests were still extensive and labor was cheap.

[1] For this quotation and the other economic facts in this paragraph, the authors are indebted to "The Planters of Colonial Virginia," Chap. I, by Thomas J. Wertenbaker, Princeton University Press, 1922.

The northern voyage was long, dangerous, and costly, the King of Denmark, who controlled the entrance to the Baltic, had it within his power at any moment to exclude the English traders; the Muscovy Company no longer enjoyed exemptions from customs in Prussia, Denmark, and Russia. In case war should break out among the northern nations this trade might for a time be cut off entirely, resulting in the strangulation of England's basic industries. . . . Her bold navigators had already crossed the Atlantic, returning with alluring stories of the limitless resources of the New World, of mighty forests spreading in unbroken array for hundreds of miles along the coast, and back into the interior as far as the eye could see. Why, it was asked, should England be forced to make the hazardous journey to the Baltic in order to procure from other nations what they might easily have for themselves by taking possession of some of the limitless unoccupied areas of America? . . . In addition to, but closely associated with, the economic causes of Anglo-Saxon expansion was the realization in England of the need for prompt action in putting a limit to the growing domains of the King of Spain. In the century which had elapsed since Columbus opened a new world to the peoples of Europe, this monarch had seized the richest part of the great prize, and was still reaching forward to the north and to the south. Unless England took advantage of the present opportunity, the vast American continents might be closed to her forever.[1]

In this juncture, charters were granted by James I to the London Company and the Plymouth Company, conveying to the incorporators great territorial areas along the Atlantic coast, which were claimed by the crown by right of discovery, and authorizing the establishment of dependent governments. At a later period similar grants authorizing the creation of

[1] *Idem.*

governments were made to individuals by royal patents, such as the grant of Pennsylvania to William Penn. When the colonies became populous, the charters to the trading companies were surrendered; in some cases, new charters that were in form and effect written constitutions were granted by the crown; in others, the colonies were taken over by the king, who ruled them as royal provinces.

In November, 1620, before the landing on Plymouth Rock, the Pilgrims made a written agreement among themselves called the Mayflower Compact, by which they pledged themselves to good behavior as members of the community they were about to establish. In 1639, the band of emigrants from Massachusetts who had established the colony of Connecticut, comprising the towns of Hartford, Windsor, and Wethersfield, adopted for the three communities a written plan of government called the Fundamental Orders. In 1643, the colonies of Massachusetts Bay, Plymouth, Connecticut, and New Haven joined in forming a league for mutual defense; it also provided for the surrender of fugitives from justice. This league, known as the New England Confederation, had a written constitution, which remained in force until 1689.

On July 4, 1776, the thirteen colonies were transformed into independent States and the United States of America was established as a sovereign, independent nation by the Declaration of Independence. From that time onward the United States had its own government carried on at first informally by the Continental Congress; afterward more regularly under the written Articles of Confederation, which became effective in 1781; and finally under the written Constitution of the United States, which became operative in 1789.   In the meantime and while the Revolution was in progress, all of the newly established States except Connecticut and Rhode Island, whose royal charters provided for independent governments, adopted written constitutions.   Since the adoption of the National Constitution, the Congress has from time to time provided written constitutions for subdivisions of the national domain in the form of Organic Acts creating territorial governments, and by Enabling Acts has admitted to the Union new States with written constitutions.   Also some of the member States of the Union have themselves adopted new and improved constitutions.

Colonial Governments.

The history of the planting of one of the first colonies and of the establishment of its first government was described as follows by Chief Justice Shaw in the case of *Commonwealth v. Roxbury*,[1] decided by the Supreme Judicial Court of Massachusetts:

At the time of the settlement of Massachusetts and the other English colonies in America, the only source of title to the vacant and unsettled lands of this portion of the continent, claimed by the crown of England by right of discovery, was a grant from the king.   It was not merely the only source of legal title to the soil, but was the only source of authority for exercising limited powers of government, in and over the lands thus granted.

The theory universally adopted, acted upon, and sanctioned by a long course of judicial decisions of the highest authority, was, that the Indians found upon this continent had no legal title to the soil . . . but only a temporary right of occupancy, for which it was perhaps equitable to make them

[1] 9 Gray (Mass.) Rep., 451, 478.

some allowance. The fee [legal title] was considered to be in the sovereign, by whose subjects it was discovered, and in whose name it was taken possession of. Under this rule, this part of North America was claimed and held by the king of England. This jurisdiction extended to all tide waters, included in said territory, in the same manner as in those held by the crown within the realm of England, subject to the public use, according to the rules of the common law. But as it was held that the king, by virtue of his prerogative, had authority to create and grant political powers, necessary to the government of these new countries, it was held, that, where charters were granted to organized bodies with power of governing the colonies to be settled, like that of Charles I to the Governor and Company of Massachusetts, they conveyed the prerogative powers of the crown . . . in trust for the public. The grantees thereby became invested with the ordinary right of property in lands for cultivation and settlement, and the extraordinary right of government, subject only to their allegiance and subordination to the parent government. . . .

Instead of resorting anew to the original charters, we will state what this court held to be the result and legal effect of them, in a recent case which was much discussed, and was decided after much consideration. *Commonwealth v. Alger*, 7 Cush., 65, 66. The Court there says: "The charters under which the Colony was formed and settled . . . first, that of James I to the Plymouth Company, and subsequently that of Charles I in 1628, reciting an assignment of part of the territory [described], which afterwards constituted the Colony of Massachusetts, to Sir Henry Roswell and his associates . . . did proceed to grant and confirm to Sir Henry Roswell and his associates all the lands described, and every part and parcel thereof. . . . This charter was not merely a grant of property within the realm of England, but it contained provisions for the establishment of a separate dependent government under the allegiance of the king; and the government thereby constituted was invested with all the civil and political powers to enable it to establish and govern the Colony, and to make laws for that purpose, not repugnant to the laws of England."

The Connecticut Constitution.

In the case of *Webster v. Harwinton,*[1] decided in 1864 by the Connecticut Supreme Court of Errors, Justice Butler described the establishment of the colony of Connecticut and of its written constitution as follows:

The free planters of Hartford, Windsor, and Wethersfield had no patent from the King. They emigrated from Massachusetts, which was then an organized commonwealth, and with the consent of that commonwealth, but they received from Massachusetts no corporate powers. They came from three different towns in as many parties, and when they settled themselves down on the banks of the Connecticut, they settled in three different places and could and did organize themselves and establish *governments* as plantations or towns, and as one colony, and with a general court or legislature for all, and thus protect themselves, and make and wage offensive and successful war against their hostile Indian neighbors. . . .

. . . That extraordinary document [the Connecticut Constitution of 1639] purports on its face to be the work of the people—the residents and inhabitants—the free planters themselves of the three towns. . . . It established a general court or assembly, and authorized the towns to send deputies to compose it, but it prescribed their number and the manner in which they should be elected; and having thus provided a legislative body it gave that body exclusively *supreme power*, their entire sovereignty and territory not possessed by individuals, in the following comprehensive words: "In which said general courts shall consist the entire power of the commonwealth, and *they*

[1] 32 Connecticut Rep., 131, 136.

only shall have power to make laws or repeal them, to grant levies, to admit freemen, dispose of lands undisposed of to several towns or persons, and shall also have power to call either court or magistrate, or any other person whatsoever, into question for any misdemeanor, and may for just cause displace or deal otherwise according to the nature of the offense; and also may *deal in any other matter that concerns the good of this commonwealth*, except election of magistrates, which shall be done by the whole body of freemen." . . . That Constitution was adopted on the 14th of January, 1639.

The New England Confederation.

The governmental purpose of the New England Confederation is set forth by Chief Justice Taney in the case of *Kentucky v. Dennison*,[1] decided in 1860 by the U. S. Supreme Court, as follows:

The necessity of [the] policy of mutual support, in bringing offenders to justice, without any exception as to the character and nature of the crime, seems to have been first recognized and acted upon by the American colonies; for we find by Winthrop's *History of Massachusetts*, vol. 2, pages 121 and 126, that as early as 1643, by "Articles of Confederation between the plantation under the government of Massachusetts, the plantation under the government of New Plymouth, the plantation under the government of Connecticut and the government of New Haven, with the plantations in common therewith," these plantations pledged themselves to each other that, "upon the escape of any prisoner or fugitive for any criminal cause, whether by breaking prison, or getting from the officer, or otherwise escaping, upon the certificate of two magistrates of the jurisdiction out of which the escape was made that he was a prisoner or such an offender at the time of

[1] 24 Howard (U. S.) Rep., 66.

the escape, the magistrate, or some of them, of the jurisdiction where, for the present, the said prisoner or fugitive
abideth, shall forthwith grant such a warrant as the case will
bear, for the apprehending of any such person, and the delivery of him into the hands of the officer or other person
who pursueth him; and if there be help required for the safe
returning of any such offender, then it shall be granted
unto him that craves the same, he paying the charges
thereof." It will be seen that this agreement gave no discretion to the magistrate of the government where the
offender was found; but he was bound to arrest and deliver,
upon the production of the certificate under which he was
demanded.

CHAPTER II

The Interregnum.

The governments that had been established by royal charters and land grants were displaced during the agitations which preceded the War for Independence. For a time, the inhabitants of the different colonies got along as well as they could without any governments at all, relying for the maintenance of order upon the control exercised in each of the towns and counties by those who had previously been public officers. The legislature of each colony, having lost its legal status under the colonial system, reassembled as a provincial congress, but was really a convention of notables rather than a governing body. These congresses sent delegates to the First Continental Congress, which met at Philadelphia in September, 1774, and to the Second Continental Congress, which declared the independence and national existence of the United States of America. This Second Continental Congress was not a government in any true sense of the word, but was really a committee composed of delegates from the newly established States. It carried on the war and made a few treaties, but did not exercise any control over the people or the States. In the case of *Penhallow v. Doane*,[1]

[1] 3 Dallas (U. S.) Rep., 54, 90.

II

decided in 1795 by the U. S. Supreme Court, Justice Paterson described as follows the political status of the Second Continental Congress:

The powers of [the Second Continental] congress were revolutionary in their nature, arising out of events adequate to every national emergency, and co-extensive with the object to be attained. Congress was the general, supreme, and controlling council of the nation, the centre of union, the centre of force, and the sun of the political system. To determine what their powers were, we must inquire what powers they exercised. Congress raised armies, fitted out a navy, and prescribed rules for their government; congress conducted all military operations both by land and sea; congress emitted bills of credit, received and sent ambassadors, and made treaties; congress commissioned privateers to cruise against the enemy, directed what vessels should be liable to capture, and prescribed rules for the distribution of prizes. These high acts of sovereignty were submitted to, acquiesced in, and approved of by the people of America. In congress were vested, because by congress were exercised with the approbation of the people, the rights and powers of war and peace. In every government, whether it consists of many states or of a few, or whether it be of a federal or consolidated nature, there must be a supreme power or will; the rights of war and peace are component parts of this supremacy, and incidental thereto is the question of prize. . . . If it be asked in whom, during our revolutionary war, was lodged, and by whom was exercised this supreme authority, no one will hesitate for an answer. It was lodged in and exercised by congress. . . . Disastrous would have been the issue of the contest, if the States separately had exercised the powers of war. For in such case there would have been as many supreme wills as there were States, and as many wars as there were wills. Happily, however, for America, this was not the case; there was but one war and one sovereign will to conduct it. The danger being imminent and common, it became necessary for the people or colonies to coalesce and act in concert, in order to divert or break the violence of the gathering storm; they accordingly grew into union, and formed one great political body, of which congress was the directing principle and soul.

The Articles of Confederation.

In 1776, the Second Continental Congress appointed a committee "to prepare and digest the form of a confederation to be entered into between these colonies." This committee drafted the Articles of Confederation, which when ratified in 1781 created a League of Friendship rather than a central government with powers of control over the States or the people. Each State retained "its sovereignty, freedom, and independence, and every power, jurisdiction, and right, which is not by this confederation expressly delegated to the United States, in Congress assembled."[1] In practice these delegated powers proved very slight indeed. The Confederation was little more than a continuation of the Second Continental Congress; it created a congress composed of delegations from each of the States, each delegation having one vote. This Congress made laws which could not be enforced unless the States and the people voluntarily obeyed them. It imposed taxes that it could not collect by compulsion. It made treaties that were not binding upon the States. It established departments of foreign affairs, of finance, and of war that could do nothing except with the co-operation of all the State governments. The Confederation Congress thus was in fact rather an assembly of

[1] Articles of Confederation, Article II.

diplomatic representatives of the States, than a federal government.

In the case of *Lane County v. Oregon*,[1] decided by the U. S. Supreme Court in 1868, Chief Justice Chase said concerning the lack of the taxing power in the Articles of Confederation:

Both the States and the United States existed before the Constitution. The people, through that instrument, established a more perfect union by substituting a national government, acting with ample power directly upon the citizens, instead of the Confederate government, which acted with powers, greatly restricted, only upon the States. . . . To the existence of the States, themselves necessary to the existence of the United States, the power of taxation is indispensable. It is an essential function of government. It was exercised by the Colonies; and when the Colonies became States, it was exercised by the new governments. Under the Articles of Confederation the government of the United States was limited in the exercise of this power to requisitions upon the States, while the whole power of direct and indirect taxation of persons and property, whether by taxes on polls, or duties on imports, or duties on internal production, manufacture, or use, was acknowledged to belong exclusively to the States, without any other limitation than that of non-interference with certain treaties made by Congress.

The Constitution of the United States.

In the case of *U. S. v. Cruikshank*,[2] decided in 1875 by the U. S. Supreme Court, Chief Justice Waite said:

Experience made the fact known to the people of the United States that they required a national government

[1] 7 Wallace (U. S.) Rep., 71, 78.
[2] 9 Wheaton (U. S.) Rep., 316, 403.

for national purposes. The separate governments of the separate States, bound together by the Articles of Confederation alone, were not sufficient for the promotion of the general welfare of the people in respect to foreign nations, or for their complete protection as citizens of the confederated States.

These impossible governmental conditions made imperative the establishment of a more effective national system. Therefore, on January 21, 1787, the Congress of the Confederation adopted the following resolution:

RESOLVED: That it is expedient that on the Second Monday in May next, a convention of delegates, who shall have been appointed by the several States, be held at Philadelphia, for the sole and express purpose of revising the Articles of Confederation, and reporting to Congress and the several legislatures such alterations and provisions therein, as shall, when agreed to in Congress, and confirmed by the States, render the Federal Constitution adequate to the exigencies of government and the preservation of the Union.

In pursuance of this authority, the legislatures of twelve of the original States sent delegates to Philadelphia to the Federal Convention, which drafted the Constitution of the United States.

In the case of *McCulloch v. Maryland*,[1] decided in 1819 by the U. S. Supreme Court, Chief Justice Marshall described the establishment of the present United States Government in the following words:

The convention which framed the Constitution was, indeed, elected in most cases by the State legislatures.

[1] 4 Wheaton, U. S. Rep., 316.

But the instrument, when it came from their hands, was a mere proposal, without obligation, or pretensions to it. It was reported to the then existing congress of the United States, with a request that it might "be submitted to a convention of delegates, chosen in each State, by the people thereof, under the recommendation of its legislature, for their assent and ratification." This mode of proceeding was adopted; and by the convention, by congress, and by the State legislatures, the instrument was submitted to the people. They acted upon it, in the only manner in which they can act safely, effectively, and wisely, on such a subject, by assembling in convention. . . . From these conventions the Constitution derives its whole authority. The government proceeds directly from the people; and is "ordained and established" in the name of the people. . . . The assent of the States, in their sovereign capacity, is implied in calling a convention, and thus submitting that instrument to the people. But the people were at perfect liberty to accept or reject it; and their act was final. It required not the affirmance, and could not be negatived by the State governments. . . . The government of the Union . . . is emphatically and truly a government of the people. Its powers are granted by them, and are to be exercised directly on them, and for their benefit.

CHAPTER III

The First State Governments.

During the agitations which preceded the War for Independence, rudimentary forms of government were established in all of the colonies except Rhode Island and Connecticut, which continued to use their old royal charters. For example, in 1772, while the tea tax was still in dispute, Governor Hutchinson refused to convene the Massachusetts legislature to decide how the salaries of public officers should be paid. Samuel Adams organized a committee of correspondence composed of residents of the different towns to consult about public affairs by means of letters. Similar committees were organized in Virginia and in other colonies. In 1774 and 1775, provincial congresses composed of members of the existing assemblies met in Massachusetts, in Virginia, in New York, and in some other colonies in defiance of royal authority, and took such measures as were necessary to continue the opposition to the British government. On May 10, 1776, the Second Continental Congress adopted a resolution recommending that such of the colonies as then had no sufficient government should adopt "such governments as should in the opinion of the representatives of the people, best conduce to the safety and happiness of their constituents in particular, and America in general." In pursuance of this resolution, except in Connecticut and Rhode Island, which used their royal charters as State constitutions, and in Massachusetts, where action was had by a regular convention composed of elected delegates, the legislatures of the different colonies, meeting as constitutional conventions, prepared constitutions establishing governments. In the case of *Kamper v. Hawkins*,[1] decided in 1793 by the General Court of Virginia, Justice Tucker described as follows the proceedings by which the people of Virginia established their first State government:

It will be remembered by all those who are conversant with the history of the rise and progress of the late glorious revolution [the War for Independence], that the measures which led to the final consummation of that important event, although they originated, in most instances, with the legal and constitutional assemblies of the different colonies, made but a small progress in that channel, particularly in this State. The dissolution of the Constitution assemblies, by the governors appointed by the Crown, obliged the people to resort to other methods of deliberating for the common good. . . . Hence the first introduction of conventions; bodies neither authorized by or known to the then constitutional government; bodies, on the contrary, which the constitutional officers of the then existing governments considered as illegal, and treated as such. Nevertheless, they met, deliberated, and resolved for the common good. They were the people, assembled by their deputies; not a legal, or constitutional assembly, or part of the government as then organized. . . . Hence, they were not, nor could

[1] 1 Virginia Cases, 20.

be deemed the ordinary legislature; that body being composed of the governor, council, and burgesses, who sat in several distinct chambers and characters; while the other was composed of a single body, having neither the character of governor, council, or legitimate representative among them; they were, in effect, the people themselves, assembled by their delegates, to whom the care of the commonwealth was especially, as well as unboundedly, confided. . . . The conventions . . . were held even whilst a legal assembly existed. Witness the Convention, held in Richmond in March, 1775, after which period, the legal, or constitutional assembly, was convened in Williamsburgh, by the governor, Lord Dunmore, and continued sitting until finally dissolved by him in June or July, 1775. No other legal assembly was ever chosen or convened under the British government.

The convention then was not the ordinary legislature of Virginia. It was the body of the people, impelled to assemble from a sense of common danger, consulting for the common good, and acting in all things for the common safety. It could not be the legitimate legislature, under the then established government, since that body could only be chosen under the permission, and assembled under the authority of the Crown of Great Britain. But although the exercise of the authority of the executive government under the Crown of Great Britain ceased altogether with the dissolution of that assembly in June, 1775, yet a constitutional dependence on the British government was never denied, until the succeeding May, nor dissolved until the moment of adopting the present constitution, or form of government; an event, which took effect by the unanimous voice of the convention (elected after the final dissolution of the general assembly, as above mentioned, and assembled in Williamsburgh), on the 29th of June, 1776, after six weeks of deliberation thereon, and eight [sic] days before the Declaration of Independence by the Congress of the United States.

The Territorial Governments.

Congress has from time to time enacted laws for the government of portions of the national domain preliminary to the formation of new States. In the case of *Downes v. Bidwell*,[1] decided in 1901 by the U. S. Supreme Court, Justice Brown described the organization of the Northwest Territory in 1787:

The Federal government was created in 1777 by the union of thirteen colonies of Great Britain in "certain articles of confederation and perpetual union," the first one of which declared that "the stile of this confederacy shall be the United States of America." Each member of the confederacy was denominated a *State*. Provision was made for the representation of each State by not less than two nor more than seven delegates; but no mention was made of territories or other lands, except in Article XI, which authorized the admission of Canada, upon its "acceding to this confederation," and of other colonies if such admission were agreed to by nine States. At this time several States made claims to large tracts of lands in the unsettled West, which they were at first indisposed to relinquish. Disputes over these lands became so acrid as nearly to defeat the confederacy, before it was fairly put in operation. Several of the States refused to ratify the articles, because the convention had taken no steps to settle the titles to these lands upon principles of equity and sound policy; but all of them through fear of being accused of disloyalty, finally yielded their claims, though Maryland held out until 1781. Most of these States in the meantime having ceded their interests in these lands, the Confederate Congress, in 1787, created the first territorial government northwest of the Ohio River, provided for local self-government, a bill of rights, a representation in Congress by a delegate, who should have a seat, "with

[1] 182 U. S. Rep., 244, 249.

a right of debating, but not of voting," and for the ultimate formation of States therefrom, and their admission into the Union on an equal footing with the original States.

Congress has from time to time established in portions of the national domain other territorial governments by what are called "organic laws," enacted for that purpose. The U. S. Supreme Court has declared that these "organic laws" are constitutions of the territories of the United States. In the case of *National Bank v. County of Yankton*,[1] decided in 1879, Chief Justice Waite said:

All territory within the jurisdiction of the United States not included in any State must necessarily be governed by or under the authority of Congress. The Territories are but political subdivisions of the outlying dominion of the United States. Their relation to the general government is much the same as that which counties bear to the respective States, and Congress may legislate for them as a State does for its municipal organizations. The organic law of a Territory takes the place of a constitution as the fundamental law of the local government. It is obligatory on and binds the territorial authorities; but Congress is supreme, and for the purposes of this department of its governmental authority has all the powers of the people of the United States, except such as have been expressly or by implication reserved in the prohibitions of the Constitution.

The Governments of New States.

Each of the States admitted to the Federal Union since the adoption of the Constitution of the United States, has a government established by a constitution.

[1] 101 U. S. Rep., 129, 133.

At first, new States were admitted somewhat informally by acts of Congress passed for that purpose. Each State which has been carved out of the Louisiana Purchase and other territory since then added to the national domain, has been established by an enabling act passed by Congress on the application of the residents of a specified portion of a territory of the United States. The procedure in the case of Nebraska is fully described in the case of *Brittle v. The People*,[1] decided by the Supreme Court of Nebraska in 1873, in which Justice Crounse said:

Nebraska, as a part of that vast tract of country ceded to the United States by France under the treaty concluded at Paris, April 30, 1803, was organized as a Territory by Congress, in the year 1854, by what is familiarly known as the Kansas-Nebraska Act. The appointment of a governor, secretary of state, judges, and marshal, and the election from time to time of a legislature, were provided for in this organic Act, and a territorial government established and conducted under it. In April, 1864, Congress passed an enabling act, providing for the election, in June of that year, of delegates who should meet in convention in July following, for the purpose of framing a constitution, with a view to the admission of Nebraska as a State into the Union. . . . Without any further act of Congress, the territorial legislature of 1866 submitted a proposed constitution to the electors, to be voted on in June of that year, with directions to choose, at the same time legislative, executive, and judicial officers, for the proposed state. The governor, secretary of state, and auditor of the Territory, were, by the act submitting the instrument, constituted a board of canvassers; and they declared the constitution adopted by a majority of a hundred.

The legislature thus chosen assembled in July, the time

[1] 2 Nebraska Rep., 198.

prescribed, and chose two senators to represent the State, who, together with the representative in Congress, took the proposed constitution to Washington, and prayed Nebraska's admission. This constitution, in prescribing the qualifications of electors, limited the right to vote to white males. To this restriction Congress took exception, and after much debate, on Feb. 9, 1867, passed an act (which provided that the proposed Constitution should not take effect except "upon the fundamental condition that, within the State of Nebraska, there shall be no denial of the elective franchise, or of any other rights, to any person, by reason of race or color, excepting Indians not taxed; and upon the further fundamental condition that the legislature of said State, by a solemn public act, shall declare the assent of said State to the said fundamental condition, and shall transmit to the President of the United States, an authentic copy of said act; upon receipt whereof, the President, by proclamation, shall forthwith announce the fact; whereupon said fundamental act shall be held as a part of the organic law of the State; and . . . its admission into the Union shall be considered as complete)." . . .

The State legislature was convened by the governor accordingly; and on the twentieth day of February, 1867, . . . declared: "*Be it enacted by the legislature of the State of Nebraska*, That the act of Congress of the United States, entitled, An Act for the Admission of the State of Nebraska into the Union, passed February 9, 1867, be, and the same is hereby ratified and accepted, and it is hereby declared that the provisions of the third section (imposing the conditions above stated) of the said Act of Congress shall be a part of the law of the State of Nebraska."

This action was certified to the President, who, on the Second day of March, 1867, made proclamation as required.

PART II

Constitutional Law

CHAPTER IV

Evolution of American Constitutions.

The chartered companies and the proprietors sent over to the colonies large numbers of colonists to protect the trading posts from the Indians and to do the work incident to the establishment of permanent communities. Afterward, larger numbers of emigrants came at their own expense to better themselves and to escape religious and political disabilities. Besides these settlers, thousands of poorer people and many criminals were transported to the colonies to be sold as indentured servants either to pay the cost of their passage or as a penalty for misdeeds. All of the colonies thus populated had to have governments to provide for the protection of the people from the attacks of savages, to punish disorderly conduct and crime, and to compel each one to do his share of the work of building houses and clearing forest lands. The government in England was three thousand miles away and could not provide for the needs of small communities existing under entirely different conditions. Consequently, the companies and the proprietors first sent over officials authorized to act as governors and to appoint advisory councils. Later on, the colonies obtained new charters which authorized the establishment of elective assem-

27

blies and otherwise modified the forms of their governments. These political conditions continued until the outbreak of the War for Independence when State governments were informally established by provincial congresses, which sent delegates to the Continental Congress. Thereafter, national and state governments were formed, modelled more or less closely upon the three-fold type of the colonial governments.

These charters, patents, and written plans of government were constitutions or laws of government and in the highest sense were laws. In the case of *Commonwealth v. Collins,*[1] decided in 1839 by the Supreme Court of Pennsylvania, Justice Huston described as follows the legal nature of a constitution:

A Constitution is but a law; it emanates from the people, the depository and the only one of all political power; it is, therefore, the supreme law. It organizes and defines the different parts of the government, confers on each department the powers and duties allotted to each, and limits the powers of every department. It has this further quality; having distributed the different powers to the different departments, it leaves those powers to be exercised by those departments, and leaves to the sovereign people themselves no other power than of choosing their own officers or representatives. The people can do no act, except make a new Constitution or make a revolution.

In the case of *Commonwealth v. Roxbury,*[2] previously referred to, Chief Justice Shaw of Massachusetts described as follows the origin and nature of the govern-

[1] 8 Watts (Penna.) Rep., 331, 409.
[2] 9 Gray (Mass.) Rep., 451, 478.

ment established by the charter of the colony of Massachusetts Bay:

The Charter [of Charles I granted in 1628] provided for the organization of the Company, by the appointment of a governor, deputy governor, and eighteen assistants, to be chosen by the freemen of the Company, after the first appointment made by the Charter itself. The governor, deputy governor, assistants and freemen were authorized to admit freemen, to elect officers for the ordering of their affairs, and to make laws and ordinances, for the good and welfare of said company, and for the government and ordering, disposition and management of the said lands and plantation, and the people inhabiting and to inhabit the same, as to them from time to time should be thought meet, not repugnant to the laws of England. Anc. Chart., 18, 9.

It is probable, as it has been suggested, that the Charter was intended to create and establish a trading corporation, to meet and act in England, with large powers to manage a planting and trading colony. But there being no restriction upon their meeting and acting anywhere within the king's dominions; in about two years, the Company, by advice of counsel, determined to remove to Massachusetts; and in 1630 the governor, deputy governor, and many of the assistants and freemen, came to Massachusetts, bringing the Charter with them. From that time all meetings were held in the Colony. For a few of the first years, and whilst the plantations and settlements were few, meetings were attended according to the Charter, by all such freemen as chose to attend; but, as early as 1634, it was provided that the freemen of each plantation might choose two or three before every general court, who should have the full voices of all the freemen to act with the governor and assistants in making laws, granting lands, etc., and other affairs, excepting elections. 1 Mass. Col. Rec. 118. Here, then, was the origin of a representative government, probably not contemplated by the Charter, but perhaps not wholly inconsistent with it, because if all freemen had a right to act, those delegated, being freemen, had that right; if repugnant at all to the Charter, it was in excluding those not appointed delegates.

In 1644, ten years later, a still more decisive step was taken. It was probably found that the delegates quite outnumbered the governor and assistants, and would of course outvote them, acting in one body. Divers inconveniencies having been found in this mode of proceeding, and accounting it wisdom to follow the laudable practice of other states, it was ordered that henceforth the two bodies shall sit and act apart, in separate bodies, each having the initiative in proposing laws and measures, and each having a negative on the other, so that no act could pass without the concurrence of both bodies. 2 Mass. Col. Rec. 58. In this we perceive the complete establishment of a representative government, with a distribution and balance of powers. Whether this was perfectly consistent with the Charter or not, it was acquiesced in, acted on, and afterwards confirmed by the Province Charter. See *Commonwealth v. Charlestown*, 1 Pick. 183.

The governments which existed under the colonial charters and patents were described as follows by Justice Iredell in his opinion in the case of *Penhallow v. Doane*,[1] decided in 1795 by the U. S. Supreme Court:

Under the British government, and before the opposition to the measures of the parliament of Great Britain became necessary, each province in America composed, as I conceive, a body politic, and the several provinces were not otherwise connected with each other than as being subject to the same common sovereign. Each province had a dis-

[1] 3 Dallas (U. S.) Rep., 54, 90.

tinct legislature, a distinct executive subordinate to the King, and a distinct judiciary.

The constitutions of the States and of the Nation have four important component parts: a preamble, a bill of rights, an assignment of powers to legislative, executive, and judicial departments of government, and an amending clause.

Preambles.

A preamble is an introduction or preface which states the purposes for which the government is to be established. The lawgivers of every age have always considered it wise to preface their edicts or decrees with general statements declaring the ends for which their mandates have been made. The English Habeas Corpus Act of 1679, for example, begins with the following words: "An Act for the better securing the Liberty of the Subject, and for the Prevention of Imprisonments beyond the Seas." For this reason, our ancestors began their instruments of government with preambles which declared the objects they had in view. The framers of the first constitution of the State of New York, for instance, intended to establish a government that would safeguard their liberty; therefore they adopted the following preamble:

We, the People of the State of New York, grateful to Almighty God for our freedom, in order to secure its blessings, do establish this constitution.

The makers of the Constitution of the United States, as a matter of form, prefaced their work with the following preamble:

We, the People of the United States, in order to form a more perfect Union, establish Justice, promote domestic Tranquillity, provide for the common Defence, promote the general Welfare, and secure the Blessings of Liberty to ourselves and our Posterity, do ordain and establish this *Constitution* for the United States of America.

The preamble of a constitution is a mere statement of objects and purposes. It does not of itself confer powers of government, though it indicates the reason for the provisions which are made to that end in the body of the instrument. In the case of *Jacobson v. Massachusetts*,[1] decided in 1905 by the U. S. Supreme Court, Justice Harlan said:

Although that Preamble indicates the general purposes for which the people ordained and established the Constitution, it has never been regarded as the source of any substantive power conferred on the Government of the United States or on any of its Departments. Such powers embrace only those expressly granted in the body of the Constitution and such as may be implied from those so granted.

Bills of Rights.

At the time of the establishment of the English colonies in this country, it was the basic principle of the English Constitution that every individual citizen, if a free man, had rights which had never been surrendered to the government. These rights, which had existed

[1] 197 U. S. Rep., 11, 22.

from time immemorial, had been re-asserted in the
Great Charter of King John, in the Petition of Right
of 1628, in the Habeas Corpus Act of 1679, and the Bill
of Rights of 1689. They were and are the principles of
that liberty upon which the English have always
insisted. These rights the colonists brought with them
to America as a part of their birthright as English
subjects.

The colonists also exercised some rights that were not
recognized in England. For example, the founders of
many of the colonies exercised the right to worship God
in certain ways and according to certain forms that were
illegal in England and in other colonies. The right of
religious liberty was a bone of contention in Virginia
just before the Revolution. Patrick Henry established
his fame as an orator by his addresses in the Church
Establishment cases, in which he vindicated the right
of each citizen to be exempt from any tax or charge
for the support of one church when he belonged to
or worshipped with another denomination. Thomas
Jefferson earned his first reputation as a statesman by
advocating the cause of freedom of religious belief
and practice in the course of the same controversy.
About this time the rights of freedom of speech and of
the press, as well as of peaceably assembling for the
discussion of grievances, were being firmly established
in Great Britain by the celebrated John Wilkes in the
course of a controversy over his right to represent in
Parliament a constituency that had elected him as their
member. Indeed, the triumphant result of that
struggle, in which the whole power of the Crown was
used against the champion of the people, encouraged
not a little the American patriots who risked "their
lives, their fortunes, and their sacred honor" in a contest

in arms against the most powerful nation in the world.

The first State constitutions contained bills of rights that were in effect declarations that as to certain specific matters, each citizen was a law unto himself; that as to those matters, the governments they established were without powers of control or regulation. The powers of self-government so reserved to individuals were enumerated to the end that the governments should know the limitations upon their powers.

When the Constitution of the United States was framed, the makers contented themselves with provisions securing the privilege of the writ of habeas corpus, exemption from prosecutions by bills of attainder and *ex post facto* laws, a clause relating to appropriations of public money, and a few limitations upon the powers of taxation and of regulating commerce.[1] They considered this moderate bill of rights sufficient because it was then generally taken for granted that the national government did not, and could not, have any powers except those which the States were called upon to surrender. For that reason they did not insert a bill of rights in the National Constitution.

When the States took up the question of the ratification of the proposed constitution, it became very evident that the people of the United States considered the omission of a bill of rights a serious defect. North Carolina refused to ratify it until it should have been amended. Many of the States ratified only after receiving assurances that a bill of rights would be proposed to the States by the first congress that should be held under the article which established the legislative power of the nation. Consequently, the First

[1] U. S. Const., Art. 1, sec. 9.

Constitutional Congress proposed and the States ratified the Bill of Rights contained in the first ten amendments.

The rights specified in these amendments are practically the same as those by which the people of the States have in their State constitutions limited the powers of their State governments. They comprise the rights of religious liberty, of freedom of speech and of the press, of meeting to discuss and if necessary of criticizing the government, of each State to have a militia, of exemption from being compelled to support and board soldiers in time of peace, of security against searches and seizures of property by public officers, of exemption from criminal prosecution except in accordance with indictments in the United States' courts (and in some States under informations duly filed by prosecutors), of immunity from being prosecuted twice for the same offense or under the same charge, of being compelled to be a witness against himself in a criminal case, of being deprived by the government or by anybody acting by its authority of life or liberty or property without due process of law, and of having his property taken by the government for public purposes without just compensation.

These rights also include the right of trial by jury in criminal cases, of being informed of the charges against him when so tried, of being confronted with the witnesses against him, of having the right to compel his own witnesses to attend and testify, and of having the assistance of counsel. They give to the parties to suits at law the right in important cases of having a trial by a jury, and provide that excessive bail shall not be required of persons charged with criminal acts, that excessive fines shall not be imposed upon persons who have been convicted of crime, and that cruel and unusual punishments shall not be inflicted upon criminals.

The additional rights secured to citizens of the United States by subsequent amendments to the National Constitution, but not secured to citizens of the States by the State constitutions, deal with the right to vote. Prior to the Civil War, the suffrage was regulated wholly by the States. When the negroes were emancipated, the Constitution of the United States was made to provide that no person shall be deprived of the right to vote because of race, color, or previous condition of servitude. More recently, the National Constitution has been so amended as to secure the suffrage to women.

In the case of *Orr v. Quimby*,[1] decided in 1874 by the Supreme Court of New Hampshire, Chief Justice Doe said:

An American bill of rights is a declaration of private rights reserved in a grant of public powers,—a reservation of a limited individual sovereignty, annexed to and made part of a limited form of government established by the independent, individual action of the voting class of the people. The general purpose of such a bill of rights is, to declare those fundamental principles of the common law, generally called the principles of English constitutional liberty, which the American people always claimed as their English inheritance, and the defence of which was their justification of the war of 1776.

In the case of *U. S. v. Cruikshank*,[2] decided in 1875 by the U. S. Supreme Court, Chief Justice Waite, said:

[1] 54 New Hampshire Rep., 590.
[2] 92 U. S. Rep., 542, 551.

The government of the United States is one of delegated powers alone. Its authority is defined and limited by the Constitution. All powers not granted to it by that instrument are reserved to the States or the people. No rights can be acquired under the constitution or laws of the United States, except such as the government of the United States has the authority to grant or secure. All that cannot be so granted or secured are left under the protection of the States.

Powers Conferred by Constitutions.

The State constitutions give the legislative power to law-making bodies composed of two houses, the members of which are elected by the people. The larger house, usually called the House of Representatives, is composed of representatives of small districts that are nearly equal in population; the smaller house, called the Senate, is composed of representatives of larger districts also as nearly as possible equal in representation. There are exceptions to this rule, especially in the older States where the equal representation of communities rather than of the people still prevails, and in others where the assignments of representation by old constitutions have been continued long after growth of population has made the original basis unequal. For example, in Connecticut, each town has two representatives in the larger house without regard to population so that little towns of a few hundred inhabitants have as much power as large cities like New Haven, Bridgeport, and Hartford. Again, New York City with a larger population than all the rest of New York State, elects less than half of the senators and assemblymen.

The National Constitution assigns the legislative power to a Congress composed of a House of Representatives in which the number of members from each State is in the proportion of its population to the populations of the other States, and a Senate in which each State is equally represented by two senators. Representatives in Congress are chosen by the people of congressional districts nearly equal in population, which have been established by the State legislatures.   Senators in Congress are chosen by the people of the States.

The legislative power of a State extends to the making of laws imposing State taxes; appropriating money to pay the expenses of the State government; defining crimes and providing for their punishment; regulating elections; regulating public service corporations, banking, and insurance; promoting public education; establishing municipal governments; modifying, altering, or improving the rules of law for the security of individual rights of person and property; and generally to the making of all kinds of laws except those which are forbidden by the bill of rights and those which can be made only by the national legislature—the Congress.

The legislative power of the United States extends to the making of laws imposing national taxes, appropriating money for governmental purposes, regulating interstate and foreign commerce and commerce with the Indians, coining money, borrowing money, regulating naturalization and bankruptcy, creating inferior national courts, providing a postal service, issuing patents and copyrights, declaring war, maintaining armies and navies, and doing everything necessary and proper for enforcing these laws and for executing the powers of the national government.

The State constitutions give the executive power to governors and other State officers elected by the people to enforce all State laws, command the militia, grant pardons, appoint under some conditions all State officers, approve or disapprove proposed laws made by legislatures, and in general manage the public business of the State.

The National Constitution gives the executive power to the President of the United States, who usually is chosen by electors, themselves elected by the people of the States, and authorizes the vice-President to succeed the President in case of his death or removal or incapacity to perform his duties. The President performs his duties through secretaries and other heads of executive departments, whom he appoints. His executive power extends to the commander in chief of the army and navy; the making of treaties if two-thirds of the Senate concur; the appointment, with the advice and consent of the Senate, of the chief officers of the national government such as ambassadors, judges of the Supreme Court, and other important officials; the performance of diplomatic duties; and the enforcement of the laws of the United States.

The National Constitution gives the judicial power or the power to judge the laws to a Supreme Court, consisting of a number of justices fixed by the Congress and appointed by the President, and to such inferior courts as Congress establishes. This power extends to the decision of all cases arising under the Constitution and laws of the United States and under its treaties; to cases affecting diplomatic representatives of other nations; to admiralty cases; to controversies in which the Nation is a party; to controversies between two or more States, between a State and citizens of another State (except cases brought by a citizen against a State or a foreign nation) and between citizens of different States; to controversies concerning land grants; and to actions between a State and its citizens and foreign States or their citizens.

A State constitution authorizes State Courts to exercise judicial powers within the State. This power extends to all cases except those that fall within the jurisdiction of the Federal Courts.

The power of the Supreme Court of the United States to judge and decide all cases arising under the Constitution and laws of the United States operates as a stabilizing device by which the balance of the Federal Union is maintained. If a State, by legislative or executive action, usurps a power that belongs exclusively to the national government or infringes any rights under the Constitution of the United States of one of its citizens, any person may, by proper legal proceeding, obtain from the Supreme Court of the United States a decision that the action complained of is null and void. The Supreme Court bases its exercise of this power upon the fact that, inasmuch as the Constitution and laws of the United States are the supreme law of the land, any act of a State which is repugnant to any provision of that constitution or of those laws is necessarily unconstitutional and unenforceable. If the Congress of the United States enacts a statute that is not authorized by the Constitution of the United States or if the President of the United States performs an unauthorized act, any person whose rights are affected can in like manner obtain a decision of the Supreme Court of the United States that the statute or the executive act complained of is unconstitutional. In such cases, the decisions of the Supreme Court, by preventing the enforcement of unauthorized statutes and the performance or repetition of unauthorized executive acts, prevents any encroachment upon the respective powers of the State and national governments, and preserves the powers of the United States for national governmental purposes and the powers of the States for local governmental purposes.

Powers Denied to the United States.

The framers of the U. S. Constitution imposed[1] a number of limitations upon the law-making powers of the Congress in order to adapt the new instrument of government to the political conditions of the Nation.

For example, the Congress was forbidden to prohibit, prior to 1808, the migration or importation of such persons as the States thought proper to admit. This prohibition referred to indentured servants who obtained passage to the United States by agreeing to be sold into service for a term of years to pay the cost, and to negroes who were imported from Africa to supply the labor needed by the plantations of the Southern States. This clause was inserted as a compromise in order to obtain the acquiescence of North Carolina, South Carolina, and Georgia, which otherwise might have refused to ratify the Constitution.

The privilege of the writ of habeas corpus was safeguarded by a provision that it should not be suspended unless, when in cases of rebellion or invasion, the public safety should require it.

Bills of attainder, inflicting punishments by act of the legislature instead of by sentences of courts of justice, and *ex post facto* laws, making unlawful acts which were lawful when performed, were prohibited.

Laws imposing direct taxes or taxes on real estate

[1] U. S. Const., Art. I., Sec. 9.

and capitation or poll taxes were forbidden unless levied upon the States in proportion to their populations in order to equalize national taxation. Any other plan of taxing real estate or individuals would have been unfair as between the States which had valuable commercial interests and those in which agriculture was the only important industry.

Taxes or duties on goods exported were prohibited because that kind of taxation is a burden upon the industries of the Nation.

The Congress was forbidden to give any preference to the ports of one State over those of another in order to prevent the national legislature from unduly favoring certain commercial centres and discriminating against others.

Another clause declared that no money should be drawn from the treasury except by appropriations made by law and that statements of the accounts of the national government should be made from time to time. This provision gives the people of the United States control over national expenditures and enables them to know how their money is spent.

The last limitation is that no titles of nobility shall be granted and that no officer of the United States shall accept any title or other gift from a foreign nation without the consent of the Congress. This prohibition prevented the establishment of a nobility in the United States, and has headed off a form of bribery.

Powers Denied to the States.

The Constitution of the United States and all laws and treaties made under its authority are the supreme law of the land of the United States.[1]   The framers

[1] U. S. Const. Art. VI., Subd. 2.

of the Constitution made binding upon the States the national government it was to create, the laws that government should make, and the treaties it might enter into with other nations. In the case of *Ex Parte Siebold*,[1] decided in 1879 by the U. S. Supreme Court, Justice Bradley said:

The true doctrine, as we conceive, is this, that whilst the States are really sovereign as to all matters which have not been granted to the jurisdiction and control of the United States, the Constitution and constitutional laws of the latter are . . . the supreme law of the land; and when they conflict with the laws of the States, they are of paramount authority and obligation. This is the fundamental principle on which the authority of the Constitution is based; and unless it is conceded in practise, as well as theory, the fabric of our institutions, as it was contemplated by its founders, cannot stand.

The framers of the Constitution of the United States specified in that instrument[2] certain powers which the States should not be allowed to exercise to the end that the United States should possess the essential attributes of sovereignty.

The first of these powers, which the States may not exercise, relates to treaties, alliances, and confederations. The States were prohibited from making any such international agreements because such acts would have been inconsistent with the sovereignty of the national government. The States were also forbidden to issue letters of marque and reprisal, that is, to commission privateers, because all war powers were given to the Nation. They were denied the power to

[1] 100 U. S. Rep., 371.
[2] U. S. Const. Art. I., Sec. 10.

coin money, emit bills of credit, or make anything except gold and silver coin, a tender in payment of debts, because the money power is an incident of sovereignty. They were prohibited from passing any bill of attainder or *ex post facto* law and from granting titles of nobility, because it would have been absurd to permit them to do the very things which the nation was not allowed to do.

The most important of these denials of power to the States is that which forbids the passage of "any law impairing the obligation of a contract." The founders of the government wished to place its foundations firmly upon honesty and good faith. Hence they declared that no State should make any law that would weaken or diminish the power of the courts to enforce contracts in existence at the time it was made, or to give a remedy by damages for failure to perform them.[1] In the case of *Sturgis v. Crowninshield*,[2] decided by the U. S. Supreme Court in 1819, it was held that a State law for the relief of insolvent debtors did not apply to debts that were in existence at the time it was passed. Chief Justice Marshall said:

Does the law of New York, which is pleaded in this case, impair the obligation of contracts, within the meaning of the Constitution of the United States? This act liberates the person of the debtor, and discharges him from all liability for any debt previously contracted, on his surrendering his property in the manner it prescribes. In discussing the question whether a State is prohibited from passing such a law as this, our first inquiry is into the meaning of words in common use. What is the obligation of a contract? and what will impair it? . . . A contract is an agree-

[1] Miller on the Constitution, 541.
[2] 4 Wheaton (U. S.) Rep., 122.

ment in which a party undertakes to do, or not to do, a particular thing. The law binds him to perform his undertaking, and this is, of course, the obligation of his contract. In the case at bar, the defendant has given his promissory note to pay the plaintiff a sum of money on or before a certain day. The contract binds him to pay that sum on that day; and this is its obligation. Any law which releases a part of this obligation, must, in the literal sense of the word, impair it. Much more must a law impair it which makes it totally invalid, and entirely discharges it. . . .

Miscellaneous Provisions of Constitutions.

Each State constitution contains special provisions authorizing laws such as those providing for the maintenance and repair of canals of the State.[1]

The Constitution of the United States contains many general provisions required by an instrument of government that establishes a system of regulation for a number of independent States, and confers no powers except those given in specific words or deduced by implication. These general provisions require that full faith and credit shall be given in each State to the public acts, records, and judicial proceedings of other States; that the citizens of each State shall be entitled to all the privileges and immunities of citizens of the other States; and that fugitives from justice shall be surrendered to the States from which they have fled, there to be tried for the crimes of which they are accused. The full faith and credit clause enables a person who has obtained a judgment in an action in a State court to enforce it in another State without trying his case over again. The privilege and immunity provision prevents a State from imposing upon citizens of other States liv-

[1] Constitution of the State of New York.

ing or doing business within its borders different taxes from those it imposes upon its own citizens. The extradition clause prevents criminals from escaping the penalties of their crimes by running away from the State in which they committed them.

Provisions for Constitutional Amendments.

The State Constitutions and the Constitution of the United States make ample provision for such alter- ations in forms of government as may be needed. An excellent authority[1] comments in the following words upon such subdivisions of the fundamental laws:

The doctrine that a constitution can be amended is of comparatively recent origin in the growth of constitu- tional government. Experience, however, taught that governments change and that their constitutions must also change to meet the requirements of new conditions and new policies. When the early charters were granted to the American colonists they were sometimes changed by the sovereign and it was understood that such power resided in the King, although to maintain the ancient rule each charter declared that its form of government should be perpetual.

The first provision for the amendment of a charter is found in the Pennsylvania Frame of April 2, 1683. That instrument contained a provision that it might be amended by the consent of the "Governor and six parts of seven of the freemen in provincial Council and General Assembly." The Pennsylvania Frame of 1696 contained a similar pro- vision.

The Pennsylvania Charter of Privileges of 1701 pro- vided that, "The First Article of this Charter relating to Liberty of Conscience, and every Part and Clause therein, according to the true Intent and Meaning thereof, shall be

[1] Watson, *The Constitution of the United States*, II., 1301.

kept and remain, without any Alteration, inviolably for ever."

In this respect the Constitution of the United States resembles this ancient instrument, for after providing for amendments it says, "No State shall without its consent, be deprived of its equal suffrage in the Senate."

The other colonial charters did not contain provisions for amendments. Franklin's Articles of Confederation of 1775 provided, "As all new institutions may have imperfections which only time and experience can discover, it is agreed that the general congress, from time to time, shall propose such amendments of this constitution as may be found necessary, which, being approved by a majority of the colony assemblies, shall be equally binding with the rest of the Articles of this Confederation." The Constitutions of Maryland, Delaware and Pennsylvania, for 1776, and those of Georgia, and Vermont, for 1777, contained provisions relative to amendments, but not by the legislatures. . . .

But by the year 1787 eight State Constitutions embodied such provisions. Three, Maryland, Delaware and South Carolina, conferred the power to amend on the legislatures under certain restrictions. The other five States, Pennsylvania, Vermont, Georgia, Massachusetts and New Hampshire, conferred the power upon conventions which should be called for the purpose.

Amendment of a State Constitution.

Each of our State constitutions contains a special provision for amendment, alteration, or revision, whenever changes of social conditions may make such action advisable. In the *Prohibitory Amendment Cases*,[1] decided in 1881 by the Supreme Court of Kansas, Justice Brewer, afterward a Justice of the U. S. Supreme

[1] 24 Kansas Rep., 700, 706, 715.

Court, passing upon the validity of the Kansas prohibitory amendment, said:

The paramount question in these cases is the validity of the prohibitory amendment submitted at the last November election. . . . On the one hand we have been told that it is the crowning effort of a brave and earnest people to free itself from the curse of intoxication; on the other, that it is a departure from the wisdom and experience of the past, a radical change of policy, trespassing upon personal liberty and rights of property. . . . Here the single question is one of power. We make no laws; we change no constitutions; we inaugurate no policy. When the legislature enacts a law, the only question which we can decide is whether the limitations of the constitution have been infringed upon. When a constitutional amendment has been submitted, the single inquiry for us is whether it has received the sanction of popular approval in the manner prescribed by the fundamental law. . . . As a court our single inquiry is, have constitutional requirements been observed, and limits of power regarded? We have no veto. The judge who casts his individual opinions of wisdom or policy into the decisions of questions of constitutional limitations and powers, simply usurps a prerogative never committed to him in the wise distribution of duties made by the people in their fundamental law. . . . The courts are to know what is and what is not a public law of the state, what is and what is not a part of the Constitution, and, to that end, must take judicial notice of everything, near or remote, that determines such fact. . . . The courts take judicial notice of what is public law, statutory or constitutional. When a majority of the electors voting on an amendment at an election properly ordered, adopts it, then it becomes a part of the Constitution. So the Constitution itself says. The courts must judicially know whether such amendment has been adopted, and is in fact a part of the constitution, and to that end, if need be, must take judicial notice of every ballot cast at that election.

Amendment of the Constitution of the United States.

An amendment becomes a part of the Constitution of the United States when it has been proposed by a two-thirds vote of both branches of Congress,[1] and has been ratified by three-fourths of the States. In the *National Prohibition Cases*,[2] decided in 1919, in which the U. S. Supreme Court ruled that the Eighteenth or Prohibitory Amendment has been added to the Constitution in due and legal form, Justice Van Devanter said:

The adoption by both Houses of Congress, each by a two-thirds vote, of a joint resolution proposing an amendment to the Constitution sufficiently shows that the proposal was deemed necessary by all who voted for it. . . . The prohibition of the manufacture, sale, transportation, importation, and exportation of intoxicating liquors for beverage purposes, as embodied in the Eighteenth Amendment, . . . by lawful proposal and ratification, has become a part of the Constitution, and must be respected and given effect the same as the other provisions of that instrument.

Ratifying Clauses of Constitutions.

A constitution becomes a law of government when it has been ratified or accepted by the people in the manner prescribed by its ratifying clause. The Constitutions of all of the original thirteen States except Rhode Island and Connecticut, which used their royal charters as constitutions, and Massachusetts, which ratified its constitution by a popular election, became

---

[1] U. S. Const. Art. V., provides for a national constitutional convention, but no such body has ever been called together.

[2] 253 U. S. Rep., 350, 386.

effective by the acceptance of the people. Some of the States admitted to the Union soon after the adoption of the U. S. Constitution also made their constitutions operative without submission to the people. All State constitutions are now voted upon at elections before going into effect.

The Constitution of the United States was established in 1788 by the ratifications of the conventions of eleven of the thirteen existing States and has since then been ratified by conventions in all of the other States.

CHAPTER V

The Constitution of the United States distinctly provides that the legislative power shall be exercised by the Congress, that the executive power shall vest in the President, and that the judicial power shall be held by a Supreme Court and such subordinate courts as the Congress shall establish. Theoretically, this assignment of the three distinct functions of government to three different departments so subdivides the powers of the National Government that the Congress shall make, but may not execute or judge, the laws; that the President shall execute, but may not make or judge, the laws; that the courts of the United States shall judge, but may not make or execute, the laws. The thought that influenced the framers of the Constitution undoubtedly was that such a distribution of governmental powers would make arbitrary government impossible. That conception was based upon the fact that, if a government could make such laws as it saw fit, could then say what those laws meant and how they applied to subsequent events, and could afterward execute them in its own way, the life, liberty, and property of every citizen would be at its mercy.

This conception of the subdivision of governmental power as a barrier against arbitrary government, which had been formulated by Montesquieu in his famous work on "The Spirit of the Laws," had been incorporated into the first Constitution of Massachusetts[1] in the following words:

> In the government of this commonwealth, the legislative department shall never exercise the executive and judicial powers, or either of them; the executive shall never exercise the legislative and judicial powers, or either of them; the judicial shall never exercise the legislative and executive powers, or either of them; to the end it may be a government of laws and not of men.

In the case of *Witter v. Cook County*,[2] decided in 1912 by the Supreme Court of Illinois, Justice Cartwright said:

> Article 3 of the Constitution [Illinois] divides the powers of the government into three distinct departments,—the legislative, executive, and judicial,—and prohibits the exercise of any power belonging to either department by any person or collection of persons belonging to another department, except as expressly directed or permitted by the constitution. The body that deliberates and enacts laws, whether of the whole State or (by delegation) for minor subdivisions and municipalities, is legislative. The executive power is that power which compels obedience to the laws and executes them. The instrumentalities employed for that purpose are officers who are elected or appointed and who are charged with the enforcement of the laws (*People v. Morgan*, 90 Ill, 558). The judicial power is that which adjudicates upon and protects the rights and interests of individual citizens and to that end construes and applies the laws. It is that power which applies the law and adjudges in particular cases.

[1] Article XXX., Part I.   [2] 256 Illinois Rep., 616, 621.

Overlapping of Powers.

In the United States Constitution, this subdivision of powers is not made exactly. The Senate exercises judicial powers when it sits as a court of impeachment at trials of public officers on charges of misconduct, and the House of Representatives performs executive functions when it prosecutes impeachment cases. The Senate exercises executive functions when it confirms the nominations of public officers made by the President and when it gives or withholds its confirmation of treaties he has negotiated. On one occasion, the Congress performed a distinctly judicial act by declaring that the bridge over the Ohio River at Wheeling should be "held and taken to be [a lawful structure], anything in the law or laws of the United States to the contrary notwithstanding."[1] The President legislates through the heads of the executive departments who make rules and regulations which, if not inconsistent with law, have the force and effect of law; and judges some cases through administrative tribunals, such as the land courts and the immigration officials who pass upon the admission or exclusion of aliens. The President also legislates when he vetoes or approves laws enacted by the Congress and presented for his approval. It might be going too far to say that the courts of the United States sometimes do legislative acts. They do, in the course of their duties, declare unconstitutional and refuse to enforce acts of Congress which they hold to be unauthorized by the provisions of the Constitution. Though savoring of the legislative character, such acts are held to be within the judicial power vested in the Courts.

Furthermore, the powers assigned by our State and

[1] *Penna. v. Wheeling &c. Bridge Co.*, 18 Howard (U. S.) Rep., 518.

national constitutions to the legislative, executive, and judicial departments of the governments they establish, are described in general words. Our State constitutions vest the legislative or law-making power in a legislature, the executive power in a governor, and the judicial power in courts, without specifying the laws the legislatures shall make or describing the executive power the governors shall exercise, or naming the kinds of cases the courts shall judge. The Constitution of the United States vests the legislative power in the Congress and describes in general words the classes or kinds of laws it may make; confers the executive power upon the President, and prescribes in general words the duties he is to perform; and gives the judicial power to the Supreme Court of the United States and inferior courts established by the Congress, and describes in general words the cases and controversies to which that power shall extend. Inasmuch as general words may always be understood in more than one way and sometimes in many ways, questions concerning the nature and extent of the powers of each of their branches have arisen from time to time, and probably will continue to arise.

Distinction Between Political and Judicial Powers.

The powers given to the three departments are radically different, those of the legislative and executive departments being powers to deal with rights which appertain to independence and sovereignty, while those of the judicial department are powers to deal with the rights of individuals. Our States maintain their rights of independent local self-government by means of legislative and executive officers and regulate the rights of individuals by means of courts and judges.

In like manner, the United States maintains its independence and sovereignty by means of the national legislature and President, and vindicates the rights of individuals by means of the Federal courts. In each case, the legislative and executive departments exercise political powers and the judiciary exercise judicial powers.

The distinction between political and judicial powers was accurately described in the case of *Kelley v. State*,[1] decided in 1869 by the Supreme Court of Arkansas, in which Justice Gregg said:

As the acquisition of *territory*, the *formation* or *recognition* of *new States*, the raising of armies, levying and carrying on war, forming alliances, and making treaties of peace, and other kindred subjects, are confided solely to the political and executive departments of the Government, we hold that the judiciary, in determining an issue at law, have nothing to do with the question as to the political status of any state or country, further than to ascertain and follow the decisions of the political departments of their Government.

In the case of *Foster v. Neilson*,[2] decided in 1829 by the U. S. Supreme Court, which hinged upon the correct boundary line of the Louisiana Territory as established by the treaty by which that territory was purchased from France in 1803, Chief Justice Marshall said:

In a controversy between two nations concerning national boundary, it is scarcely possible that the courts of either should refuse to abide by the measures adopted by

[1] 25 Arkansas Rep., 392, 398.
[2] 2 Peters (U. S.) Rep., 253, 307.

its own government. There being no common tribunal to decide between them, each determines for itself on its own rights, and if they cannot adjust their differences peaceably, the right remains with the strongest. The judiciary is not that department of the government to which the assertion of its interests against foreign powers is confided; and its duty, commonly, is to decide upon individual rights according to those principles which the political departments of the nation have established.

Another decision describing this distinction was given in the case of *Georgia v. Stanton*,[1] decided in 1867 by the U. S. Supreme Court, in which the question was whether the judicial branch of the National Government could issue an injunction restraining Secretary of War E. M. Stanton from enforcing the Reconstruction Acts adopted by Congress after the Civil War by which the Southern States had been divided into military districts to be governed by military officers until loyal State governments could be legally established. In the opinion of a majority of the justices that the court had no power to interfere with the executive department of the government in the execution of political powers conferred by acts of Congress, Justice Nelson said:

It is claimed that the court has no jurisdiction either over the subject matter set forth in the bill or over the parties defendants. And, in support of the first ground, it is urged that the matters involved, and presented for adjudication, are political and not judicial, and, therefore, not the subject of judicial cognizance.

This distinction results from the organization of the government into three great departments, executive, legislative, and judicial, and from the assignment and limitation of the powers of each by the Constitution.

[1] 6 Wallace (U. S.) Rep., 50, 71.

The judicial power is vested in one supreme court, and in such inferior courts as Congress may ordain and establish; the political power of our government in the other two departments.

The distinction between judicial and political power is . . . generally acknowledged. . . .

The case bearing most directly on the one before us is *The Cherokee Nation v. The State of Georgia* (12 Peters U. S. Rep., 752). . . . Chief Justice Marshall, who delivered the opinion of the majority . . . observed . . . "The bill requires us to control the legislature of Georgia, and to restrain the exertion of its physical force. The propriety of such an interposition by the Court may be well questioned. It savors too much of the exercise of political power, to be within the province of the judicial department." . . .

In respect to the prayers of the bill. The first is, that the defendants may be enjoined against doing or permitting any act or thing, within or concerning the State, which is or may be directed, or required of them, by or under the two acts of Congress complained of; and the remaining four prayers are of the same character. . . .

That these matters . . . call for the judgment of the court upon political questions, and upon rights, not of persons or property, but of a political character, will hardly be denied. For the rights for the protection of which our authority is invoked, are the rights of sovereignty, of political jurisdiction, of government, of corporate existence as a State, with all its constitutional powers and privileges. . . . This court possesses no jurisdiction over the subject matter presented in the bill for relief.

The boundary lines between the political power of legislatures and the judicial power of courts have been established from time to time in decisions of cases in which the validity of statutes by which legislatures have attempted to exercise judicial powers has been challenged.

In the case of *Merrill v. Sherburne*,[1] decided in 1818 by the Superior Court of Judicature of New Hampshire, it was shown to the court that, in 1806, Nathaniel Ward had died leaving a will by which he gave all his property to Benjamin Merrill, who had had the will probated and had taken possession of the estate. In 1812, on the petition of the heirs at law of Ward, the Court of Probate affirmed its decree allowing the will. Ward's heirs then appealed to the Superior Court, which reversed the decree of the probate court, and Merrill then applied to the State Legislature, asking that it direct a new trial of the case. The legislature, in 1817, passed an act giving Merrill's administratrix (he having died meanwhile) the right to re-enter the case in the Superior Court and have it retried like an ordinary case of review or appeal. Ward's heirs thereupon moved to quash the proceedings on the ground that the act was unconstitutional. The court, in deciding the question thus raised, pointed out the distinction between the functions of the legislature and those of the courts. Justice Woodbury said:

Since the adoption of our constitution, courts of justice, as well as legislative bodies, have furnished some complaints, that their jurisdiction has been violated, when those complaints were not founded on sound principles or respectable precedents. . . . It must be admitted that Courts ought to decide, according "to the laws of the land," all cases, which are submitted to their examination. To do this, however, we must examine those laws. The constitution is one of them, and "is in fact, and must be regarded by

[1] 1 N. H. Rep., 199, 201, 203.

the judges as a fundamental law." It was created by the people, who in our republics, are "the supreme power," and, it being the expression of their will, their agents, as are all the branches of the governments, can perform no act which, if contrary to that will, should be deemed lawful. "To deny this, would be to affirm that the deputy is greater than his principal; that the servant is above his master; that the representatives of the people are superior to the people themselves; that men acting by virtue of power may do, not only what their powers do not authorize, but what they forbid." Their oaths of office too, prohibit, and the constitution itself, in express terms, prohibits the legislative from making "laws repugnant to or contrary to the constitution." "If then there should happen to be an irreconcileable variance between the constitution and a statute, that which has the superior obligation and validity ought of course to be preferred"; in other words, "the intention of the people ought to be preferred to the intention of their agents." "Nor does this conclusion by any means suppose a superiority of the judicial to the legislative power. It only supposes, that the power of the people is superior to both; and that where the will of the legislature, declared in its statutes, stands in opposition to that of the people, declared in the constitution, the judges ought to be governed by the latter, rather than by the former. They ought to regulate their decision by the fundamental laws, rather than by those, which are not fundamental." [Cases cited]. . . . It becomes proper to examine [the act].

First, whether the passage of it was not an exercise of judicial powers. . . .

No particular definition of judicial powers is given in the constitution; and considering the general nature of the instrument, none was to be expected. . . . But "powers judicial," "judicial powers," and "judicatories" are all phrases used in the constitution; and though not particularly defined, are still so used to designate with clearness, that department of government, which it was intended should interpret and administer the laws. On general principles therefore, those enquiries, deliberations, orders and decrees, which are peculiar to such a department, must in their nature be judicial acts. Nor can they be both judicial and legislative; because a marked difference exists between the employments of judicial and legislative tribunals. The former decide upon the legality of claims and conduct; the latter make rules, upon which, in connection with the constitution, those decisions should be founded. It is the province of judges to determine what is the law upon existing cases. In fine, the law is *applied* by the one and *made* by the other.

In the *Sinking Fund Cases*,[1] decided in 1878 by the U. S. Supreme Court, Justice Field in a dissenting opinion said:

The distinction between a judicial and a legislative act is well defined. The one determines what the law is, and what the rights of parties are, with reference to transactions already had; the other prescribes what the law shall be in future cases arising under it. Wherever an act undertakes to determine a question of right or obligation, or of property, as the foundation upon which it proceeds, such act is to that extent a judicial one, and not the proper exercise of legislative functions. Thus an act of the legislature of Illinois authorizing the sale of the land of an intestate, to raise a specific sum, to pay certain parties their claims against the estate of the deceased for moneys advanced and liabilities incurred, was held unconstitutional, on the ground that it involved a judicial determination that the estate was indebted to those parties for the money advanced and liabilities incurred. The ascertainment of indebtedness from one party to another, and a direction for its payment, the court considered to be judicial acts which

[1] 99 U. S. Rep., 700, 761.

could not be performed by the legislature. 3 *Scam.* 238. So also an act of the legislature of Tennessee authorizing a guardian of infant heirs to sell certain lands of which their ancestor died seized, and directing the proceeds to be applied to the payment of the ancestor's debts, was, on similar grounds, held to be unconstitutional, *Jones v. Perry,* 10 Yerg. (Tenn.), 59.

This assignment of governmental powers to three distinct departments does not so operate as to establish an equilibrium of authority between them. On the contrary, there has never been a time since our government had its beginnings when one of the branches has not exercised greater power than the others. President Washington, with the aid of Hamilton who was his Secretary of the Treasury, was able to establish our industrial, commercial, and financial systems on lines that were unsatisfactory to the majority in the First Congress which met after the Constitution had been adopted. President Jackson defeated the efforts of the Bank of the United States to obtain a renewal of its charter though the Congress was uniformly on the other side and the Supreme Court, so far as its power went, stood by the Bank. President Lincoln was able to enforce a suspension of the writ of habeas corpus without an act of Congress during the first part of the Civil War, though the Supreme Court, in the person of its chief justice, declared that he had no authority to do so. Throughout that great struggle, he enforced an act of Congress that suspended the same right, not only in the States where military operations were going on, but also in the States that had not taken up arms against the nation. After the war had ended, the Supreme Court ruled that the suspension of the writ in States where the authority of the courts of the United

States was not obstructed could not be authorized even by an act of Congress.[1]   President Roosevelt was the dominant force in our government so long as he was in the White House.

Other considerations have at different times given more power to one of the branches of the National Government than to the other two.   During the first period of our national history, security of property in the form of negro slaves was the dominant issue.   The advocates of the abolition of slavery were numerous in the Northern and Middle-western States.   The Southern States insisted upon guaranties for the safety of that institution.   All parties relied upon the courts, which then as always enforced the laws that safeguard rights of every kind as established by law.   Hence, until the result of the Civil War put an end to the slavery question, the Supreme Court of the United States was the most important department of the National Government.   During the period of industrial and commercial development that followed the War between the States, the business men of the nation looked to Congress for the enactment of legislation that might help forward the development of the material resources of the United States.   From that source only could they obtain laws that would promote the construction of trans-continental railroads, laws that would protect by tariffs the struggling industries, and laws that would regulate commerce among the States. In satisfying these needs, the Congress naturally assumed a leadership that it never before had attained. During the last years of the nineteenth century and the first decade of the twentieth, it became increasingly evident that trusts, monopolies, combinations, and

[1] Ex parte Milligan, 4 Wallace (U. S.) Rep., 2.

contracts in restraint of trade and commerce had grown to such proportions that the curb rather than the spur was needed.   In that emergency, the people looked for help, not to Congress, which was too large a body to be easily accessible, nor to the courts which act only upon disputes brought before them for judgment, but to the President, in whom they saw a power of immediate action that could grapple with the problem.   It is not too much to say that since the beginning of this century, the executive branch of our National Government has, with the consent of the people, been much more powerful than the other departments.

This predominance of power in one or another department of the government does not show that our governmental system is defective.   On the contrary, it shows that as now organized, it responds almost automatically to the force of public opinion.   At the present moment, our people believe that the President can direct the destinies of the nation better than either the Congress or the courts.   If at any time in the future, the people believe that constructive legislation is needed more than executive direction, it is quite certain that the center of political power will be transferred to the Congress. Again, if stabilization becomes more necessary than either executive direction or legislative modification of social and economic conditions, it is quite as certain that the judicial department will take over the leadership.   Thus our national plan of assigning to three departments of the government the three functions of governmental regulation is a means of giving to the people a greater measure of control over their public business.

The nature and effect of this three-fold distribution of governmental powers have been discussed at length by the Courts. In the case of *Crane v. Meginnis,*[1] decided in 1829 by the Court of Appeals of Maryland, Justice Earle said:

The enactment of the third section of the act of 1823 [granting.a divorce], being in our opinion an exercise by the legislature of judicial power, our attention will now be engaged . . . with the enquiry, whether the exercise by the legislature of judicial power in the passage of the law, is repugnant to the constitution. The decision of this point must depend upon .the sound construction of the *sixth section* of the bill of rights [of the Maryland Constitution], which says, "that the legislative, executive, and judicial powers of government, ought to be forever separate and distinct from each other." This political maxim made its appearance, in some form, in all the state constitutions formed about the time of the war of the revolution, and is said to have been borrowed by them of the celebrated *Montesquieu's Spirit of Laws*, vol. 1, p. 181 . . . upon a full consideration of each of them, it seems to us to have been the intent to ingraft this invaluable maxim of political science on their respective systems, only as far as comported with free government, and to prohibit the exercise by one department of the powers of another department, or to confine each department to the exclusive exercise of its own powers. This last is admirably expressed in the Constitution of *Massachusetts*, and evinces a perfect acquaintance of its framers with the pages and doctrines of Baron Montesquieu. It is worded thus: "That the legislative department shall never exercise the executive and judicial powers, or either of them; the executive shall never exercise the legislative and judicial powers, or either of them; the judicial shall never exercise the legislative and executive powers or either of them." The inhibition goes to the *practical* exercise of powers conferred by the con-

[1] 1 Gill and Johnson (Md.) Rep.. 463, 475.

stitution, and to be used after it is in operation, and does not apply singly to the original distribution of powers among the departments of the government. In the same sense we construe the *sixth* article of our bill of rights, which has the same objects in view with the Constitution of *Massachusetts*, although somewhat different terms are used to express them. The one imitates the language, and the other dives into and expresses the meaning of the venerated author from which they both copied. Their common purpose is to confine in practice, the action of each department to its own appropriate sphere, by forbidding to it the use of powers allotted to the co-ordinate departments.

In the case of *Kilbourn v. Thompson,*[1] decided in 1880 by the U. S. Supreme Court, Justice Miller said:

It is believed to be one of the chief merits of the American system of written constitutional law, that all the powers entrusted to government, whether State or national, are divided into three grand departments, the executive, the legislative, and the judicial. That the functions appropriate to each of these branches of government shall be vested in a separate body of public servants, and that the perfection of the system requires that the lines which separate and divide these departments shall be broadly and clearly defined. It is also essential to the successful working of this system that the persons entrusted with power in any one of these branches shall not be permitted to encroach upon the powers confided to the others, but that each shall by the law of its creation be limited to the powers appropriate to its own department and to no other. . . . That instrument [the Constitution], the model on which are constructed the fundamental laws of the States, has blocked out with singular precision, and in bold lines, in its three primary articles, the allotment of power to the executive,

[1] 103 U. S. Rep., 168, 190.

the legislative, and the judicial departments of the government. It also remains true, as a general rule, that the powers confided by the Constitution to one of these departments cannot be exercised by another.

CHAPTER VI

Permanence of Constitutional Guaranties.

The constitutions of the States and the Constitution of the United States contain provisions that no person shall be deprived of life, liberty, or property without due process of law.[1] The Constitution of the United States provides that no State shall pass any law impairing the obligation of contracts[2] or any law which shall abridge the privileges or immunities of citizens of the United States[3] and declares that no State shall deprive any person of life, liberty, or property without due process of law or deny to any person within its jurisdiction the equal protection of the laws.[4]

These provisions in the form of limitations upon the powers of the State legislatures and of the Congress of the United States, guarantee the rights of liberty and property of citizens of the United States. Although social and economic conditions have changed with the growth of the nation, these guaranties mean now what they meant when they were made. The constitutional grants of legislative power and the provisions of con-

---

[1] Bills of Rights of State Constitutions; U. S. Const. Amendment V.
[2] Art. I., Sec. 10.
[3] U. S. Const. Art. I., Sec. 10., Amendment XIV.
[4] U. S. Const. Amendment XIV.

stitutional guaranties of rights are made in general terms which cover all new social conditions that come within their scope. They apply from generation to generation to all things to which they are in their nature applicable.[1] The makers of the constitutions intended to provide for the welfare of the people, not only under existing social and economic conditions but under any new conditions that might afterward arise. Consequently, the courts, in determining cases under statutes dealing with new social conditions, have ruled that the constitutional guaranties of liberty and property are not limited to rights of liberty and property under social conditions, existing when the constitutions were made, but extend to such rights existing under subsequent social conditions.

The United States was at first a farming nation in which every farm was an industrial center. The farmer with his sons or relatives tilled the soil, made farming tools in his blacksmith shop, made his meal and flour, and carried on a number of other trades. The farmer's wife and daughters wove cloth with yarn spun by themselves from wool clipped from his sheep. The only things he had to buy were sugar, molasses, and salt. Living healthy outdoor lives, working in a leisurely way except when planting and harvesting, the farmer asked from the State governments nothing more than protection from violence and robbery, and justice in the determination of his rights.

Mining and manufacturing, then and for many years afterward, were carried on in such a small way that no special State laws for the protection of miners and factory operatives were needed.

[1] See opinion of Justice Brewer in *So. Carolina v. United States*, 199 U. S. Rep., 437.

Commerce among the States consisted largely of the interchange of articles that had been imported from other countries for distribution and sale. Importers doing business in one State could sell on credit to persons living in other States so long as they could be sure that no State could pass any law that would affect the legal obligation to pay debts. Until the abolition of slavery and the enfranchisement of the negroes at the end of the Civil War, there was no need of any constitutional provision to prevent the States from violating the rights of citizens of the United States or denying to any person the equal protection of the laws.

During the first part of the nineteenth century, some of the States, in order to safeguard public health, began to regulate burials in city cemeteries by means of laws that limited the property rights of owners of plots. After the introduction of railroads and steamboats, the States, in order to protect the rights of passengers and shippers, enacted new laws that deprived those common carriers of a part of their property right to manage their business as they saw fit. When the growth of manufacturing caused an influx of working people who lived in unsanitary tenements that were a menace to public health, some of the States enacted sanitary laws that affected the property rights of the owners of tenement houses. The employment of women and children in industry led to the enactment of State health laws regulating the sanitary conditions of factories, prohibiting the employment of children of school age, and limiting the hours of labor of women and children workers. These laws affected the right of the factory owners to manage their business as they saw fit, denied to women citizens the right to earn their living by certain kinds of work, and limited the right of parents to the earnings of their children. Many of the States limited the hours of labor in mines by laws that impaired the property rights of mine owners and of mine workers alike. In course of time, the States and the United States regulated the rates to be charged and the service to be rendered by railroad and other public service corporations by laws that deprived the owners of their property right to carry on their business in their own way. The States and United States enacted quarantine laws; laws declaring unlawful contracts in restraint of trade and commerce and suppressing monopolies; pure food and drug laws; white slave laws; and many other laws that affected constitutional guaranties.

Application of Constitutional Guaranties.

In deciding cases in which the validity of State statutes to protect public health, to promote public morality, and to regulate commerce has been challenged on the ground that in their operation, they either deprived persons of their property without due process of law or impaired the obligation of contracts or abridged the privileges or immunities of citizens of the United States or denied to persons the equal protection of the laws, the courts have ruled uniformly that, under their *police power*,[1] the State governments have always had the power to provide for public health and public morality, and, under their *commerce power*, have had power to regulate trade and industry within their borders. The courts also in determining the validity

---

[1] The police power is so called because it originated in cities which in old times were the only communities that needed health and morality regulations. The Greek word for city—πολις— was applied to all city laws, which were called police laws. It is now used for similar laws of the larger communities.

of such State statutes have constantly declared that the constitutional guaranties of liberty and property are to be construed in the light of the social and economic conditions which existed when the statutes were made, not in the light of such conditions existing when the constitutions were made. In like manner, the courts in dealing with acts of Congress for the regulation of commerce among the States and with foreign countries have held that the United States has power to regulate such commerce in all ways that are not forbidden by the Constitution of the United States, and that the guaranties of liberty and property contained in that instrument and in the amendments, so far as they affect the validity of such acts of Congress, are to be construed in the light of the social and economic conditions that existed when the acts were passed, not in the light of such conditions existing when the guaranties were made.

The courts, in determining the applicability of constitutional guaranties to statutes, have constantly ruled that, as those guaranties are intended to promote the welfare of society, statutes made to promote social welfare under new social conditions are not invalid, although under previous social conditions such statutes would have been repugnant to those guaranties. The courts in applying the constitutional guaranties follow one principle so long as that principle is reasonable. When new social conditions have called for different statutory enactments and the former principle is no longer reasonable, they apply new principles so that the aims and purposes of the constitutional guaranties may not be defeated.

Many good authorities hold that in thus disregarding rules of laws that have ceased to be reasonable and in making new rules to give effect to the objects of con-

stitutional guaranties, the courts have legislated.[1]
Other jurists believe that such rulings show, instead of a
close adherence by the courts to the words of constitutional provisions, a distinct movement on the part
of the courts toward a recognition of the effect in practice of constitutional provisions, in place of a close
adherence to their terms.[2] The courts generally regard
their new constructions of such guaranties as judicial
acts done in the strict performance of the judicial duty
to construe and interpret general constitutional
provisions so as to effect the great object for which
they were made—the welfare of society.

[1] "I recognize without hesitation that judges must and do legislate,
but they can do so only interstitially; they are confined from molar to
molecular motions." Justice Holmes in *So. Pacific Co. v. Jensen*, 244
U. S. Rep. 205.

[2] "Perhaps the most significant advance in the modern science of law
is the change from the analytical to the functional attitude. . . . The
emphasis has changed from the content of the precept and the existence
of the remedy to the effect of the precept in action and the availability
and efficiency of the remedy to attain the end for which the precept
was devised." Pound *Administrative Application of Legal Standards.*
Proceedings of American Bar Association, 1919, pp. 441, 449.

CHAPTER VII

Validity of Welfare Legislation.

In the case of *Holden v. Hardy*,[1] decided in 1898, in which the U. S. Supreme Court sustained the constitutionality of an act of the Utah legislature making eight hours a working day in underground mines. Justice Brown explained as follows the origin and nature of the police powers of the States.[2]

While the people of each State may . . . adopt such systems of laws as best conform to their own traditions and customs, the people of the entire country have laid down in the Constitution of the United States certain fundamental principles to which each member of the Union is bound to accede as a condition of its admission as a State. Thus, the United States are bound to guarantee to each State a republican form of government, and the tenth section of the first article contains certain other specified limitations upon the power of the several States, the object of which was to secure to Congress paramount authority with respect to matters of universal concern. In addition, the Fourteenth Amendment contains a sweeping provision forbidding the States from abridging the privileges and immunities of citizens of the United States, and denying them the benefit of due process or the equal protection of the laws.

This court has never attempted to define with precision

[1] 169 U. S. Rep., 366, 395.

[2] Justices Brewer and Peckham dissented.

the words "due process of law," nor is it necessary to do so in this case. It is sufficient to say that there are certain immutable principles of justice which inhere in the very idea of free government which no member of the Union may disregard, as that no man may be condemned in his person or property without due notice and an opportunity of being heard in his defence. . . .

The right of contract, however, is itself subject to certain limitations which the State may lawfully impose in the exercise of its police powers. While this power is inherent in all governments, it has doubtless been greatly expanded during the past century, owing to an enormous increase in the number of occupations which are dangerous, or so far detrimental to the health of employees as to demand special precautions for their well-being and protection, or the safety of adjoining property.

While this power is necessarily inherent in every form of government, it was, prior to the adoption of the Constitution, sparingly used in this country. As we were then almost purely an agricultural people, the occasion for any special protection of a particular class did not exist. Certain profitable employments such as lotteries and the sale of intoxicating liquors, which were then considered to be legitimate, have since fallen under the ban of public opinion, and are now either altogether prohibited, or made subject to stringent police regulations. The power to do this has been repeatedly affirmed by this court [cases cited].

While the business of mining coal and manufacturing iron began in Pennsylvania as early as 1716, and in Virginia, North Carolina, and Massachusetts even earlier than this, both mining and manufacturing were carried on in such a limited way and by such primitive methods that no special laws were considered necessary, prior to the adoption of the Constitution, for the protection of the operatives; but in the vast proportions which these industries have since assumed, it has been found that they can no longer be carried on with due regard to the safety and health of those engaged in them, without special protection against the dangers necessarily incident to these employments. In consequence of this, laws have been enacted in most of the States designed to meet these exigencies and to secure the safety of persons peculiarly exposed to these dangers. Within this general category are ordinances providing for fire escapes for hotels, theatres, factories, and other large buildings, a municipal inspection of boilers, and appliances designed to secure passengers upon railways and steamboats against the dangers necessarily incident to these methods of transportation. In States where manufacturing is carried on to a large extent, provision is made for the protection of dangerous machinery against accidental contact, for the cleanliness and ventilation of working rooms, for the guarding of well holes, stairways, elevator shafts, and for the employment of sanitary appliances. In others, in which mining is the principal industry, special provision is made for the shoring up of dangerous walls, for ventilation shafts, bore holes, escapement shafts, means of signalling the surface, for the supply of fresh air and the elimination, as far as possible, of dangerous gases, for safe means of hoisting and lowering cages. . . .

These statutes have been repeatedly enforced by the Courts of the several States, their validity assumed, and, so far as we are informed, they have been uniformly held to be constitutional. . . .

If it be within the power of a legislature to adopt such means for the protection of the lives of its citizens, it is difficult to see why precautions may not also be adopted for the protection of their health and morals. . . . With this end in view, quarantine laws have been enacted in most if not all of the States. . . . In other States, laws have been enacted limiting the hours during which women and children shall be employed in factories; and while their constitutionality, at least as applied to women, has been doubted in some of the States, they have been generally upheld. . . .

Upon the principles above stated, we think the act in question may be sustained as a valid exercise of the police power of the State. The enactment does not profess to limit the hours of all workmen, but merely those who are employed in underground mines, or in the smelting, reduction or refining of ores or metals. These employments, when too long pursued, the legislature has judged to be detrimental to the health of the employes, and, so long as there are reasonable grounds for believing that this is so, its decision upon this subject cannot be reviewed by the Federal Courts.

Sanitary Legislation.

One of the first cases in which the police power of a State was made the basis of a judicial decision is *Coates v. Mayor and Aldermen of New York City*[1] decided in 1827, by the New York Courts, in which the question was upon the validity of a city ordinance[2] prohibiting burials of the bodies of deceased persons in congested parts of the city of New York. An action to recover the penalty of $250 prescribed by the ordinance had been brought against Mr. Coates, the Sexton of Trinity Church, who had buried a body in the churchyard. His defence was that he had acted under the orders of the rector and other officers of the church who had a legal right to inter bodies in this churchyard and to receive fees and perquisites for so doing. Mr. Coates claimed that this right was a contract, the obligation of which could not, under the Constitution of the United States, be impaired by the State of New York. In the decision that the city ordinance was a valid police law, the Court said:

[1] 7 Cowen (N. Y.) Rep., 585, 604.

[2] A city ordinance is a State law applying to a city, made by the city government under legislative power delegated by the State government.

It was conceded, on the argument, that the corporation [City of New York] have, in general, power so to order the use of private property in the city, as to prevent its proving pernicious to the citizens generally. A contrary doctrine would strike at the root of all police regulations. . . . A lot is granted as a place of deposit for gunpowder, or other purpose, innocent, in itself, at the time; it is devoted to that purpose, till, in the progress of population, it becomes dangerous to the property, the safety, or the lives of hundreds; it cannot be, that the mere form of the grant, because the parties choose to make it particular, instead of general and absolute [that is, saying that it is to be used for a certain purpose, instead of saying nothing about what it is to be used for], should prevent the use to which it is limited being regarded and treated as a nuisance, when it becomes so in fact. . . . Every right, from an absolute ownership in property, down to a mere easement [right to use property for some purpose such as a pathway], is purchased and holden subject to the restriction, that it shall be so exercised as not to injure others. . . . No property has, in this instance, been entered upon or taken. None are benefited by the destruction, or rather the suspension of the rights in question, in any other way than citizens always are, when one of their number is forbidden to continue a nuisance. For the same reason, there is nothing impairing the obligation of a contract within the sense of the Constitution of the United States.

In the *Slaughter House Cases*,[1] decided in 1872, the U. S. Supreme Court held constitutional as an exercise of the police power by the State of Louisiana a statute that gave to a corporation for twenty-five years the right to maintain and carry on slaughter houses, landings for cattle, and cattle yards in the city of New Orleans. It was contended that the law creating this monopoly

[1] 16 Wallace U. S. Rep., 35.

was void under the provisions of the Fourteenth Amendment of the Constitution of the United States which provides that no State shall pass any law abridging the privileges and immunities of citizens of the United States. It is undoubtedly true that when the Constitution of the United States was adopted and the first ten amendments declaring the rights of citizens of the United States were added to that instrument, there were no restrictions upon the right to carry on the slaughtering trade anywhere. But in the passage of the years, New Orleans had become a great city in which such an occupation could not be carried on without annoyance and injury to the health of the people. For this reason, the court sustained the power of the State in this particular in a decision in which Justice Miller said:

The power here exercised by the legislature of Louisiana is, in its essential nature, one which has been, up to the present period in the constitutional history of this country, always conceded to belong to the States, however it may now be questioned in some of its details. "Unwholesome trades, slaughter-houses, operations offensive to the senses, the deposit of powder, the application of steam power to propel cars, the building with combustible materials, and the burial of the dead, may all," says Chancellor Kent (2 *Commentaries*, 340), "be interdicted by law, in the midst of dense masses of population, on the general and rational principle, that every person ought so to use his property as not to injure his neighbors; and that private interests must be made sub-servient to the general interests of the community." . . . The power is, and must be from its very nature, incapable of any very exact definition or limitation. Upon it depends the security of social order, the life and health of the citizen, the comfort of an existence in a thickly populated community, the enjoyment of private and social life, and the beneficial use of property.

In the case of *Fertilizing Co. v. Hyde Park*,[1] decided in 1878, the U. S. Supreme Court sustained as an exercise of the police power, an Illinois statute which prohibited the manufacture of fertilizers in densely populated localities. Justice Swayne said:

That a nuisance of a flagrant character existed . . . is not controverted. We cannot doubt that the police power of the State was applicable and adequate to give an effectual remedy. That power belonged to the States when the Federal Constitution was adopted. They did not surrender it, and they all have it now. It extends to the entire property and business within their local jurisdiction. Both are subject to it in all proper cases. It rests upon the fundamental principle that every one shall so use his own as not to wrong and injure another. To regulate and abate nuisances is one of its ordinary functions. . . .

The charter [of the Fertilizing Company] was a sufficient license until revoked; but we cannot regard it as a contract, guaranteeing, in the locality originally selected, exemption for fifty years from the exercise of the police power of the State, however serious the nuisance might become in the future, by reason of the growth of population around it. The owners had no such exemption when they were incorporated, and we think the charter did not give it to them.

The Supreme Court of the United States in the case of *Barbier v. Connolly*,[2] decided in 1885, interpreted the clause of the 14th Amendment of the U. S. Constitution that "No State . . . shall deny to any person within

[1] 97 U. S. Rep., 659.   [2] 113 U. S. Rep., 27.

its jurisdiction the equal protection of the laws" to mean that a State policing statute that applies equally to all persons affected by it does not deny to any of such persons the equal protection of the laws. On April 8, 1884, the city of San Francisco, California, enacted a municipal ordinance, making it unlawful to carry on a laundry business in certain parts of the city without first obtaining one certificate from the city health officer that the sanitary arrangements of the laundry were good, and another from the Board of Fire Wardens that the stoves and appliances for heating smoothing irons were so managed as not to be a source of danger from fire to surrounding property. A Mr. Barbier, who had a laundry within the city limits, was sentenced to imprisonment for five days for violation of this ordinance. He petitioned the United States court for release on the ground that his constitutional right to the equal protection of the laws had been violated and afterward appealed to the U. S. Supreme Court. Justice Field, in giving the opinion of the Supreme Court, said that Mr. Barbier had no just cause for complaint because he had received the same protection of the laws as all the other laundrymen of San Francisco, and, therefore, had been punished under a law which did not violate this clause of the Fourteenth Amendment. The decision is in part as follows:

Neither the [Fourteenth] amendment—broad and comprehensive as it is—nor any other amendment, was designed to interfere with the power of the State, sometimes termed its police power, to prescribe regulations to promote the health, peace, morals, education, and good order of the people, and to legislate so as to increase the industries of the State, develop its resources, and add to its wealth and prosperity. Regulations for these purposes may press

with more or less weight upon one than upon another, but
they are designed, not to impose unequal or unnecessary
restrictions upon any one, but to promote, with as little
individual inconvenience as possible, the general good.
Though, in many respects, necessarily special in their
character, they do not furnish just ground for complaint,
if they operate alike upon all persons and property under the
same circumstances and conditions. Class legislation, discriminating against some and favoring others, is prohibited,
but legislation which, in carrying out a public purpose, is
limited in its application, if within the sphere of its operation it affects alike all persons similarly situated, is not within the amendment.

Prohibition Laws.

The police power of the States was invoked in the
case of *Mugler v. Kansas*,[1] decided in 1887, in which the
U. S. Supreme Court held constitutional a Kansas statute prohibiting the manufacture and sale of intoxicating
liquors. In the opinion of the Court, Justice Harlan
said:

It is contended [by the brewers] that as the primary and
principal use of beer is as a beverage; as their respective
breweries were erected when it was lawful to engage in the
manufacture of beer for every purpose; as such establishments will become of no value as property, or, at least,
will be materially diminished in value, if not employed in
the manufacture of beer for every purpose; the prohibition
upon their being so employed is, in effect, a taking of property for public use without compensation, and depriving
the citizen of his property without due process of law. In
other words, although the State, in the exercise of her
police powers, may lawfully prohibit the manufacture and
sale, within her limits, of intoxicating liquors to be used as

[1] 123 U. S. Rep., 623, 664. Justice Field dissented.

a beverage, legislation having that object in view cannot be enforced against those who, at the time, happen to own property, the chief value of which consists of its fitness for such manufacturing purposes, unless compensation is first made for the diminution in the value of their property, resulting from such prohibitory amendments. . . .

It is difficult to perceive any ground for the judiciary to declare that the prohibition by Kansas of the manufacture or sale, within her limits, of intoxicating liquors for general use there as a beverage, is not fairly adapted to the end of protecting the community against the evils which confessedly result from the excessive use of ardent spirits. There is no justification for holding that the State, under the guise merely of police regulations, is here aiming to deprive the citizen of his constitutional rights; for we cannot shut out of view the fact, within the knowledge of all, that the public health, the public morals, and the public safety, may be endangered by the general use of intoxicating drinks; nor the fact established by statistics accessible to every one that the idleness, disorder, pauperism, and crime existing in the country are, in some degree at least, traceable to this evil. If, therefore, a State deems the absolute prohibition of the manufacture and sale, within her limits, of intoxicating liquors, for other than medical, scientific, and manufacturing purposes, to be necessary to the peace and security of society, the courts cannot, without usurping legislative functions, override the will of the people as thus expressed by their chosen representatives. . . .

The conclusion is unavoidable, unless the Fourteenth Amendment of the Constitution takes from the States of the Union those powers of policing that were reserved at the time the original Constitution was adopted. But this Court has declared upon full consideration, in the case of *Barbier v. Connolly*, 113 U. S. 27, 31, that the Fourteenth Amendment had no such effect.[1]

[1] See *ante*, p. 79.

CONSTITUTIONAL LAW 83

Labor Laws.

In the case of *Lochner v. New York*,[1] decided in 1905, in which the U. S. Supreme Court declared unconstitutional as to male employees a State law regulating hours of labor in bakeries, Justice Holmes filed a dissenting opinion in which he laid down rules of law that have since been followed by that court in many decisions upon similar State policing laws. He said:

This case is decided on an economic theory which a large part of the country does not entertain. . . . It is settled by various decisions of this court that State constitutions and State laws may regulate life, in many ways which we as legislators might think as injudicious or if you like as tyrannical as this, and which equally interfere with the liberty of contract. Sunday laws and usury laws are ancient examples. A more modern one is the prohibition of lotteries. The liberty of the citizen to do as he likes so long as he does not interfere with the liberty of others to do the same, which has been a shibboleth for some well-known writers, is interfered with by school laws, by the Post Office, by every state or municipal institution which takes his money for purposes thought desirable, whether he likes it or not. The Fourteenth Amendment does not enact Mr. Herbert Spencer's *Social Statics*. The other day we sustained the Massachusetts vaccination law, *Jacobson v. Massachusetts*, 197 U. S. 11. United States and state statutes and decisions cutting down the liberty to contract by way of combination are familiar to this court. *Northern Securities Co. v. United States*, 193 U. S. 197. Two years ago we upheld the prohibition of sales of stock on margins or for future delivery in the constitution of California. *Otis v. Parker*, 187 U. S. 606. The decision sustaining an eight hour law for miners is still recent, *Holden v. Hardy*, 169 U. S. 366. Some of these laws embody convictions or

[1] 198 U. S. Rep., 49, 74.

prejudices which judges are likely to share. Some may not. But a constitution is not intended to embody a particular economic theory, whether of paternalism and the organic relation of the citizen to the State, or of *laissez faire*. It is made for people of fundamentally differing views, and the accident of our finding certain opinions natural and familiar, or novel and even shocking, ought not to conclude our judgment upon the question whether statutes embodying them conflict with the Constitution of the United States. . . .

Every opinion tends to become a law. I think the word liberty in the Fourteenth Amendment is perverted when it is held to prevent the natural outcome of a dominant opinion, unless it can be said that a rational and fair man necessarily would admit that the statute proposed would infringe fundamental principles as they have been understood by the traditions of our people and our law. It does not need research to show that no such sweeping condemnation can be passed upon the statute before us. A reasonable man might think it a proper measure on the score of health. Men whom I certainly could not pronounce unreasonable would uphold it as a first instalment of a general regulation of the hours of work.

In the case of *People v. Charles Schweinler Press*,[1] decided in 1915, the New York Court of Appeals held constitutional a State statute which provided that no woman should be employed or allowed to work in any factory in the State before six o'clock in the morning and after ten o'clock at night. The same court in the case of *People v. Williams*,[2] decided in 1907, had ruled that a similar law was void because it deprived women of their property right in their own labor. In this second case, the court decided that the protection of the

[1] 214 N. Y. Rep., 395, 410.   [2] 189 N. Y. Rep., 131.

health and morals of women working in factories was a part of the police power of the State. Judge Hiscock said:

The statute under consideration in the *Williams* case, like the present one, prohibited night work by women in factories, and while its provisions were somewhat more drastic than those of the present one, it may be conceded that these differences were of details and would not serve to distinguish that statute from the present one in respect of its constitutionality. But the facts on which the former statute might rest as a health regulation and the arguments made to us in behalf of its constitutionality were far different than those in the present case.

That statute bore on its face no clear evidence that it was passed for the purpose of protecting the health and welfare of women working in factories, and while of course the presence or absence of such a label would not be controlling in determining the purposes and validity of the statute, it still was in that case an incident of some importance as leading to the conclusions finally expressed by Judge Gray and adopted by the court. . . .

While theoretically we may have been able to take judicial notice of some of the facts and of some of the legislation now called to our attention as sustaining the belief and opinion that night work in factories is widely and substantially injurious to the health of women, actually very few of these facts were called to our attention, and the argument to uphold the law on that ground was brief and inconsequential.

Especially and necessarily was there lacking evidence of the extent to which during the intervening years the opinion and belief have spread and strengthened that such night work is injurious to women; of the laws as indicating such belief, since adopted by several of our own states and by large European countries, and the report made to the legislature by its own agency, the factory investigating commission, based on investigation of actual conditions and study of scientific and medical opinion that night work by women in factories is generally injurious and ought to be prohibited. . . .

So, as it seems to me, in view of the incomplete manner in which the important question underlying this statute—the danger to women of night work in factories—was presented to us in the *Williams* case, we ought not to regard its decision as any bar to a consideration of the present statute in the light of all the facts and arguments now presented to us and many of which are in addition to those formerly presented, not only as a matter of mere presentation, but because they have been developed by study and investigation during the years which have intervened since the *Williams* decision was made. There is no reason why we should be reluctant to give effect to new and additional knowledge upon such a subject as this even if it did lead us to take a different view of such a vastly important question as that of public health or disease than formerly prevailed. Particularly do I feel that we should give serious consideration and great weight to the fact that the present legislation is based upon and sustained by an investigation by the legislature deliberately and carefully made through an agency of its own creation, the present factory investigating commission.

In the case of *Muller v. Oregon*,[1] decided in 1908 by the U. S. Supreme Court, the question was upon the constitutionality of a State law providing that "no female shall be employed in any mechanical establishment or factory or laundry, . . . more than ten hours during any one day." The plaintiff in error (Muller) had been convicted and sentenced in the trial court for violation of the act and had appealed to the Supreme

[1] 208 U. S. Rep., 412.

Court of the State which also had decided against him. He then took the case to the Supreme Court of the United States upon the ground that his rights of contract as an employer and those of his employees had been violated by the act, thus in effect relying upon the ruling of the court in the *Lochner Case*.[1] The highest court sustained the validity of the law upon the ground that woman's physical structure and the performance of maternal functions place her at a disadvantage which justifies the exercise of the police power for the protection of public health. In the decision of the court, Justice Brewer said:

We held in *Lochner v. New York*, 198 U. S. 45, that a law providing that no laborer shall be required or permitted to work in a bakery more than sixty hours in a week or ten hours in a day was not as to men a legitimate exercise of the police power of the State, but an unreasonable, unnecessary and arbitrary interference with the right and liberty of the individual to contract in relation to his labor, and as such was in conflict with, and void under, the Federal Constitution.

That woman's physical structure and the performance of maternal functions place her at a disadvantage in the struggle for subsistence is obvious. This is especially true when the burdens of motherhood are upon her. Even when they are not, by abundant testimony of the medical fraternity, continuance for a long time on her feet at work, repeating this from day to day, tends to injurious effects upon the body, and as healthy mothers are essential to vigorous offspring, the physical well-being of woman becomes an object of public interest and care in order to preserve the strength and vigor of the race. . . .

Though limitations upon personal and contractual rights [of women] may be removed by legislation, there is

[1] See *ante*, p. 83.

that in her disposition and habits of life which will operate against a full assertion of those rights. She will still be where some legislation to protect her seems necessary to secure a real equality of right. Doubtless there are individual exceptions, and there are many respects in which she has an advantage over him; but looking at it from the viewpoint of the effort to maintain an independent position in life, she is not upon an equality [with man]. . . . It is impossible to close one's eyes to the fact that she still looks to her brother and depends upon him. Even though all restrictions in political, personal and contractual rights were taken away, and she stood, so far as statutes are concerned, upon an absolutely equal plane with him, it would still be true that she is so constituted that she will rest upon and look to him for protection; that her physical structure and a proper discharge of her maternal functions, . . . having in view not merely her own health, but the well-being of the race, . . . justify legislation to protect her from the greed as well as the passion of man. The limitations which this statute places upon her contractual powers, upon her right to agree with her employer as to the time she shall labor, are not imposed solely for her benefit, but also largely for the benefit of all. . . . The two sexes differ in structure of body, in the functions to be performed by each, in the amount of physical strength, in the capacity for long continued labor, particularly when done standing, the influence of vigorous health upon the future well-being of the race, the self-reliance which enables one to assert full rights, and in the capacity to maintain the struggle for subsistence. The difference justifies a difference in legislation and upholds that which is designed to compensate for some of the burdens which rest upon her. . . .

For these reasons, and without questioning in any respect the decision in *Lochner v. New York*, we are of the opinion that it cannot be adjudged that the act in question is in conflict with the Federal Constitution, so far as it respects the work of a female in a laundry.

In the case of *Bunting v. Oregon,*[1] decided in 1917, the U. S. Supreme Court ruled that a State law limiting to ten hours in any one day, the hours of labor of employees in factories was constitutional,[2] Justice McKenna said:

The consonance of the Oregon law with the Fourteenth Amendment [of the U. S. Constitution] is the question in the case, and this depends upon whether it is a proper exercise of the police power of the State, as the Supreme Court of the State decided that it is.

That the police power extends to health regulations is not denied, but it is denied that the law has such purpose or justification. It is contended that it is a wage law, not a health regulation, and takes the property of plaintiff in error without due process. The contention presents two questions: (1) Is the law a wage law, or an hours of service law? And (2) if the latter, has it equality of operation?

Section 1 of the law expresses the policy that impelled its enactment to be the interest of the State in the physical well-being of its citizens and that it is injurious to their health for them to work "in any mill, factory, or manufacturing establishment more than ten hours in any one day"; and Sec. 2 . . . forbids their employment in those places for a longer time. If, therefore, we take the law at its word, there can be no doubt of its purpose, and the Supreme Court of the State has added the confirmation of its decision, by declaring that "the aim of the statute is to fix the maximum hours of service in certain industries. The act makes no attempt to fix the standard of wages. No maximum or minimum wage is named. This is left wholly to the contracting parties." . . . We cannot know all the conditions that impelled the law or its particular form.

[1] 243 U. S. Rep., 426.
[2] The court was divided; five judges for affirming the Oregon courts, three dissenting, and one not taking part in the decision.

The Supreme Court, nearer to them, describes the law as follows: "It is clear that the intent of the law is to make 10 hours a regular day's labor in the occupations to which reference is made. Apparently the provisions for permitting labor for the overtime on express conditions were made in order to facilitate the enforcement of the law, and in the nature of a mild penalty for employing one not more than three hours overtime. It might be regarded as more difficult to detect violations of the law by an employment for a shorter time than for a longer time. The penalty also goes to the employee in case the employer avails himself of the overtime clause." . . .

It is enough for our decision if the legislation under review was passed in the exercise of an admitted power of government; and that it is not as complete as it might be, not as rigid in its prohibitions as it might be, gives perhaps evasion too much play, is lighter in its penalties than it might be, is no impeachment of its legality. . . . Our judgment is that it [the law] does not transcend constitutional limits.

In the case of *Stettler v. O'Hara*,[1] decided in 1914 by Supreme Court of Oregon, the question was upon the constitutionality of an Oregon statute enacted in 1913, making unlawful the employment of women and minors in the State of Oregon for unreasonably long hours, the employment of women for wages inadequate for the cost of living, and of minors for unreasonably low wages, and establishing an industrial welfare commission authorized to prescribe the hours of employment for women and children and the standards of wages for women workers declaring what wages are inadequate for the necessary cost of living, and the standards of minimum wages for minors in any occupation in the

[1] 69 Oregon Rep., 519, 534.

State. This suit was brought by one Stettler to vacate and annul an order of the commission fixing nine hours a day or fifty hours a week as maximum hours of service for women in the City of Portland and $8.64 as the minimum weekly wage for woman factory workers, "any lesser amount being declared inadequate to supply the necessary cost of living to such women factory workers, and to maintain them in health." Justice Eakin, delivering the opinion of the majority of the court sustaining the validity of the act, said:

"Common sense" and "common knowledge" are sufficient to make it palpable and beyond doubt that the employment of female labor as it has been conducted is highly detrimental to public morals and has a strong tendency to corrupt them. Elizabeth Beardsley Butler, in her "Women of the Trades," says:

"Yet the fact remains that, for the vast bulk of salesgirls, the wages paid are not sufficient for self-support, and, where girls do not have families to fall back on, some go undernourished, some sell themselves. And the store employment which offers them this two horned dilemma is replete with opportunities which in gradual, easy, attractive ways beckon to the second choice; a situation which a few employers not only seem to tolerate, but to encourage."

The legislature of the State of Massachusetts appointed a commission known as the Commission on Minimum Wage Boards to investigate conditions. In the report of that commission in January, 1912, it is said:

"Women in general are working because of dire necessity, and in most cases the combined income of the family is not more than adequate to meet the family's cost of living. In these cases it is not optional with the woman to decline low-paid employment. Every dollar added to the family income is needed to lighten the burden which the rest are carrying. . . . Wherever the wages of such a woman are less than the cost of living and the reasonable provision for maintaining the worker in health, the industry employing her is in receipt of the working energy of a human being at less than its cost, and to that extent is parasitic. The balance must be made up in some way. It is generally paid by the industry employing the father. It is sometimes paid in part by future inefficiency of the worker herself, and by her children, and perhaps in part ultimately by charity and the State. . . ."

Many more citations might be made from the same authorities and from such students of the question as Miss Caroline Gleason, of Portland, Oregon, Louise B. More, of New York, Irene Osgood, of Milwaukee, and Robert C. Chapin, of Beloit College. With this common belief, of which Mr. Justice Harlan says "we take judicial notice," the courts cannot say beyond all question that the act is a plain, palpable invasion of rights secured by the fundamental law, and has no real or substantial relation to the protection of public health, the public morals or public welfare. Every argument put forward to sustain the maximum hours of law, or upon which it was established, applies equally in favor of the constitutionality of the minimum wage law as also within the police power of the State and as a regulation tending to guard the public morals and the public health.[1]

The police power of a State, however, does not, according to the most recent decisions of the U. S. Supreme Court, extend to a law that will either compel an employer to continue a business in which minimum wage rates have been fixed, nor can it be used to prevent working people from combining together to obtain higher wages. In the case of *Wolff Packing Co. v. Court*

[1] This decision was affirmed without an opinion by the U. S. Supreme Court in 1917 by an equally divided court. *Stettler v. O'Hara*, 243 U. S. 629. Brandeis, J., took no part.

of Industrial Relations of Kansas,[1] decided June 11, 1923, the U. S. Supreme Court declared unconstitutional so much of the Industrial Relations Act of Kansas, passed in 1890, as declares that the manufacture and preparation of food for human consumption is affected with a public interest and gives to an industrial court power to fix wages and make other terms for the conduct of such business. In 1921, at the instance of the Meat Cutters' Union, the Industrial Court made an order increasing the rate of wages paid by the Wolff Packing Company, with which the packing company refused to comply. Thereupon proceedings were brought against it in the Kansas courts which confirmed the action of the Industrial Court. The packing company then took the case to the U. S. Supreme Court upon the ground that the Industrial Court Act was unconstitutional by reason of conflict with the provision of the 14th Amendment that "no State shall deprive any person of liberty or property without due process of law." In the decision that the act was unconstitutional, Chief Justice Taft said:

The necessary postulate of the Industrial Court Act is that the State representing the people is so much interested in their peace, health, and comfort that it may compel those engaged in the manufacture of food and clothing, and the production of fuel, whether owners or workers, to continue in their business and employment on terms fixed by an agency of the State. . . .

It is manifest from an examination of the cases cited [by the Kansas court] that the mere declaration by a legislative body, that a business is affected with a public interest is not conclusive of the question whether its attempted regulation on that ground is justified. The circumstances

[1] 262 U. S. Rep. 522.

of its alleged change from the status of a private business and its freedom from regulation into that in which the public have come to have an interest are always a subject of judicial inquiry. . . .

The avowed object [of the Industrial Court Act] is continuity of food, clothing and fuel supply. By Section 6, reasonable continuity and efficiency of the interests specified are declared to be necessary for the public peace, health, and general welfare, and all are forbidden to hinder, limit or suspend them. Section 7 gives the Industrial Court power in case of controversy between employers and workers which may endanger the continuity or efficiency of service, to bring the employer and employees before it and after hearing and investigation to fix the terms and conditions between them. The employer is bound by this Act to pay the wages fixed and while the worker is not required to work, he is forbidden, on penalty of fine or imprisonment, to strike against them, and thus is compelled to give up that means of putting himself on an equality with his employer which action in concert with his fellows gives him. . . .

We are considering the validity of the Act as compelling the employer to pay the adjudged wages, and as forbidding the employees to combine against working and receiving them. The penalties of the Act are directed against effort of either side to interfere with the settlement by arbitration. Without this joint compulsion the whole theory and purpose of the Act would fail. . . .

The power of a legislature to compel continuity in a business can only arise where the obligation of continued service by the owner and its employees is direct and is assumed when the business is entered upon. A common carrier which accepts a railroad franchise is not free to withdraw the use of that which it has granted to the public. Not so the owner when by mere changed conditions his business becomes clothed with a public interest. He may stop at will whether the business be losing or profitable.

The minutely detailed government supervision, including that of their relations with their employees, to which the railroads of the country have been gradually subjected by Congress through its power over interstate commerce, furnishes no precedent for regulation of the business of the plaintiff in error whose classification as public is at the best doubtful. . . .

We think the Industrial Relations Act, in so far as it permits the fixing of wages in plaintiff in error's packing house, is in conflict with the Fourteenth Amendment and deprives it of its property and liberty of contract without due process of law.

In the case of *Baltimore & Ohio R. R. Co. v. Interstate Commerce Commission*,[1] decided in 1910, the U. S. Supreme Court sustained the constitutionality of an act of Congress entitled "An act to promote the safety of employes and travelers upon railroads by limiting the hours of service of employes," upon the ground that the United States has power so to regulate interstate commerce as to provide for the safety of travelers and of employees of railroads. Justice Hughes said:

By virtue of its power to regulate interstate and foreign commerce, Congress may enact laws for the safeguarding of the persons and property that are transported in that commerce, and of those who are employed in transporting them. [Cases cited.] The fundamental question here is whether a restriction upon the hours of labor of employes who are connected with the movement of trains in interstate transportation is comprehended within this sphere of authorized legislation. This question admits of but one answer. The length of hours of service has direct relation to the efficiency of the human agencies upon which protection to life and property necessarily depends. This has been

[1] 221 U. S. Rep., 612.

repeatedly emphasized in official reports of the Interstate Commerce Commission, and is a matter so plain as to require no elaboration. In its power suitably to provide for the safety of employes and travelers, Congress was not limited to the enactment of laws relating to mechanical appliances, but it was also competent to consider, and to endeavor to reduce, the dangers incident to the strain of excessive hours of duty on the part of engineers, train dispatchers, telegraphers, and other persons embraced within the class defined by the Act. And in imposing restrictions having reasonable relation to this end, there is no interference with liberty of contract as guaranteed by the Constitution. *Chicago, Burlington & Quincy Railroad Company v. McGuire*, 219 U. S. 549.[1]

The United States, unlike the States, has never had the police power in the ordinary sense of the words. In the cases of *Adkins v. Commrs. of Children's Hospital* and *Adkins v. Willis A. Lyons*,[2] decided April 9th, 1923, the U. S. Supreme Court passed upon the validity of a national statute that established a board of three persons to investigate the rates of wages paid to women and minors in different occupations in the District of Columbia, to ascertain and declare standards of minimum wages for women workers in the District and what wages are inadequate to maintain them in good health and protect their morals; and standards of minimum wages for minors within the District and what wages are unreasonably low for such minor workers. The act also provided for procedure by conferences of employers and employees and for public hearings upon recommendations made by such conferences. The law authorizes

[1] The case here cited was upon validity of the Employers Liability Law of Iowa.
[2] 261 U. S. Rep., 525.

the board to make such orders as may be necessary to carry into effect such recommendations of the conferences as it approves, and makes unlawful and punishable by fine and imprisonment any violation by any employer of any provision of any such order. The first of the two cases was a suit in equity by which a corporation maintaining a hospital for children at Washington asked the Supreme Court of the District to restrain the board from enforcing an order fixing the wages of women whom it employed at less than the minimum wage that had been fixed by such board. The second case was brought by a woman who wished to keep her position as an elevator operator in a hotel at a salary of thirty-five dollars a month and two meals a day. The hotel was willing to keep her, but had to let her go because it was unwilling to incur the penalties incident to violating an order of the board. The Supreme Court of the District denied the injunctions and dismissed the bills in each case and appeals were taken to the U. S. Supreme Court. In the decision holding the law invalid for unconstitutionality,[1] Justice Sutherland said:

The statute now under consideration is attacked upon the ground that it authorizes an unconstitutional interference with the freedom of contract included within the guaranties of the due process clause of the Fifth Amendment. That the right to contract about one's affairs is a part of the liberty of the individual protected by this clause, is settled by the decisions of this Court and is no longer open to question. [Cases cited.] . . .

The feature of the statute which, perhaps more than any other, puts upon it the stamp of invalidity is that it exacts from the employer an arbitrary payment for a pur-

[1] Chief Justice Taft and Justice Holmes dissenting.

pose and upon a basis having no causal connection with his business, or the contract or the work the employee engages to do. The declared basis . . . is not the value of the service rendered, but the extraneous circumstance that the employee needs to get a prescribed sum of money to insure her subsistence, health, and morals. The ethical right of every worker, man or woman, to a living wage may be conceded. . . . And with that principle and with every legitimate effort to realize it in fact, no one can quarrel; but the fallacy of the proposed method of attaining is that it assumes that every employer is bound at all events to furnish it. The moral requirement implicit in every contract of employment, viz., that the amount to be paid and the service to be rendered shall bear to each other some relation of just equivalence, is completely ignored. The necessities of the employee are alone considered and these arise outside of the employment, and are as great in one occupation as in another. Certainly the employer by paying a fair equivalent for the service rendered, though not sufficient to support the employee, has neither caused nor contributed to her poverty. . . . In principle, there can be no difference between the case of selling labor and the case of selling goods. . . . Should a statute undertake to vest in a commission power to determine the quantity of food necessary for individual support and require the shopkeeper, if he sell to the individual at all, to furnish that quantity at no more than a fixed maximum, it would undoubtedly fall before the constitutional test. . . . The argument in support of that now being considered is equally fallacious, though the weakness of it may not be so plain. A statute requiring an employer to pay in money, to pay at prescribed and regular intervals, to pay the value of the services rendered, even to pay with fair relation to the extent of the benefit obtained from the service would be understandable. But a statute which prescribes payment without regard to any of these things and solely with relation to circumstances apart from the contract of employment, the business affected by it and the work done under it, is so clearly the product of a naked, arbitrary exercise of power that it cannot be allowed to stand under the Constitution of the United States. . . .

To sustain the individual freedom of action contemplated by the Constitution, is not to strike down the common good but to exalt it; for surely the good of society as a whole cannot be better served than by this preservation from arbitrary restraint of the liberties of its constituent members.

It follows . . . that the act in question passes the limit prescribed by the Constitution.

CHAPTER VIII

Commerce Laws.

The States and the United States have made extensive use of their commerce powers in order to promote the general welfare of society. The State legislatures have enacted statutes fixing the charges for carrying passengers and goods and the service to be rendered by railroads operating wholly within their limits, regulating gas and electric light service and charges, supervising and controlling banking and insurance, and otherwise controlling businesses affected by a public interest. The Congress has made many statutes regulating interstate and foreign commerce, such as the Interstate Commerce Commission Act, the Sherman Anti-Trust and Anti-Monopoly Act, the Hepburn Railroad Rate Law, the Clayton Fair Trade Commission Law, the Meat Inspection and Pure Food and Drug Law, the White Slave Act, the Lottery Law, and the acts to prevent the use of the post office for immoral and fraudulent purposes.

These statutes have from time to time been challenged in the courts on allegations that they operate to deprive citizens of the United States of the benefit of the constitutional rights of liberty and property. In all cases so arising, the courts have held that, as the purpose of the guaranties is to secure the welfare of society, they are to be applied according to the social conditions which existed when the statutes were made, not according to the social conditions that existed when the guaranties were created.

State and Federal Railroad Commission Acts.

During the period of expansion that followed the Civil War, the railroad systems of the United States increased their mileage by almost one half, and their competition for freight shipments became ruinous to themselves and in the end disastrous to the shippers. The railroads underbid each other on through shipments and made good their losses by overcharges on local traffic. In order to avoid this unreasonable competition, the railroads began to make pooling agreements by which they fixed passenger and freight rates and divided their total receipts in proportionate shares agreed upon among themselves. But they did this with an eye to their own profits only and without regard to the interests of passengers and shippers. They charged "what the traffic would bear," granted rebates to favored shippers, and as a means of getting contracts sometimes divided with the big shippers the profits they made on freights of smaller shippers in the same lines of business. Where there were no competing lines, the railroads sometimes charged higher rates for hauling freight short distances than long distances. The big shippers, like the Standard Oil Company, drove their competitors out of business. Local industries were often paralyzed.

The first result of these impossible business conditions was the enactment by State legislatures of statutes

establishing railroad commissions which were authorized to regulate the rates to be charged and prescribed
the service to be rendered by railroads operating within
State boundaries. The second result was the passage
by Congress in 1887 of the Interstate Commerce Commission Act, which prohibited discriminatory rates,
made unlawful the charging of higher rates for short
than for long hauls, and required railroads and other
carriers to publish rate schedules and file them with
the commission.

The United States Supreme Court has repeatedly held
that State statutes establishing railroad commissions
with authority to fix railroad rates and train service do
not deprive the railroad companies of their property
rights without due process of law, provided the authority is not so exercised as to amount to a confiscation of
property.[1]

The United States Supreme Court has also ruled that
the Interstate Commerce Commission Act, which
undoubtedly deals with property rights after a fashion
which the makers of the Constitution of the United
States could not have understood, is a valid exercise
of the commerce powers of the nation.

The *Granger Cases*,[2] decided in 1876 by the United
States Supreme Court created a sensation that is not
easily understood at the present time. The people as a
rule had taken it for granted that a railroad, like an
individual, could charge for the service it rendered

---

[1] *Railroad Commission Cases*, 116 U. S. Rep., 307; *Minneapolis etc.
R. Co. v. Minnesota*, 186 U. S. Rep., 257; *Smith v. Alabama*, 124 U. S.
Rep., 465.

[2] *C. B. & Q. R. R. Co. v. Iowa*, 94 U. S. Rep., 155; *Peik v. C. & N. W. R.
R. Co.*, 94 U. S. Rep., 164; *C. M. & St. Paul R. R. Co., v. Ackley*, 94 U. S.
Rep., 179; *Winona & St. Peter R. R. Co. v. Blake*, 94 U. S. Rep., 180;
Stone v. Wiseman, 94 U. S. Rep., 180.

whatever rate it chose to fix; that if those who travelled in its cars or shipped merchandise over its lines did not like to pay what it demanded, there was no way to compel it to make reasonable rates. There seemed to be something revolutionary in judicial decisions which held that the States which had given the railroads their charters could tell the companies they were charging more than the service was worth and that their rates must be lowered. Such decisions rendered by the highest courts of Iowa, Minnesota, and Wisconsin were sustained by the United States Supreme Court in a series of cases which created much alarm at the time, but now would not excite surprise.

These decisions have been qualified to some extent by subsequent cases,[1] which hold that the charges fixed by the authorities of the States must be reasonable, but the principle remains unchanged.

The case of *Interstate Commerce Commission v. Baltimore and Ohio Railroad Company*,[2] decided in 1892 by the U. S. Supreme Court, was a proceeding to compel the Baltimore and Ohio Railroad Company to withdraw from its lines upon which business competition existed with the Pittsburgh, Cincinnati and St. Louis Railroad Company certain so-called "party rates" and excursion tickets, without posting those rates in its offices as required by the law. The Commission after hearing the parties decided that the "party rates" constituted an unjust discrimination under the act and ordered the Baltimore and Ohio Company to cease giving them. The Baltimore & Ohio Company refused to obey the order and the Commission filed a petition for an

---

[1] *C. M. & St. Paul R. R. Co. v. Minnesota*, 134 U. S. Rep., 418; *Budd v. New York*, 143 U. S. Rep., 517.

[2] 145 U. S. Rep., 263, 275.

injunction in the U. S. Circuit Court for the Southern District of Ohio. This petition was dismissed and the Commission then took the case to the U. S. Supreme Court, which affirmed the decision of the lower court. In the course of the opinion of the Court, Justice Brown explained the objects of the Interstate Commerce Act in the following words:

Prior to the enactment of the act of February 4, 1887, to regulate commerce, commonly known as the Interstate Commerce Act, 24 Stat. 379, c. 104, railway traffic in this country was regulated by the principles of the common law applicable to common carriers, which demanded little more than that they should carry for all persons who applied, in the order in which the goods were delivered at the particular station, and that their charges for transportation should be reasonable. It was even doubted whether they were bound to make the same charge to all persons for the same service [cases cited]; though the weight of authority in this country was in favor of an equality of charge to all persons for similar service. In several of the States acts had been passed with the design of securing the public against unreasonable and unjust disciminations; but the inefficiency of these laws beyond the lines of the State, the impossibility of securing concerted action between the legislatures toward the regulation of traffic between the several States, and the evils which grew up under a policy of unrestricted competition, suggested the necessity of legislation by Congress under its constitutional power to regulate commerce among the several States. These evils ordinarily took the shape of inequality of charges made, or of facilities furnished; and were usually dictated by or tolerated for the promotion of the interests of the officers of the corporation or of the corporation itself, or for the benefit of some favored persons at the expense of others, or of some particular locality or community, or of some local trade or commercial connection, or for the destruction or crippling of some rival or hostile line.

The principal objects of the Interstate Commerce Act were to secure just and reasonable charges for transportation; to prohibit unjust discriminations in the rendering of like services under similar circumstances and conditions; to prevent undue or unreasonable preferences to persons, corporations, or localities; to prohibit greater compensation for a shorter than for a longer distance over the same line: and to abolish combinations for the pooling of freights. It was not designed, however, to prevent competition between different roads, or to interfere with the customary arrangements made by railway companies for reduced fares in consideration of increased mileage, where such reduction did not operate as an unjust discrimination against other persons travelling over the road. In other words, it was not intended to ignore the principle that one can sell cheaper at wholesale than at retail. It is not all discriminations and preferences that fall within the inhibition of the statute; only such as are unjust or unreasonable.

The Sherman Anti-Trust Law.

On July 2, 1890, Congress passed the famous Sherman Act which declared unlawful every contract, combination in the form of trust or otherwise, or conspiracy in restraint of trade or commerce among the several States or with foreign nations, and made guilty of misdemeanor "every person who shall monopolize or attempt to monopolize, or combine, or conspire, with any other person or persons, to monopolize any part of the trade or commerce among the several States or with foreign nations." This drastic law was an attempt to deal with a number of great "trusts" that had been formed in the cordage, meat, cottonseed, sugar, whiskey and other industries. It has been enforced by a series

106 THE REASONABLENESS OF THE LAW

of great decisions in which the U. S. Supreme Court
has established the rule that a contract in restraint of
trade is one which is contrary to the public welfare;
that a contract which merely facilitates business by
improving business methods is not a contract in
restraint of trade because it is advantageous to the
public[1]; but that a contract which operates to the
prejudice of the public interests by unduly and injuriously restricting trade or commerce is a contract in
restraint of trade.[2]

In *U. S. v. E. C. Knight Co.*,[3] the U. S. Supreme
Court held that the commerce power of the United
States does not extend to manufacturing, because
manufacturing is not commerce, but has ruled in
Addyston Pipe and Steel Co. v. U. S.[4] that a combination
of manufacturers to restrain trade by fixing prices is
within that power. It ruled in *U. S. v. Trans-Missouri
Freight Association*[5] and in *U. S. v. Joint Traffic Association*,[6] that agreements to fix passenger and freight
rates in territory controlled by certain railroads are
conspiracies in restraint of trade, but in *Standard Oil
Co. v. U. S.*[7] and in *U. S. v. American Tobacco Co.*[8] it
held that in order to be in restraint of trade, a contract
must be injurious to the public interests because contracts in partial restraint of trade that are "necessary
to the freedom of trade" are not really contracts in
restraint of trade. Its decision in the *Northern Securities Case*[9] that a holding company which controls a
majority of the stock of two railroad companies that

---

[1] *Standard Oil Co. v. U. S.*, 221, U. S. Rep. 1.
[2] U. S. v. American Tobacco Co., 221, U. S. Rep. 106.
[3] 156 U. S. Rep., 1.   [4] 175 U. S. Rep., 211.
[5] 166 U. S. Rep., 290.   [6] 171 U. S. Rep., 505.
[7] 221 U. S. Rep., 1.   [8] 221 U. S. 106.
[9] 193 U. S. Rep., 197.

together furnish the only service in a section of the United States is a contract in restraint of trade; but its decision in *U. S. v. U. S. Steel Corporation*,[1] is that the mere fact that a combination of manufacturing corporations controls the greater part of an industry does not make it unlawful. In *Hopkins v. U. S.*[2] the court decided that a voluntary association of commission merchants engaged in buying and selling live stock at the Kansas City stock yards was not a contract in restraint of interstate commerce, and in *Anderson v. U. S.*[3] it held that the Traders' Live Stock Association of Kansas City composed of dealers in live stock also was not a combination in restraint of interstate commerce. On the other hand, in *Swift & Co. v. U. S.*[4] it ruled that a combination of corporations and individuals to refrain from bidding against one another at the stockyards at Chicago, Omaha, East St. Louis, and St. Paul was an unlawful contract in restraint of trade.

These decisions extending over a period of twenty-five years have not been uniform, but they have been governed at least in the final result by the rule that constitutional guaranties are to be applied with a view to the best interests of the people.

[1] 251 U. S. Rep., 417.   [2] 171 U. S. Rep., 578.
[3] 171 U. S. Rep., 604.   [4] 196 U. S. Rep., 375.

CHAPTER IX

THE CONSTRUCTION AND INTERPRETATION OF CONSTITUTIONS

In the course of trials of cases in which the constitutional rights of individuals are at stake, there frequently arise questions either concerning the objects and purposes of constitutional provisions or concerning the meaning of the words in which those provisions are set forth. In such cases, the courts must either determine by construction the application of the clauses in dispute or fix by interpretation the meaning of the words and phrases in which they are expressed. When the courts construe a constitutional provision, they take into consideration the social and political conditions that existed when it was framed and thus ascertain how it applies to the controversy. When they interpret a constitutional provision, they ascertain and declare the sense in which the words used were spoken and understood when it was framed.

In the case of *South Carolina v. U. S.*,[1] decided by the U. S. Supreme Court in 1905, Justice Brewer, in order to determine whether under that power Congress could levy taxes upon the dispensaries by which South Carolina regulated the sale of intoxicating liquors, construed the clause of the Constitution of the United

[1] 199 U. S. Rep., 437, 448, 456.

States which confers upon Congress power to lay and collect taxes. It was admitted that the national government could not tax the agencies and instrumentalities of a State government because under our Federal system such taxation would impair the efficiency of its administration. The only question was whether the national government could tax those agencies and instrumentalities when employed in carrying on a business for profit. The court decided that the tax could be levied. Justice Brewer said:

The Constitution is a written instrument. As such its meaning does not alter. That which it meant when adopted it means now. Being a grant of powers to a government its language is general, and as changes come in social and political life it embraces in its grasp all new conditions which are within the scope of the powers in terms conferred. In other words, while the powers granted do not change, they apply from generation to generation to all things to which they are in their nature applicable. This in no manner abridges the fact of its changeless nature and meaning. Those things which are within its grants of power, as those grants were understood when made, are still within them, and those things not within them remain still excluded. . . .

It must also be remembered that the framers of the Constitution were not mere visionaries, toying with speculations or theories, but practical men, dealing with the facts of political life as they understood them, putting into form the government they were creating, and prescribing in language clear and intelligible the powers that government was to take. . . .

To determine the extent of the grants of power we must, therefore, place ourselves in the position of the men who framed and adopted the Constitution, and inquire what they must have understood to be the meaning and scope of those grants. . . . The exemption of the State's property and its functions from Federal taxation is implied from the dual character of our Federal system and the necessity of preserving the State in all its efficiency. In order to determine to what extent that implication will go we must turn to the condition of things at the time the Constitution was framed. What, in the light of that condition, did the framers of the convention intend should be exempt? Certain it is that modern notions as to the extent to which the functions of a State may be carried had then no hold. Whatever Utopian theories may have been presented by any writers were regarded as mere creations of fancy, and had no practical recognition. . . . While many believed that the liberty of the people depended on the preservation of the rights of the States, they had no thought that those States would extend their functions beyond their then recognized scope, or so as to imperil the life of the Nation.

In the case of *Gibbons v. Ogden*,[1] decided in 1824 by the U. S. Supreme Court, Chief Justice Marshall interpreted the word "commerce" in the clause of the Constitution of the United States which gives Congress power "to regulate commerce with foreign nations, and among the several States, and with the Indian tribes." The question before the Court was whether an exclusive right to navigate the waters within the State of New York by vessels propelled by steam, which had been given by a New York statute to Robert Fulton and Robert R. Livingston was inconsistent with the clause of the Constitution of the United States that gives Congress power to regulate commerce.

An action had been brought by Robert R. Livingston to assert his and Fulton's joint rights under the New York statute. This was the case of *Livingston v. Van Ingen*,[2] in which Chancellor Kent said:

[1] 9 Wheaton (U. S.) Rep., 1, 188
[2] 9 Johnson (N. Y.) Rep., 589.

Congress, indeed, has not any direct jurisdiction over our interior commerce or waters. Hudson River is the property of the people of this State, and the legislature have the same jurisdiction over it that they have over the land, or over any of our public highways, or over the waters of any of our rivers or lakes. They may, in their sound discretion, regulate and control, enlarge or abridge the use of its waters, and they are in the habitual exercise of that sovereign right. If the Constitution had given to Congress exclusive jurisdiction over our navigable waters, then the argument of the respondents would have applied; but the people never did, nor ever intended to grant such a power; and Congress have concurrent jurisdiction over the navigable waters no further than may be incidental and requisite to the due regulation of commerce between the States and with foreign nations.

Fulton and Livingston assigned to Aaron Ogden a part of their rights covering the privilege of conducting a steamboat line between Elizabethtown, New Jersey, and New York City. Thomas Gibbons started an opposition line with two steamboats called *The Stoudinger* and *The Bellona*, whereupon Ogden brought an action in equity and obtained a temporary injunction. Gibbons answered the bill in equity by urging that his boats were duly enrolled and licensed to engage in the coastwise trade under the laws of the United States; and this he claimed gave him a right superior to Ogden's right under a State law. The New York courts ruled in Ogden's favor. Gibbons then took the case to the Federal Supreme Court, where the New York injunction was annulled on the ground that the Act of Congress under which Gibbons' steamboats had been enrolled and licensed to be employed in the coastwise trade, gave those vessels full authority to navigate the waters of the United States by steam or otherwise, "any laws of the State of New York to the contrary notwithstanding." In the decision reversing the New York Court, Chief Justice Marshall declared that commerce includes navigation. In reading this conclusion, he explained the rule of interpretation as follows:

The words [giving Congress power to regulate commerce] are: "Congress shall have power to regulate commerce with foreign nations, and among the several States, and with the Indian tribes." The subject to be regulated is commerce; and our Constitution being, as was aptly said at the bar, one of enumeration and not of definition, to ascertain the extent of the power, it becomes necessary to settle the meaning of the word. The counsel for the appellee would limit it to traffic, to buying and selling, or to the interchange of commodities, and do not admit that it comprehends navigation. . . . All America understands, and has uniformly understood, the word "commerce" to comprehend navigation. It was so understood, and must have been so understood, when the constitution was framed. The power over commerce, including navigation, was one of the primary objects for which the people of America adopted their government, and must have been contemplated in forming it. The convention must have used the word in that sense, because all have understood it in that sense; and the attempt to restrict it comes too late.

RULES OF CONSTRUCTION AND INTERPRETATION

The courts are guided in determining the nature of constitutional powers and the meaning of constitutional declarations by rules of construction and interpretation, which form a body of substantive law much like the common law,[1] in that it exists, not in the form of acts of legislatures, but in the form of precedents. The most important of these rules are given in the following pages.[2]

A Constitution is to be so Construed and Interpreted as to Carry Out the Intent of its Framers.

The case of *Prigg v. Pennsylvania*,[3] decided in 1842 by the U. S. Supreme Court, had to do with the alleged kidnapping of a negro woman, who had escaped from her owner, a citizen of Maryland, and had taken refuge in Pennsylvania. She had been arrested as a fugitive slave under the old fugitive slave law, and had been taken before a magistrate who had refused to act. Thereupon Edward Prigg, the agent of the owner, had taken her back to Maryland and delivered her to her owner. Prigg was then indicted in Pennsylvania under a statute of that State which prohibited the taking by fraud or false pretense of any negro from the State of Pennsylvania with intent to cause such negro to be detained as a slave or servant. The jury by which he was tried found a special verdict that one of the slave woman's children had been born in Pennsylvania after her escape from Maryland. Upon this verdict, he was adjudged guilty. He then took the case to the U. S. Supreme Court by means of a writ of error, assigning as error that, under the Constitution of the United States, Congress had exclusive jurisdiction

[1] See p. 143.
[2] The words "construction" and "interpretation" are frequently used by our courts as if they had the same meaning. Hence, the distinction between them should be had in mind by all who read decisions of constitutional cases.
[3] 16 Peters (U. S.) Rep., 539, 611.

in all matters relating to the rendition of fugitive slaves to their owners, and that the Pennsylvania statute under which he had been tried was void by reason of inconsistency with the national constitution. The Court ruled that the Pennsylvania statute was unconstitutional in a decision in which Justice Story construed and interpreted the constitutional provisions concerning fugitive slaves as follows:

There are two clauses in the constitution upon the subject of fugitives, which stand in juxtaposition with each other, and have been thought mutually to illustrate each other. They are both contained in the 2nd section of the 4th article, and are in the following words: "A person charged in any State with treason, felony, or other crime, who shall flee from justice, and be found in another State, shall, on demand of the executive authority of the State from which he fled, be delivered up, to be removed to the State having jurisdiction of the crime."

"No person held to service or labor in one State under the laws thereof, escaping into another, shall in consequence of any law or regulation therein, be discharged from such service or labor; but shall be delivered up, on claim of the party to whom such service or labor may be due."

The last clause is that, the true interpretation whereof is directly before us. Historically, it is well known that the object of this clause was to secure to the citizens of the slaveholding States the complete right and title of ownership in their slaves, as property, in every State in the Union into which they might escape from the State where they were held in servitude. The full recognition of this right and title was indispensable to the security of this species of property in all the slaveholding States; and, indeed, was so vital to the preservation of their domestic interests and institutions, that it cannot be doubted that it constituted a fundamental article, without the adoption of which the Union could not have been formed. Its true design was to guard against the doctrines and principles prevalent in the non-slaveholding States, by preventing them from intermeddling with, or obstructing, or abolishing the rights of the owners of slaves.

By the general law of nations, no nation is bound to recognize the state of slavery, as to foreign slaves found within its territorial dominions, when it is in opposition to its own policy and institutions, in favor of the subjects of other nations, where slavery is recognized. . . . It is manifest from this consideration, that if the constitution had not contained this clause, every non-slaveholding State in the Union would have been at liberty to have declared free all runaway slaves coming within its limits, and to have given them entire immunity and protection against the claims of their masters; a course which would have created the most bitter animosities, and engendered perpetual strife between the different States. The clause was, therefore, of the last importance to the safety and security of the southern States, and could not have been surrendered by them without endangering their whole property in slaves. The clause was accordingly adopted into the Constitution by the unanimous consent of the framers of it; a proof at once of its intrinsic and practical necessity.

How, then, are we to interpret the language of the clause? The true answer is, in such manner, as, consistently with the words, shall fully and completely effectuate the whole objects of it. If by one mode of interpretation the right must become shadowy and unsubstantial, and, without any remedial power adequate to the end, and by another mode it will attain its just end and secure its manifest purpose, it would seem upon principles of reasoning absolutely irresistible that the latter ought to prevail. No court of justice can be authorized so to construe any clause of the Constitution as to defeat its obvious ends, when another construction, equally accordant with the words and sense thereof, will enforce and protect them.

The Whole of a Constitution must be Considered when the Meaning of Particular Words and Phrases is to be Ascertained.

In the case of *Manly v. State*,[1] decided by the Court of Appeals of Maryland in 1854, the State's attorney contested the right of the Court of Appeals to hear and determine an appeal from a judgment of the lower court that the defendant was guilty of the crime of assault with intent to kill, upon the ground that the constitution of Maryland had not conferred the right to grant writs of error to the court in which he had been convicted. The constitutional clause referred to provided that "the judges [of the circuit courts] in their respective circuits shall have and exercise all the power, authority, and jurisdiction of the present Court of Chancery." In construing this sentence, Justice Tuck ruled that the whole State constitution showed that the framers did not intend to deprive defendants in criminal cases of the right of appeal by words which taken by themselves seemed to indicate that writs of error could be granted only in matters of equity. He said:

We have no idea that the convention [which framed the Constitution of Maryland] intended to deprive the people of the State, of the benefit of this process, nor do we think that by any reasonable interpretation of the constitution, such a purpose can be deduced. The chancery court was abolished, but the system of equity jurisprudence was not otherwise disturbed, than by transferring the jurisdiction to other courts. As to the circuit courts for the counties this was done in the most ample manner. Not content with

[1] 7 Maryland Rep., 135, 145, 147.

devolving upon these courts all the powers, authority and jurisdiction which the county courts then exercised, the constitution expressly declares, that the *"judges* in their respective circuits shall have and exercise all the power, authority and jurisdiction of the present [former] court of *chancery."* . . . The argument is, that the eleventh section of the judiciary article, by which the superior court for Baltimore city was created, only confers "equity jurisdiction" within the limits of that city; and that as the right to grant this writ was no part of the chancellor's equity jurisdiction, but was vested in him as the depository of a portion of the supreme power, after the manner that this officer represented the king, at common law, it does not appertain to the judge of the Superior Court, as a portion of his equity jurisdiction. It is not necessary to inquire into the origin and nature of this writ. It is enough for us to know that it has always been considered in this State, as belonging to the applicant as a matter of right; and believing, as we have said, that the framers of the constitution had no intention to impair it in any degree, we are clear in the opinion that the judge of the Superior Court possessed the power equally with the judges of the circuit courts.

It is true that the same comprehensive language is not employed as to both these courts. But constitutions are not to be interpreted according to the words used in particular clauses. The whole must be considered, with a view to ascertain the sense in which the words were employed, and its terms must be taken in their ordinary and common acceptation, because they are presumed to have been so understood by the framers and by the people who adopted it. This is unquestionably the correct rule of interpretation. It, unlike the acts of our legislature, owes its whole force and authority to its ratification by the people, and they judged of it by the meaning apparent on its face, according to the general use of the words employed, where they do not appear to have been used in a legal or technical sense.

Constitutions are so Construed as to Operate Prospectively, not Retrospectively.

In the case of *Shreveport v. Cole*,[1] decided in 1889 by the U. S. Supreme Court, the plaintiffs claimed that a provision of a new constitution of the State of Louisiana, adopted in 1879, after a contract made by them with the City of Shreveport had been performed, prevented the city from paying what was justly due them by limiting municipal taxation to ten mills on the dollar of assessed valuation of property, at which rate the city could not raise by taxation money enough to pay its obligations. The court ruled that this claim was not well founded because the constitutional clause in question was to be interpreted as a provision for the future not applicable to the past. Chief Justice Fuller said:

Constitutions as well as statutes are to be construed to operate prospectively only, unless, on the face of the instrument or enactment, the contrary intention is manifest beyond reasonable question. There is nothing on the face of Article 209 [the clause in question] evidencing an intention that it should be applied to antecedent contracts, and the highest tribunal of the State has declared that it cannot be so applied. It is impossible, under these circumstances, to sustain the jurisdiction of the Circuit Court upon the ground, not that the city had been, but that it might perhaps be, allowed to interpose to defeat the enforcement, by the appropriate means, of payment of an alleged indebtedness, a constitutional provision inapplicable by the ordinary rules of law.

Constitutions must be Construed and Interpreted Uniformly.

Our courts will not construe or interpret a written law in one way at one time and in another way afterward,

[1] 129 U. S. Rep., 36, 43.

even if public opinion or public feeling about the morality or justice of its provisions has in the meantime completely changed. For example, at the time of the adoption of our national Constitution most of our people believed that negro slavery was justifiable. It had died out in the Northern States, where it was unprofitable. It had flourished in the Southern States, where it was apparently necessary for the production of cotton on a large scale. Prior to the Civil War, however, a strong anti-slavery sentiment grew up in the North, and when in 1856, the famous case of *Dred Scott v. Sandford,*[1] came up for hearing in the U. S. Supreme Court, public opinion in the free States favored some ruling which would vary from the original rulings of our courts upon the political status of the negroes.

Dred Scott, a negro slave, had been taken by his master, an army surgeon, to Fort Snelling, now St. Paul, Minn., then a part of the territory of the United States in which, by the provisions of the Missouri Compromise Act of 1820, slavery had been abolished. A few years afterward, he was brought to Missouri, in which slavery was allowable. He then brought in the United States Circuit Court an action to recover his liberty against a Mr. Sandford, a citizen of New York, to whom he had been sold, alleging that by reason of his residence in free territory he had become a citizen of the United States and of the State of Missouri and as such could sustain an action in the federal courts against a citizen of the State of New York. The court was thus called upon to construe and interpret the provisions of the U. S. Constitution concerning the qualifications of citizens. Six of the nine justices rendered opinions to the effect that a negro could not be a citizen; three dissented.

[1] 19 Howard (U. S.) Rep., 393, 416, 426.

Chief Justice Taney, in the course of his opinion, reviewed the previous decisions of the courts upon the political status of negroes and then ruled that the Constitution must be construed and interpreted according to the rules thus laid down. He said:

The legislation of the States . . . shows, in a manner not to be mistaken, the inferior and subject condition of that [negro] race at the time the constitution was adopted, and long afterwards, throughout the thirteen States by which that instrument was framed; and it is hardly consistent with the respect due to these States, to suppose that they regarded at that time, as fellow citizens and members of the sovereignty, a class of beings whom they had thus stigmatized; . . . and upon whom they had impressed such deep and enduring marks of inferiority and degradation; or, that when they met in convention to form the constitution, they looked upon them as a portion of their constituents, or designed to include them in the provisions so carefully inserted for the security and protection of the liberties and rights of their citizens. It cannot be supposed that they intended to secure to them rights and privileges, and rank, in the new political body throughout the Union, which everyone of them denied within the limits of its own dominion. More especially, it cannot be believed that the large slaveholding States regarded them as included in the word citizens, or would have consented to a constitution which might compel them to receive them in that character from another State. . . .

No one, we presume, supposes that any change in public opinion or feeling, in regard to this unfortunate race, in the civilized nations of Europe or in this country, should induce the court to give to the words of the constitution a more liberal construction in their favor than they were intended to bear when the instrument was framed and adopted. Such an argument would be altogether inadmissible in any tribunal called upon to interpret it. If any of its provisions are deemed unjust, there is a mode prescribed in the instrument itself by which it may be amended; but while it remains unaltered, it must be construed now as it was understood at the time of its adoption.

The Words of a Constitution must be Interpreted According to their Natural Significance, unless such Construction and Definition be Repugnant to Public Policy.

The case of *People v. May*,[1] decided by the Supreme Court of Michigan in 1855, turned upon the meaning of the word "attorney" in a section of the Michigan constitution of 1850, which provided that there should be a "prosecuting attorney" in each organized county of the State, chosen by the electors once in two years. At the election in 1852, the whole number of votes given for that office in Calhoun County was 3914. Of these, C. S. May received 2027 and D. D. Hughes received 1887. The Board of Canvassers awarded a certificate of election to May, who thereupon entered upon the duties of the office. Hughes then brought this action by an information in which he claimed that May had not been licensed and admitted to practice as an attorney in any of the courts of Michigan; that he was therefore ineligible for the office; and that the certificate of election had been wrongfully awarded to him. The court ruled in favor of Hughes in a decision in which Justice Martin said:

Among the well settled rules of construction of statutes, are these: 1st, the natural import of the words of any legislative act, according to the common use of them when applied to the subject matter of the act, is to be taken as expressing the intention of the legislature, unless the in-

[1] 3 Michigan Rep., 605.

tention so resulting from the ordinary import of the words be repugnant to sound acknowledged principles of public policy; and 2nd, if the subject of the statute relates to courts or legal proofs, the words of the legislature are to be construed technically, unless from the statute it appears that the terms were used in a more popular sense. These words are equally applicable in the construction of a constitution—as the constitution is law, the people having been the legislators—as much as a statute is law, the senators and representatives being legislators.

The *natural* import of words is that which their utterance promptly and uniformly suggests to the mind—that which common use has affixed to them; the *technical* is that which is suggested by their use in reference to a science or profession—that which particular use has affixed to them; and when the natural and technical import unite upon a word, both these rules combine to control its construction, and indeed it is difficult to understand how any other signification than that which they suggest can be affixed to it, unless upon the most positive declaration that a different one was designed.

The Words of a Constitution must be Interpreted in the Sense in which they were Generally Understood at the Time it was Made.

The question at issue in the case of *Chesapeake and Ohio Railway Co. v. Miller, Auditor,*[1] decided by the Supreme Court of Appeals of West Virginia in 1882, was whether the property in West Virginia of the railway company was entitled to exemption under a statute which provided that it should not be taxed until its profits should amount to ten per cent upon its capital stock. The railroad claimed that this statute had been properly passed under the authority of an article in the

[1] 19 West Virginia Rep., 408, 420, 435.

State constitution, which provided that "property used for educational, literary, scientific, religious, or charitable purposes, and public property may by law be exempted from taxation." The State auditor urged that it was void under another section of the same article which declared that "taxation shall be equal and uniform throughout the State." In reaching a decision upon the meaning of the exemption provision, President Johnson (the Chief Justice) said:

If the clause to be construed is ambiguous or obscure and leaves room for doubt as to what was really intended by it, then we may report to other and extrinsic lights to aid us in giving it a correct interpretation; then and only then are we warranted in seeking elsewhere for aid. Where the text is obscure or ambiguous, we may look to the proceedings of the constitutional convention, which framed the instrument (Cooley *Const. Lim.*, 66); but even in such case we must remember, that the Constitution does not derive its force from the convention, which framed, but from the people, who ratified it. Judge Cooley, page 67, says: "The intent to be arrived at is that of the people; and it is not to be supposed, that they have looked for any dark or abstruse meaning in the words employed, but rather that they have accepted them in the sense most obvious to the common understanding, and ratified the instrument in the belief, that that was the sense designed to be conveyed." Also in case of doubtful meaning in the words used, we may look to contemporaneous and practical construction. "Contemporaneous construction may consist simply in the understanding, with which the people received it at the time, or in the acts done in putting it in operation, and which necessarily assume, that it is to be construed in a particular way." (Cooley, *Const. Lim.* 67). . . . No authority, to which we have been cited, or which we have found, sustains the constitutionality of so much of . . . the act . . . as exempts the property therein mentioned from taxation.

A Constitutional Provision, which has Received a Settled Judicial Construction or Interpretation will, if Reenacted or Incorporated into the Constitution of another State, be Presumed to have the Same Meaning as it Originally Had.

In the case of *Atty. Gen. v. Brunst,*[1] decided in 1854 by the Supreme Court of Wisconsin, the question before the court was upon the construction of a section of the State constitution concerning the election of county officers, which had been copied from the constitution of the State of New York where its meaning had been determined by the courts. Justice Smith in the decision that the construction of the phrase adopted by the New York courts was that which the framers of the Wisconsin constitution had had in mind, said:

The language of the section is precisely like to a similar clause in the constitution of the state of New York . . . and there can be no doubt that it was adopted by the convention from that instrument. And there can scarcely be a doubt that the members of the convention were familiar with the judicial decision in that state, which had settled the construction of the language used, and that in adopting the language of the section, the judicial construction was likewise adopted. If this be so, then it would seem that the case of *The People ex rel. Galup v. Green,* 2 Wend. 266, is conclusive.

A Constitutional Clause will not be Extended beyond its Strict Purpose by Construction and Interpretation.

In the case of *Brown v. Fifield,*[2] decided in 1856 by the Supreme Court of Michigan, the question at issue

[1] 3 Wisconsin Rep., 787, 790.   [2] 4 Michigan Rep., 322, 326.

was whether a married woman without the consent of
her husband had a right to sell a house that had belonged to her before her marriage. Under the rule of
the common law, the house became the property of her
husband when she married; but there was a provision
in the Michigan constitution that the real and personal
property of a female acquired before marriage, and all
property which she might acquire while married should
not be liable for the debts of her husband and might be
devised or bequeathed by her as if she were unmarried.
The court held that the meaning of this constitutional
provision was that the wife's property should not be
liable for his debts, but did not give her a right to sell it.
Justice Green said:

Has the constitution removed the disability to contract,
which resulted from the coverture [marriage relation] by
the common law? It certainly has not done so in express
terms, nor do we discover anything in its language which
seems to imply such an intention. She is expressly em-
powered to devise and bequeath the property as if she were
unmarried, and it may fairly be inferred that if it had been
intended to enable her to sell and dispose of it by contract
during the coverture, such intent would have been mani-
fested in express terms. It is a familiar rule, that a statute
in contravention of the common law ought not to be
extended by construction, and the rule is equally applicable
to a constitutional provision of this character.

Constitutional Provisions are Mandatory, and Not merely Rules of Procedure.

The question in the case of *People v. Lawrence*,[1] decided by the New York Supreme Court in 1862, was
upon the validity of an act of the State legislature di-

[1] 36 Barbour (N. Y.) Rep., 177, 185.

recting the appointment of commissioners who should make a contract with the Long Island Railroad Company for closing a tunnel, restoring the street to grade, and constructing a horse railroad between South Ferry and Jamaica, Long Island. The railroad company for relinquishing its property and rights was to receive $125,000, which was to be assessed upon the property benefited. The constitutionality of this act was challenged upon the ground that it was repugnant to the last part of a provision of the State constitution which declared that "no private or local bill which may be passed by the legislature shall embrace more than one subject, and that shall be expressed in the title." In giving the decision of the court, Justice Emott said:

It is said that this provision of the constitution is merely directory, and only establishes a rule of legislative practice. . . . I am not aware that any court in this state has yet felt constrained or authorized to hold any provision of the constitution to be merely directory. . . . The clause now in question relates to the form and substance of the bill itself, and refers to it as and after it is passed by the legislature. I think it will be found, upon full consideration, to be difficult to treat any constitutional provision as merely directory and not mandatory.

A Constitutional Provision that Confers Powers, Confers also by Implication the Right to Adopt the Means of Exercising those Powers.

In the case of *McCulloch v. Maryland*,[1] decided in 1819 by the U. S. Supreme Court, Chief Justice Marshall said:

It may, with great reason, be contended, that a government, intrusted with such ample powers, on the due execu-

[1] 4 Wheaton (U. S.) Rep., 316, 408.

tion of which the happiness and prosperity of the nation so vitally depends, must also be intrusted with ample means for their execution. The power being given, it is the interest of the nation to facilitate its execution. . . . It is not denied, that the powers given to the government imply the ordinary means of execution. . . . But it is denied that the government has its choice of the means; or, that it may employ the most convenient means, if, to employ them, it be necessary to erect a corporation. On what foundation does this argument rest? On this alone; The power of creating a corporation, is one appertaining to sovereignty, and is not expressly conferred on Congress. This is true. But all legislative powers appertain to sovereignty. The original power of giving the law on any subject whatever, is a sovereign power; and if the government of the Union is restrained from creating a corporation, as a means of performing its functions, on the single reason that the creation of a corporation is an act of sovereignty; if the sufficiency of this reason be acknowledged, there would be some difficulty in sustaining the authority of Congress to pass other laws for the accomplishment of the same objects.

The government which has the right to do an act, and has imposed on it the duty of performing that act, must, according to the dictates of reason, be allowed to select the means.

PART III

The American Common Law: An Unwritten Law of Government

CHAPTER X

Evolution of the Common Law.

In the case of *Jacob v. State*,[1] decided in 1842 by the Supreme Court of Tennessee, Justice Turley said:

The common law has been aptly called the "*lex non scripta*," because it is a rule prescribed by the common consent and agreement of the community, as one applicable to its different relations, and capable of preserving the peace, good order, and harmony of society, and rendering unto everyone, that which of right belongs to him. Its sources are found in the usages, habits, manners and customs of a people. Its seat is in the breast of the judges who are its expositors and expounders. Every nation must of necessity have its common law, let it be called by what name it may, and it will be simple or complicated in its details, as society is simple or complicated in its relations. A few plain and practical rules will do for a wandering horde of savages, but they must and will be much more extensively ramified when civilization has polished, and commerce, and arts and agriculture enriched a nation. The common law of a country will, therefore, never be entirely stationary, but will be modified, and extended by analogy, construction and custom, so as to embrace new relations, springing up from time to time, from an amelioration or change of society.

[1] 3 Humphrey (Tenn.) Rep., 493, 514.

The present common law of England is as dissimilar from that of Edward the 3d, as is the present state of society. And we apprehend that no one could be found to contend that hundreds of principles, which have in more modern times, been examined, argued and determined by the judges, are not principles of the common law because not found in the books of that period. They are held to be great and immutable principles, which have slumbered in their repositories, because the occasion that called for their exposition, had not arisen. The common law, then, is not like the statute law, fixed, and immutable but by positive enactment, except where a principle has been adjudged as the rule of action.

Chancellor Kent says in his *Commentaries:*[1]

The common law includes those principles, usages, and rules of action applicable to the government and security of person and property which do not rest for their authority upon any express and positive declaration of the will of the legislature. A great proportion of the rules and maxims which constitute the immense code of the common law grew into use by gradual adoption, and received, from time to time, the sanction of our courts of justice, without any legislative act or interference. It was the application of the dictates of natural justice, and of cultivated reason, to particular cases. In the just language of Sir Matthew Hale, the common law of England is not the product of some one man, or society of men, in any one age, but of the wisdom, counsel, experience, and observation of many ages of wise and observing men.

In the case of *People v. Randolph,*[2] decided by the Supreme Court of New York in 1855, Justice Greene said:

[1] 2 Kent Comm., 471.
[2] 2 Parker (N. Y.) Crim. Rep., 174.

The common law consists of those principles and maxims, usages, and rules of action which observation and experience of the nature of man, the constitution of society, and the affairs of life have commended to enlightened reason, as best calculated for the government and security of persons and property. Its principles are developed by judicial decisions as necessities arise from time to time demanding the application of those principles to particular cases in the administration of justice. The authority of its rules does not depend upon positive legislative enactment, but upon the principles which they are designed to enforce, the nature of the subject to which they are to be applied, and their tendency to accomplish the ends of justice. It follows that these rules are not arbitrary in their nature nor invariable in their application, but, from their nature as well as the necessities in which they originate, they are and must be susceptible of a modified application suited to the circumstances under which that application is to be made. The principles of the common law, as its theory assumes and its history proves, are not exclusively applicable or suited to one country or condition of society, but on the contrary, by reason of their properties of expansibility and flexibility their application to many is practicable.

In the case of *Sayward v. Carlson*,[1] decided in 1890 by the Supreme Court of the State of Washington, Justice Stiles described the evolution of the common law in England and in America as follows:

The common law grew with society, not ahead of it. As society became more complex, and new demands were made upon the law by reason of new circumstances, the courts originally, in England, out of the storehouse of reason and good sense, declared the "common law." But since courts have had an existence in America they have never hesitated

[1] 1 Washington Rep., 29, 40.

to take upon themselves the responsibility of saying what is the "common law." . . . Therefore we have the "common law" as declared by the highest courts of this, that, and the other State, and by the courts of the United States, sometimes varying in each. And we understand . . . that where there are no governing provisions of the written laws, the courts . . . are, in all matters coming before them, to endeavor to administer justice according to the promptings of reason and common sense, which are the cardinal principles of the common law.

The Common Law in the Colonies.

The common law of England is the basis of the law of all the States of the Union, except Florida, Louisiana, and Texas.[1] It is a body of rules for the punishment of crimes and the protection of rights. These rules were established by English courts long prior to the first English settlements in America. They are based upon customs and usages that had been generally followed by the members of English communities in their relations or dealings with one another. They may have been survivals of forgotten statutes. They may have had their origin in conceptions of right and justice, or in their usefulness as a means of maintaining order and safeguarding rights. For example, the common law rule that a party to an action has the right of trial by a jury, which existed long before *Magna Carta*, may either have been established because the people thought it promoted the cause of justice, or may have been an edict of Alfred the Great, or may have been adopted because it was a satisfactory device for the arbitration of disputes.[2]

---

[1] See post, page 140.

[2] There are three conceptions of law: first, as a rule of right and justice, which prevailed while the courts were administered by ecclesias-

The Common Law of the Original States.

The common law of the States is partly English and partly American. The English element comprises the common law of England as amended by English statutes in force at the beginning of the era of colonization, a few English statutes passed afterward that were applicable to the colonies, some decisions of English courts, and some customs and usages of government followed by the colonists before the establishment of the regular colonial governments and courts. The American element consists of acts of the colonial legislatures and provincial congresses and since then, of customs and usages of the American people in dealing with new conditions resulting from such inventions as steam power, electric transmission, submarine and aërial transportation, and the like.

In the case of *Commonwealth v. Knowlton*,[1] decided in 1807, the Supreme Judicial Court of Massachusetts described as follows the law of that State when it became independent:

Our ancestors, when they came into this new world, claimed the common law as their birthright, and brought it with them, except such parts as were judged inapplicable to their new state and condition. The common law, thus claimed, was the common law of their native country, as it was amended or altered by *English* statutes in force at the time of their emigration. Those statutes were never re-enacted in this country, but were considered as incorporated into the common law. Some few other *English*

---

tics; second, as a rule founded upon commands of the supreme authority; and third, as a rule based upon utility. The definition of law based upon authority has been urged by an English jurist named Austin; the utilitarian theory was presented by Bentham, an English philosopher.

[1] 2 Mass. Rep., 530, 534.

statutes, passed since their emigration, were adopted by our courts, and now have the authority of law derived from long practice. To these may be added some ancient usages, originating probably from laws passed by the legislature of the colony of *Massachusetts Bay*, which were annulled by the repeal of the first charter, and, from the former practice of the colonial courts, accommodated to the habits and manners of the people. So much, therefore, of the common law of *England*, as our ancestors brought with them, and of the statutes then in force, amending or altering it,—such of the more recent statutes as have been since adopted in practice,—and the ancient usages aforesaid,—may be considered as forming the body of the common law of *Massachusetts* which has submitted to some alteration by the acts of the provincial and State legislatures and by the provisions of our constitutions.

Continuance of Existing Law.

After the Declaration of Independence and until the adoption of new constitutions by the States, the provisional State governments continued to enforce the colonial laws and made such new laws as were needed. The new State constitutions contained provisions in their bills of rights for the continuance of all existing laws, although such provisions were not strictly necessary, the rule being that the laws do not cease to be valid when a revolution takes place. A good example of the way in which laws are continued in force is found in Sections 16 and 17 of Article I of the Constitution of the State of New York, which read as follows:

Such parts of the common law, and of the acts of the Legislature of the colony of New York, as together did form the law of the said colony, on the nineteenth day of April, one thousand seven hundred and seventy-five, and the resolutions of the Congress of the said colony, and of the convention of the State of New York, in force on the twentieth day of April, one thousand seven hundred and seventy-seven, which have not since expired, or been repealed or altered; and such acts of the Legislature of this State as are now in force, shall be and continue the law of this State, subject to such alterations as the Legislature shall make concerning the same. But all such parts of the common law, and such of the said acts, or parts thereof as are repugnant to this Constitution, are hereby abrogated.

All grants of land within this State, made by the king of Great Britain, or persons acting under his authority, after the fourteenth day of October, one thousand seven hundred and seventy-five, shall be null and void; but nothing contained in this Constitution shall affect any grants of land within this State, made by the authority of the said king or his predecessors, or shall annul any charters to bodies politic and corporate, by him or them made before that day; or shall affect any such grants or charters since made by this State, or by persons acting under its authority; or shall impair the obligation of any debts, contracted by the State or individuals, or bodies corporate, or any other rights of property, or any suits, actions, rights of action, or other proceedings in courts of justice.[1]

In the case of *Commonwealth v. Chapman*,[2] decided in 1847 by the Supreme Judicial Court of Massachusetts, Justice Shaw described as follows the effect of the clause in the Massachusetts Constitution which continued existing laws:

[1] On April 19, 1775, the Provincial Congress of the Colony of New York begun to act independently of the colonial governor. On April 20, 1777, the first Constitution of the State of New York, which displaced the Provincial Congress, was adopted. On October 14, 1775, Governor Tryon left the colony and took refuge on board the British frigate *Asia* in New York harbor. This act was as an abdication by the British government of its authority in the colony.

[2] 13 Metcalf (Mass.) Rep., 68, 71.

The clause [in the Massachusetts Constitution of 1780] is this . . . "all the laws which have been adopted, used, and approved in the province, colony or state of Massachusetts Bay, and usually practiced on in the courts of law, shall still remain and be in full force until altered or repealed by the legislature; such parts only excepted as are repugnant to the rights and liberties contained in this constitution." . . . We take it to be a well settled principle, acknowledged by all civilized states governed by law, that by means of a political revolution, by which the political organization is changed, the municipal laws, regulating their social relations, duties and rights are not necessarily abrogated. They remain in force, except so far as they are repealed or modified by the new sovereign authority. Indeed, the existence of this body of laws, and the social and personal rights dependent upon them, from 1776, when the declaration of independence was made, and our political revolution took place, to 1780, when this constitution was adopted, depend on this principle. The clause in the constitution, therefore, though highly proper and expedient to remove doubts, and give greater assurance to the cautious and timid, was not necessary to preserve all prior laws in force, and was rather declaratory of an existing rule, than the enactment of a new one.

The English statutes that were incorporated into the laws of the States by their first constitutions have been described as follows:[1]

The position among the English colonists in what is now the United States of the statutes passed by the English or British Parliament, whether before or after their departure from the mother country, presents an interesting question. Undoubtedly the principles embodied in those statutes were largely applied as rules by the American

[1] Gray, *The Nature and Sources of the Law* (New Edition, Macmillan Co., N. Y., 1922), p. 196.

courts, but they were applied not as commands of the English or British Parliament, for no Acts of Parliament extended to the colonies unless they were expressly mentioned, but as a part of a body of rules, known as the Common Law, which were, in fact, applied by the English courts, and which the courts in the colonies took over from them; and they dealt with these rules much more freely than they would have felt at liberty to do, had the statutes been made by their own legislatures.   They said that they would consider as furnishing rules for decision only those English statutes which were "suited to our condition," a phrase giving them a wide discretion, of which they did not hesitate to avail themselves.

The decisions of the English courts were also used as rules of law in the colonial courts.   Professor Gray says:[1]

As to the decisions [of English courts] made before the establishment of the English colonies in America, there seems to be little doubt that, in the absence of legislation to the contrary, they must be considered as Judicial Precedents. It is true that only so much of the English Law as was applicable to the altered conditions of life was adopted here. This doctrine, which is generally approved, leaves a wide door for judicial discretion to abrogate or alter the Common Law, but does not affect this part of the Law more than any other, the Statute Law, for instance. . . .

In the intervening period between the settlement of the country and the Revolution, there lay, in general, no appeal to the English courts, nor to any tribunal having a control at the same time over the English and the Colonial courts, and it seems, therefore, that the decisions of the English courts during this period were strictly not precedents, but were admissible only upon the grounds just stated [as opinions of learned men as to what the Law was

[1] See footnote, p. 138.

or ought to be] for considering decisions of the English courts subsequent to the Revolution.

The Common Law of the New States.

The common law of the States formed in territory that was already under a civilized government when acquired by the United States is based, either on the common law of England, or on the customs and laws of the European country that had settled it originally. Thus, while the common law of Oregon is of English origin, that of Louisiana is of French origin, and that of Florida and Texas, of Spanish origin.

In the case of *Norris v. Harris*,[1] decided in 1860 by the Supreme Court of California, Chief Justice Field said:

There is no doubt that the common law is the basis of the laws of those States which were originally colonies of England, or carved out of such colonies. It was imported by the colonies and established so far as it was applicable to their institutions and circumstances, and was claimed by the Congress of the United Colonies in 1774 as a branch of those "indubitable rights and liberties to which the respective colonies" were entitled. (Kent's Com. Vol. I, 343.) . . .

A similar presumption must prevail as to the existence of the common law in those States which have been established in territory acquired since the Revolution, where such territory was not at the time of its acquisition occupied by an organized and civilized community; where, in fact, the population of the new State upon the establishment of government was formed by emigration from the original States. As in British Colonies, established in uncultivated regions by emigration from the parent country, the subjects are considered as carrying with them the

[1] 15 California Rep., 226, 252.

common law, so far as it is applicable to their new situation, so when American citizens emigrate into territory which is unoccupied by civilized man, and commence the formation of a new government, they are equally considered as carrying with them so much of the same common law, in its modified and improved condition under the influence of modern civilization and republican principles, as is suited to their new condition and wants.

But no such presumption can apply to States in which a government already existed at the time of their accession to the country, as Florida, Louisiana, and Texas. They had already laws of their own, which remained in force until by the proper authority they were abrogated and new laws were promulgated. With them there is no more presumption of the existence of the common law than of any other law. They were independent of the English law in their origin, and hence no presumption of the existence of the common law of England can be indulged.

In the case of *Browning v. Browning*,[1] decided in 1886 by the Supreme Court of New Mexico, Justice Bunker said:

There are three classes of common law as recognized in the United States of America: (1) In those states which were a part of the original colonies, and which have not by legislation adopted statutes passed prior to a particular date, the unwritten law, and such general British statutes applicable to their condition as were in force at the time of the formation of the colonial governments, and such as were afterward adopted, expressly or tacitly, constituted the common law; (2) in those states which have adopted the common law and the British statutes passed and enforced prior to the date fixed in the act of adoption, and were of a general nature and suitable to their situation, such common law and statutes constitute their common law;

[1] 3 New Mexico Rep., 659, 674.

and (3) in those states and territories which were not of the original colonies, and which have not in terms adopted any English statutes, but have adopted the common law, the unwritten or common law of England and the acts of Parliament of a general nature, not local to Great Britain, which had been passed and were in force at the date of the war of the revolution, and not in conflict with the constitution or laws of the United States, nor of the state or territory, and which were suitable to the wants and conditions of the people, are the common law of such states and territories.

The Common Law of the United States.

The common law of the United States is not a national customary law separate and distinct from the common law of the States. It consists of principles established by judicial decisions interpreting the Constitution of the United States and its treaties with other nations and applying general rules to commercial transactions.

In the case of *Smith v. Alabama*,[1] decided in 1887 by the Supreme Court of the United States, Justice Matthews said:

There is no common law of the United States, in the sense of a national customary law, distinct from the common law of England as adopted by the several States each for itself, applied as its local law, and subject to such alterations as may be made by its own statutes. . . .

There is . . . one clear exception to the statement that there is no national common law. The interpretation of the Constitution of the United States[2] is necessarily influenced by the fact that its provisions are framed in the language of the English common law, and are to be read

[1] 124 U. S. Rep., 465, 478.
[2] Cross Reference to Chapter on Construction, etc.

in the light of its history. The code of constitutional and statutory construction which, therefore, is gradually formed by the judgments of this court, in the application of the Constitution and the laws and treaties made in pursuance thereof, has for its basis so much of the common law as may be implied in the subject, and constitutes a common law resting on national authority.

The case of *Western Union Telegraph Co. v. Call Publishing Co.*,[1] decided in 1900 by the U. S. Supreme Court, was an action which the publisher of a newspaper had brought in the courts of Nebraska to recover sums of money alleged to have been unjustly charged for telegraphic service in excess of the rates charged to another newspaper in the same place and at the same time. The telegraph company contended that inasmuch as the services it had rendered were wholly a matter of interstate commerce and thus exclusively under the jurisdiction of Congress, which had prescribed no rules or regulations concerning its charges, the state court of Nebraska had no right to judge or decide the case. The courts of Nebraska ruled in favor of the newspaper, and the telegraph company took the case to the U. S. Supreme Court, which sustained that ruling in an opinion, in the course of which Justice Brewer said:

There is no body of Federal common law separate and distinct from the common law existing in the several States in the sense that there is a body of statute law enacted by Congress separate and distinct from the body of statute law enacted by the several States. But it is an entirely different thing to hold that there is no common law in force generally throughout the United States, and that the countless multitude of interstate commercial

[1] 181 U. S. Rep., 92.

transactions are subject to no rules and burdened by no restrictions other than those expressed in the statutes of Congress. . . .

Can it be that the great multitude of interstate commercial transactions are freed from the burdens created by the common law, as so defined, and are subject to no rule except that to be found in the statutes of Congress? We are clearly of the opinion that this cannot be so, and that the principles of the common law are operative upon all interstate commercial transactions except so far as they are modified by Congressional enactment. . . .

In *Interstate Commerce Commission v. Baltimore and Ohio Railroad*, 145 U. S. 263, 275, . . . it was said by Mr. Justice Brown, speaking for the court: "Prior to the enactment of the act of February 4, 1887, to regulate commerce, commonly known as the interstate commerce act, . . . railway traffic in this country was regulated by the principles of the common law applicable to common carriers." . . .

Reference may also be had to the elaborate opinion of District Judge Shiras, holding the Circuit Court in the Northern District of Iowa, in *Murray v. Chicago & Northwestern Railway*, 62 Fed. Rep., 24, in which is collated a number of extracts from opinions of this court, all tending to show the recognition of a general common law existing throughout the United States, not, it is true, as a body of law distinct from the common law enforced in the States, but as containing the general rules and principles by which all transactions are controlled, except so far as those rules and principles are set aside by express statute.

CHAPTER XI

Establishment of Common Law Rules.

Principles of justice are vague and uncertain so long as they exist only in the minds and hearts of the people. They become more definite by usage; that is, being used continuously by the people in settling disputes about business and property without going to law. They become rules of the common law when they have been applied and accepted by the courts.

A court of justice for the trial of cases is composed of a judge, who decides questions of law, and a jury, which decides questions of fact. In declaring a rule of the common law, the judge acts upon evidence of the law in the form of customs and usages, precedents established by decisions of previous cases, and statutes. He then declares the rule of law which governs the jury in deciding the matters of fact about which the parties to an action disagree. In deciding questions of fact, the jury acts upon evidence in the form of written documents presented by the parties in support of their contentions and in the form of testimony by word of mouth given by witnesses who know about the matters which are in dispute. Whenever, in a number of trials of similar cases, the same principle of law is applied, a rule of the common law is said to be established.

The establishment of a rule of the common law is explained in the case of *Norway Plains Co. v. Boston and Maine Railroad*,[1] decided in 1854 by the Supreme Judicial Court of Massachusetts, in which it was shown to the court and the jury that the railroad had received a shipment of goods directed to the Norway Plains Company and that a truckman sent by the plaintiff had been told that they were on the last car of the train and were at a place on the tracks where they were inaccessible so that delivery had to be postponed until the next day.. The truckman went away, and the goods were destroyed by fire during the night. The question of law to be decided by the court was whether the railroad ought to be compelled to pay for the goods. The questions of fact to be decided by the jury were whether the truckman had actually called for the goods and been told that he could not get them and whether the goods had actually been burned up. Inasmuch as railroads were then a new means of transportation and there were no decided cases declaring the rule of law to be applied, the court, in deciding the question of law, was obliged to refer to the principles of right and wrong that were involved and to the usages, practices and rules of the common law that governed the liability of carriers of merchandise by older methods. Chief Justice Shaw said:

The liability of carriers of goods by railroads, the grounds and precise extent and limits of their responsibility, are coming to be subjects of great interest and importance to the community. It is a new mode of transportation, in some respects like the transportation by ships, lighters, and canal boats on water, and in others like that by wagons on land; but in some respects it differs from both. Though the

[1] 1 Gray (Mass.) Rep., 263, 266.

practice is new, the law, by which the rights and obligations of owners, consignees, and of the carriers themselves, are to be governed, is old and well established. It is one of the great merits and advantages of the common law, that, instead of a series of detailed practical rules, established by positive provisions, and adapted to the precise circumstances of particular cases, which would become obsolete and fail, when the practice and course of business to which they apply, should cease or change, the common law consists of a few broad and comprehensive principles, founded on reason, natural justice, and enlightened public policy, modified and adapted to the circumstances of all the particular cases which fall within it. These general principles of equity and policy are rendered precise, specific, and adapted to practical use, by usage, which is the proof of their general fitness and common convenience, but still more by judicial exposition; so that, when in a course of judicial proceeding, by tribunals of the highest authority, the general rule has been modified, limited and applied, according to particular cases, such judicial exposition, when well settled and acquiesced in, becomes itself a precedent, and forms a rule of law for future cases, under like circumstances. The effect of this expansive and comprehensive character of the common law is, that whilst it has its foundations in the principles of equity, natural justice, and that general convenience which is public policy; although these general considerations would be too vague and uncertain for practical purposes, in the various and complicated cases, of daily occurrences, in the business of an active community; yet the rules of the common law, so far as cases have arisen and practices actually grown up, are rendered in a good degree, precise and certain, for practical purposes, by usage and judicial precedent. Another consequence of this expansive character of the common law is, that when new practices spring up, new combinations of facts arise, and cases are presented for which there is no precedent in judicial decision, they must be governed by the general principle, applicable to cases most nearly analogous, but modified and adapted to new circumstances, by considerations of fitness and propriety, of reason and justice, which grow out of these circumstances. The consequence of this state of the law is, that when a new practice or new course of business arises, the rights and duties of parties are not without a law to govern them; the general considerations of reason, justice and policy, which underlie the particular rules of the common law, will still apply, modified and adapted, by the same considerations, to the new circumstances. If these are such as give rise to controversy and litigation, they soon, like previous cases, come to be settled by judicial exposition, and the principles thus settled soon come to have the effect of precise and practical rules. Therefore, although steamboats and railroads are but of yesterday, yet the principles which govern the rights and duties of carriers of passengers, and also those which regulate the rights and duties of carriers of goods, and of the owners of goods carried, have a deep and established foundation in the common law, subject only to such modifications as new circumstances may render necessary and mutually beneficial.

Application of Common Law Rules.

The decisions of courts are not the law, but evidence of the law. Since the common law consists of "broad and comprehensive principles, founded on reason, natural justice, and enlightened public policy, modified and adapted to the circumstances of all the particular cases which fall within it,"[1] its applications may vary with the courts that render the decisions. For this reason it has become the rule in ascertaining the common law applicable to cases for the courts of a State to follow their own precedents and for a Federal court that

---

[1] See *Norway Plains Co. v. B. & M. R. R.*, 1 Gray (Mass.) Rep., 263.

has concurrent jurisdiction with the courts of a State to follow Federal precedents.

In the case of *St. Nicholas Bank v. State Bank*,[1] decided in 1891 by the New York Court of Appeals, Justice Earl said:

> The defendant . . . claims that the contract with the plaintiff is to be treated as a Tennessee contract, and that by the law of that state, it cannot be made liable for this loss [on which suit had been brought]. Upon the trial, for the purpose of showing the law of that state, it put in evidence a decision of the Supreme Court [of Tennessee]. . . . That decision was not based upon any statute law, but upon the principles of the common law supposed to be applicable to the facts of the case. It did not make or establish law, but expounded the law, and furnished some evidence of what the law applicable to that case was—evidence which other courts might or might not take and receive as reliable and sufficient, and even the same court, upon fuller discussion and more mature consideration, might in some subsequent case refuse to take the same view of the law. There is no common law peculiar to Tennessee. But the common law there is the same as that which prevails here and elsewhere, and the judicial expositions of the common law there do not bind the courts here. The courts of this state and of the United States would follow the courts of that state in the construction of its statute law. But the courts of this state will follow its own precedents in the expounding of the general common law applicable to commercial transactions.

In the case of *Smith v. Alabama*,[2] decided in 1887 by the U. S. Supreme Court, Justice Matthews said:

> A determination in a given case of what that law [the common law] is, may be different in a court of the United

[1] 128 New York Rep., 26, 33.   [2] 124 U. S. Rep., 465, 478.

States from that which prevails in the judicial tribunals of a particular State. This arises from the circumstance that the courts of the United States, in cases within their jurisdiction, where they are called upon to administer the law of the State in which they sit or by which the transaction is governed, exercise an independent though concurrent jurisdiction, and are required to ascertain and declare the law according to their own judgment. This is illustrated by the case of *Railroad Co. v. Lockwood*, 17 Wall., 357, where the common law prevailing in the State of New York, in reference to the liability of common carriers for negligence, received a different interpretation [by the U. S. Supreme Court], from that placed upon it by the judicial tribunals of the State; but the law as applied was none the less the law of that State.

RULES OF THE COMMON LAW

The following rules of the common law illustrate concretely the general nature and the particular applications of the common law.

A Party to an Action is Entitled to a Trial by Jury.

In old times, when the common law was growing into form, crimes were acts that were so dangerous to the safety of all of the people that those who committed them had to be deprived of their right to live in the community, whereas lesser offenses, which merely made other people uncomfortable, could be suppressed by disciplinary punishments. Thieves and robbers, murderers, rebels and traitors, whose acts injured the community, were tried by all of the people at their smaller or larger assemblies; while loafers, drunkards, and quarrelsome folk were dealt with by the lord of the manor or by the sheriff. In the one case, the assembly either put the offender to death or banished him from the community; in the other, the magistrate put the offender in the stocks, or on a pillory, or had him well whipped. The distinction thus made still exists. Those who are accused of serious crimes called felonies, are tried in courts of justice by juries of twelve men, who are representatives of all the members of a community; those who are charged with minor offenses amounting to little more than bad behavior, called misdemeanors, are tried by magistrates.

Theoretically, a party to a civil case always has the right to a trial by jury; but in practice unimportant cases, such as actions for small debts or for the enforcement of property rights of small value, are usually tried in magistrates' courts without the aid of a jury. In very old times, the headmen of each community adjusted such little disputes; and the poorer people, who could not have afforded to employ lawyers and pay the heavy expenses of lawsuits, were glad to submit their controversies to the lord of the manor, or to the mayor of the city, or to some justice of the peace who had authority to judge such cases. This practice still continues, though the right of trial by jury is now fixed by the State and national constitutions and is regulated by statutes. Important cases are tried in courts in which the parties to an action have a trial by jury unless they agree to a trial before a judge, and smaller litigations are tried in justices' courts, in which a trial by a jury is not usual, but may be had if either of the parties so desire.

Trial by jury in both criminal and civil cases had existed in England in one form or another from the time of King Alfred. It assumed its present form of a trial by a jury of twelve men under the supervision of a judge in the time of Edward I.

In the case of *U. S. v. Reid,*[1] decided in 1851 by the U. S. Supreme Court, Chief Justice Taney said:

The colonists who established the English colonies in this country, undoubtedly brought with them the common and statute laws of England, as they stood at the time of their emigration, so far as they were applicable to the situation and local circumstances of the colony. And among the most cherished and familiar principles of the common law was the trial by jury in civil, and still more especially in criminal cases. And however the colonies may have varied in other respects in the modifications with which the common or statute law was adopted, the trial by jury in all of them of English origin was regarded as a right of inestimable value, and the best and only security of life, liberty and property.

But as the law formerly stood, the value of this right was much impaired by the mode of proceeding in criminal cases. For when a person was accused of a capital crime, and his life depended upon the issue of the trial, he was denied compulsory process for his witnesses; and when they voluntarily appeared in his behalf, he was not permitted to examine them on oath, nor to have the aid of counsel in his defense, except only as regarded the questions of law. . . .

This oppressive mode of proceeding had been abolished in England and the colonies also by different statutes before the declaration of independence. But the memory of the abuses which had been practiced under it had not passed away. And the thirteen colonies, . . . as soon as they became States, placed in their respective constitutions or fundamental laws, safeguards against the restoration of proceedings which were so oppressive and odious while they remained in force. It was the people of these thirteen States which formed the constitution of the United States, and ingrafted on it the provision which secures the trial

[1] 12 Howard (U. S.) Rep., 361, 363.

by jury [in the Federal courts], and abolishes the old common law proceeding which had so often been used for the purposes of oppression. And the provisions in the constitution of the United States in this respect are substantially the same with those which had been previously adopted in the several States. They were overlooked in the constitution of the United States as originally framed. But as soon as the public attention was called to the fact, that the securities for a fair and impartial trial by jury in criminal cases had not been inserted among the cardinal principles of the new government, they hastened to amend it, and to secure to the party accused of an offense against the United States, the same mode of trial and the same mode of proceeding, that had been previously established and practiced in the courts of the several States. It was for this purpose that the 5th and 6th amendments were added to the constitution.

Matters in Dispute in Law Suits shall be Determined upon such Evidence as will Prove the Facts.

The rules of the common law provide that matters in dispute in criminal and civil cases shall be determined upon such evidence as will prove the facts. For example, witnesses can testify only about what they know of their own knowledge, and are not allowed to tell the jury what some one has told them. Again, a witness is not allowed to testify about what is contained in a letter or other written document; the written evidence itself, or a properly proved copy, must be produced and offered in evidence. When such primary evidence cannot be presented, as in cases where those who know the facts of their own knowledge are dead or where original written evidence has been lost or destroyed, secondary[1] evidence may be offered.

[1] See *Matter of Smart*, p. 155.

In the case of *Patterson v. Winn*,[1] decided by the U. S. Supreme Court in 1831, the question was whether a copy of a land grant authenticated by the secretary of state of Georgia under the great seal of that State, could be used in evidence in court, until it had been proved that the original document had been lost or destroyed, or the failure to produce it had been explained. The court decided that a document so authenticated was admissible in evidence by the rules of the common law. Justice Story said:

The common law is the law of Georgia, and the rules of evidence belonging to it are in force there, unless so far as they have been modified by statute, or controlled by a settled course of judicial decisions and usage. . . . It does not appear that Georgia has ever established any rules at variance with the common law. . . . We think it clear that by the common law, as held for a long period, an exemplification [authentication] of a public grant under the great seal, is admissible in evidence, as being record proof of as high a nature as the original. It is a recognition, in the most solemn form, by the government itself, of the validity of its own grant, under its own seal, and imports absolute verity as matter of record. . . . There was in former times a technical distinction existing on this subject which deserves notice. As evidence, such exemplifications of letters-patent seem to have been generally deemed admissible. But where, in pleading, a profert [offer] was made of the letters-patent, there, upon the principles of pleading, the original under the great seal was required to be produced. . . . It was to cure this difficulty that the statutes of 3 Edw. VI. c. 4, and 13 Elizab. c. 6, were passed, by which patentees, and all claiming under them, were enabled to make title in pleading by showing forth an exemplification of the letters-patent, as if the original were

[1] 5 Peters (U. S.) Rep., 233, 241.

pleaded and set forth. These statutes being passed before the emigration of our ancestors, being applicable to our situation, and in amendment of the law, constitute a part of our common law.

The Genuineness of a Will is to be Determined by the Evidence of the Subscribing Witnesses.

According to the rules of the common law, a will must be proved by the testimony of the persons who subscribed their names as witnesses to its execution, not by the evidence of persons who may have been present when the testator signed it and declared that it was his will, or by persons familiar with his signature who were not present.

In *Matter of Smart*,[1] a proceeding in New York City for the probate or proving of a will made in Australia by a person who lost his life at sea, decided in 1914 by the Surrogate's Court of New York County, N. Y., the attorney general, who represented the rights of the State of New York, contended that the will presented did not bear the signature of the testator. He did not cross-examine the subscribing witnesses that testified that they saw the deceased sign it, but called to the stand two persons that were familiar with his signature. One of these said that the signature did not look like that of the testator; the other testified that it was not his signature. Surrogate Fowler held that, by the rule of the testamentary common law of England, attesting witnesses were presumed to be competent, and that as they had not been cross-examined, their testimony could not be impeached. He then showed that the testamentary common law of England was a part of the common law of the State of New York, saying:

[1] 84 Miscellaneous (N. Y.) Rep., 336.

The testamentary common law, as part of the common law in force in the province of New York, was continued in force by the first Constitution of the state, since several times readopted and confirmed by amended Constitutions. Chancellor Kent's decision in relation to the continuance of the old *equity* jurisprudence as part of the *common law*, adopted by the Constitution, covers that point. *Manning v. Manning*, 1 Johns. Ch., 529–531. It would be flying in the face of all principle to exclude the testamentary common law. *Manning v. Manning* was perhaps the most important cause ever decided by Chancellor Kent, for it fixed the boundaries of equity jurisdiction in this country. Why should the Constitution be taken to have adopted the old rules of chancery as part of the common law of the State and to have rejected the old testamentary law, always admitted to be part of the common law and placed solely on that foundation after the reign of Henry VIII? It would be difficult to give a reason. . . . It has for ages past been the rule in courts of this character that where the evidence of the attesting witnesses stands uncontradicted the will must prevail.

A Debt upon which no Action or Attempt to Recover has been Made for Twenty Years is Presumed to have been Paid.

At first sight this seems to be a mere repetition of the statute of limitations. It differs, however, in this,— that it applies in cases where that statute does not apply, as, for example, when the debtors have been absent from the State and the process of the courts could not be enforced against them.

The case of *Courtney v. Staudenmayer*,[1] decided in 1896 by the Supreme Court of Kansas, was an action to foreclose a mortgage upon which no part of the

[1] 56 Kansas Rep., 392, 396, 397.

principal and no interest had been paid for twenty-seven years. The court ruled that the debt secured by the mortgage was presumed to have been paid. Chief Justice Martin said:

At the common law, a presumption of payment arises after the lapse of 20 years. . . . The presumption of payment from lapse of time differs essentially from a statute of limitations. The presumption may be rebutted by sufficient evidence, no matter how long the time may be; but a statute of limitations cuts off the right of action, although it may be admitted that no payment has ever been made. The presumption of payment is based upon the experience of mankind that vouchers, acquittances, and evidences of payment are not usually preserved from one generation to another; that creditors usually desire their own without waiting a score of years upon their debtors; and that, where there has been no recognition of the claim by the debtor, and the creditor has forborne to assert a right for so long a time, it is most probable that his claim has been in some way satisfied.

No Action will lie to Recover Damages for the Killing of a Human Being.

This rule of the common law, now changed by statutes, was based upon the theory that when a human being was killed, the act of the person committing the homicide was an offense against the king, and the right of the heirs of the person killed to recover damages was merged in the higher right of the crown to prosecute a charge of felony.

In the case of *Grosso v. D. L. & W. R. R. Co.*,[1] decided by the Supreme Court of New Jersey in 1888, the husband of a woman who had been killed in a railroad

[1] 50 New Jersey Law Rep., 317, 318, 320, 323.

accident sought to recover damages upon the ground that her death had been caused by the negligence of the employees of the railroad. In the decision of the case, Justice Magie said:

In the very ingenious argument submitted by counsel for the plaintiff in error it seems to be admitted that the current of English authority indicates that such an action could not be brought at common law. In 1607 it was held that a husband could not recover for the injury he sustained by the death of his wife, occasioned by the battery of the defendant. *Higgins v. Butcher*, Yelv., 89. In deciding the case, Tanfield, J., expressed this opinion: "If a man beat the servant of S., so that he die of that battery, the master shall not have an action for that battery and loss of service, because the servant dying of the extremity of the battery, it is now become an offence to the crown, being converted into a felony, and that drowns the particular offence and private wrong offered to the master before, and his action is thereby lost." . . .

Many reasons have been suggested for the rule. It has been said that it is inconsistent with the policy of the law to permit the value of human life to become the subject of judicial computation [case cited]; that upon the principle which would allow an action to those who have been deprived of the services of deceased, an action would lie in favor of those entitled to the protection or interested in the life of deceased as dependents or even creditors [case cited]; that there is a natural and universal repugnance among enlightened nations to setting a price on human life. . . . .

We have the common law rule forbidding an action for damages occasioned by the death of a human being, except in cases where a statute gives a remedy by action, acknowledged in Massachusetts, . . . in Kentucky, . . . in New York, . . . in Michigan, . . . in Indiana, . . . in Con-

necticut, . . . in the Supreme Court of the United States,
. . . in Maine, . . . in Pennsylvania, . . . and in Georgia,
. . .

The conclusion I have reached is that the rule of the common law was that no action would lie to recover damages for the killing of a human being.

A Deed or Will Conveying Real Estate to a Person and his Heirs gives the Holder Absolute Ownership.

The most important difference between personal property such as money, cattle, furniture, and other things that can be taken from place to place, and real property such as lands, buildings on lands, and rights to the use of lands, is that personal property can be sold or transferred from hand to hand by the person who has it in possession, while real property can be sold only in accordance with the provisions of the deed or will by which the holder obtained it. The tenures or conditions of ownership of real estate contained in such deeds or wills vary greatly. In some cases, they give rights of ownership for life or for a term of years. In others, they give such rights to a person and to the heirs of his body. In still other instances, and most commonly, they convey it to the new holders and their heirs. This last form of ownership is known as an estate in fee simple and is the most complete title known to the common law.

In former times, an estate given or conveyed to a man and his heirs could not be sold or transferred absolutely because when the holder died, his rights went to his heirs, who could take it away from any person that had bought it from him. In the time of Queen Elizabeth, however, the English courts, in what is known as "Shelley's Case," formulated a rule of the common law that the limitation "to the heirs" in a deed gives the holder the whole estate so that he can sell it or give it away as he may see fit, without regard to any claims of his heirs. In nearly all of our States, statutes have been made by which estates for life with remainder to heirs are made estates in fee simple or complete ownership, and the rule is no longer of much importance. Nevertheless, it is a part of the common law except as abrogated by statute.

In the case of *Hardage v. Stroope*,[1] decided in 1893 by the Supreme Court of Arkansas, the question was upon the effect of a deed to a woman named Tennessee M. Carroll "to have and to hold the said land unto the said Tennessee M. Carroll for and during her natural life, and then to the heirs of her body, in fee simple; and if, at her death, there are no heirs of her body to take the said land, then, in that case, to be divided and distributed according to the laws for distribution in this State." It was claimed on one side that this gave her only a right to have the land during her life time; and on the other, that it gave her full and complete ownership. Justice Battle, in the decision of the court that she held full title, said:

The rule in Shelley's Case, as stated by Mr. Preston, which Chancellor Kent says is full and accurate, is as follows: "When a person takes an estate of freehold, legally or equitably, under a deed, will, or other writing, and in the same instrument there is a limitation by way of remainder, either with or without the interposition of another estate, of an interest of the same legal or equitable quality, to his heirs, or heirs of his body, as a class of persons to take in succession, from generation to generation, the limitation to the heirs entitles the ancestor to the whole estate." 4 Kent Com., 215. Its origin is enveloped in the mists of

[1] 58 Arkansas Rep., 303, 307.

antiquity. It was laid down in Shelley's Case in the 23rd year of the reign of Queen Elizabeth, upon the authority of a number of cases in the year-books. . . . Whatever may have been the cause of its origin, its effect has been "to facilitate the alienation" of land "by vesting the inheritance in the ancestor, instead of allowing it to remain in abeyance until his decease." Its operation in that respect has commended it to the favorable consideration of the most learned and able men of Great Britain and the United States, and, doubtless, contributed to its preservation and continuance, and enabled it to survive the innovations of legislation and the changes and fluctuations of centuries. Based upon the broad principles of public policy and commercial convenience, which abhor locking up and rendering inalienable any class of property, it has ever been in harmony with the genius of the institutions of our country and with the liberal and commercial spirit of the age. Hence it has been recognized and enforced as a part of the common law of nearly every State where it has not been repealed by statute.

Judicial Proceedings on Sunday are Void.

Sunday at the common law is a day on which judicial proceedings are suspended. The first day of the week is "observed by the Christian world as holy and set apart for the purposes of rest and worship."[1] In old times in England, even the orders of a court such as writs and executions could not be enforced on Sunday by the arrest of defendants in proceedings to recover debts or by the seizure of property owned by one person but in the possession of another. At the common law the day was not regarded as existing at all for ordinary legal purposes. Hence persons that were in debt, and were afraid of being arrested and imprisoned under

[1] 1 Am. & Eng. Ency. of Law, XXIV., 528.

the old common law rule that a creditor could satisfy his judgment by confining the debtor until he paid the debt, had to keep out of the way of the sheriff on week days, but could go where they pleased on Sunday. This common law rule, though for the most part superseded in our country by acts of legislatures, is still to some extent in force.

In the case of *City of Parsons v. Lindsay*,[1] decided in 1889 by the Supreme Court of Kansas, the validity of a judgment was challenged on the ground that it had been rendered on a Sunday. Chief Justice Horton ruled that the common law on the subject, as modified by law and custom in the State of Kansas, was still recognized and followed by the courts of that State. He said:

> By the common law, Sunday is *dies non juridicus* [not a judicial day], and therefore all judicial proceedings which take place on that day where the common-law rule is in force are void. The common-law rule of the invalidity of judicial proceedings on Sunday is impliedly recognized by our [Kansas] statute [cases cited]. The common law, as modified by constitutional and statutory law, judicial proceedings, and the condition and wants of the people, is enforced in this state in aid of the general statutes.

Common Carriers are Liable to Passengers and Shippers of Goods for Injuries caused by Acts of Negligence or Carelessness.

Common carriers are persons or corporations that make a business of transporting passengers and articles of merchandise and other property. When the common law was established in England and afterward when it was transplanted to the colonies, passengers and goods were transported from place to place by wagons, stage

[1] 41 Kansas Rep., 336.

coaches, and merchant ships. The owners of each of these instruments of trade were common carriers either of passengers or of such articles of property as they might choose to transport. The proprietor of a stage line engaged in passenger traffic did not carry merchandise unless he chose to engage in that kind of business. Wagoners and ship owners were equally free to choose the articles of commerce or other property that they would take from one place to another. Each of the three was under the law in duty bound to do his work carefully so that neither passengers nor property should be injured while in transit. If either passengers or property were injured or damaged by the carelessness either of the owners or of their employees, the owners were responsible for the injuries suffered and could be made to compensate persons injured or pay for property damaged. If, by careless driving, a stage coach was upset and the passengers were hurt, they could sue the owner of the stage line. If by careless packing or other neglect articles in transit were damaged, the owner could sue the carrier. This rule of the common law continued in force after the introduction of railroads.

In the case of *Kansas Pacific R. R. Co. v. Nichols*,[1] decided in 1872 by the Supreme Court of Kansas, the question at issue was whether a railroad company that had received a shipment of cattle was bound to transport them safely and expeditiously though no special agreement for such safe and expeditious transportation had been made. There was no statute governing the liability of a railroad in such a case. Therefore the question had to be decided according to the rules of the common law. This was not easy. At the time of the first

[1] 9 Kansas Rep., 236, 253.

settlements in this country, when the common law was introduced here, cattle were taken from place to place in droves, or very rarely were transported in ships. Railroads had not been invented. The railroad company interposed the defense that there was under these circumstances no rule of the common law applicable to the case. In overruling this contention, Justice Valentine said:

At common law no person was a common carrier of any article unless he chose to be, and unless he held himself out as such; and he was a common carrier of just such articles as he chose to be, and no others. If he held himself out as a common carrier of silk and laces, the common law would not compel him to be a common carrier of agricultural instruments such as plows, harrows, etc. . . . And it seems to us clear, beyond all doubt, that if a person had, in England, prior to the year 1607, held himself out as a common carrier of cattle and live stock by land, the common law would have made him such. If so, where is the valid distinction that is attempted to be made between the carrying of live stock and the carrying of any other kind of personal property? . . . At common law, any person could be a common carrier of all kinds, of any kind, or of just such kinds, of personal property as he chose; no more, no less. Of course, it is well known that at the time when our common law had its origin, that is, prior to the year 1607, railroads had no existence. But when they came into existence it must be admitted that they would be governed by the same rules so far as applicable which govern other carriers of property. . . . In this state, it must be presumed that they were created for the purpose of carrying all kinds of personal property. . . . Railroads are undoubtedly created for the purpose of carrying all kinds of property, which the common law would have permitted to be carried by common carriers in any mode, either by land or water. . . . Our decision, then, upon this question is that whenever a railroad company receive cattle or live stock to be transported over their road from one place to another, such company assume all the responsibilities of a common carrier, except so far as such responsibilities may be modified by special contract.

Marriage is a Contract.

According to the common law, a marriage is a contract or agreement to live together made by a man and woman of proper age, not too nearly related by blood or otherwise incapacitated, and made effective by their living together as husband and wife. Though usually made by a religious ceremony, a marriage contract made by agreement by word of mouth and consummated by the parties by living as husband and wife, is valid unless there is some statute which prescribes a particular way and manner for making it.

In the case of *Port v. Port*,[1] decided by the Supreme Court of Illinois in 1873, Justice Scholfield said:

We are inclined to the opinion, supported as it is by the statements of many of the most eminent text writers, as well as by the decisions of courts of the highest respectability, that, inasmuch as our statute does not prohibit or make void a marriage not solemnized in accordance with its provisions, a marriage without observing the statutory regulations, if made according to the common law, will still be a valid marriage, and that, by the common law, if the contract be made *per verba de presenti*, it is sufficient evidence of a marriage.

A Marriage Contract may be Annulled.

Under the rules of the common law, a marriage contract may be annulled and set aside by a divorce,

[1] 70 Illinois Rep., 484, 486.

though in its nature it is intended to be permanent. The power so to annul marriage is vested in courts of justice. At the time of the colonizing of this country, it was exercised in England by the ecclesiastical courts. In this country, originally by custom and usage and later on by the authority of statutes of legislatures, it has been exercised by common law courts or equity tribunals.

In the case of *Le Barron v. Le Barron*,[1] decided in 1862 by the Supreme Court of Vermont, Chief Justice Poland said:

The legal power to annul marriages has been recognized as existing in England from a very early period, but its administration, instead of being committed to the common law courts, was exercised by their spiritual or ecclesiastical courts. Under the administration of those courts, for a long period of time, the principles and practice governing this head of their jurisdiction, ripened into a settled course and body of jurisprudence, like that of the courts of chancery and admiralty, and constituted, with those systems, a part of the general law of the realm, and in the broad and enlarged use of the term, a part of the common law of the land, and was so held by the courts of that country.

This country having been settled by colonies from that, under the general authority of its government, and remaining for many years a part of its dominion, became and remained subject and entitled to the general laws of the government, and they became equally the laws of this country, except so far as they were inapplicable to the new relation and condition of things. This we understand to be well settled, both by judicial decision and the authority of eminent law writers. But if this were not so, the adoption of the common law of England, by the legislature of

[1] 35 Vermont Rep., 365.

the state, was an adoption of the whole body of the law of that country (aside from their parliamentary legislation), and included those principles of law administered by the courts of chancery and admiralty, and the ecclesiastical courts.

CHAPTER XII

Actions at Common Law.

Nearly all of the acts that are now forbidden by statute law and are punished as crimes, are also punishable under the rules of the common law. The common law likewise enables the supreme power in the community to maintain order and protect the people from acts not specifically prohibited by statute. In like manner, the rights of property of individuals are protected by processes that have long existed under the unwritten law, though now superseded by forms of procedure ordained by statutes. These common law actions are either criminal or civil according to the objects for which they are used.

Criminal Actions.

All actions at the common law that are brought to enforce penalties for acts which endanger the safety of members of the community are criminal actions. Such actions at common law exist solely under the laws of the States. There are no crimes under the laws of the United States except those which are denounced by written laws. In the case of *Ames v. Kansas*,[1] decided in 1884 by the U. S. Supreme Court, Chief Justice

[1] 111 U. S. Rep., 449, 460.

Waite, commenting upon the Code of Civil Procedure of Kansas, said:

A criminal action is one prosecuted by the State as a party, against a person charged with a public offence.

Civil Actions.

The jurisdiction given to the courts of the United States by Article III of the U. S. Constitution enables all persons engaged in certain classes of controversies to assert their rights in the Federal Courts. For that reason, the seventh article of the bill of rights provides for the trial by jury of suits at common law. Hence, in the United States courts as well as in the State courts, all actions arising under common law rules that safeguard the property rights of citizens may be determined. In the case of *Jefferson County v. Philpot*,[1] decided in 1899 by the Supreme Court of Arkansas, Justice Battle said: .

A civil action . . . is an ordinary proceeding in a court of justice by one party against another for the enforcement or protection of a private right, or the redress or prevention of a private wrong. Sand. & H. Dig., Sec. 5602. It is variously defined to be: "The rightful method of obtaining in a court what is due to any one; the lawful demand of one's right in a court of justice; the lawful demand of one's rights in the form given by law; the form of a suit given by law for the recovery of that which is one's due; the lawful demand of one's rights, a remedial instrument of justice, whereby redress is obtained for any wrong committed or right withheld; any judicial proceeding which, conducted to a termination, will result in a judgment." Winfield's Adjudged Words and Phrases, p. 16.

[1] 66 Arkansas Rep., 243, 245.

Kinds of Civil Actions.

Civil actions may be classified as actions of contract, actions of tort, actions of replevin, actions *in rem*, and real actions.

Actions of Contract.

The members of a community, living together and doing business with one another, are constantly making contracts. Some of these are formal agreements, in which one person agrees to do some work or perform some service for another and the other agrees to pay for such work or service. Others are implied agreements, in which one person does something for another for which he expects to be paid though the other person may not promise in words to make any such payment. In each case, the person who does the work or performs the service can bring an action of contract if the other person refuses or neglects to make the payments. Actions of contract, therefore, are those which grow out of contracts.

Actions of Tort.

It often happens that one person, either intentionally, or unintentionally does an act that injures another. For example, a man may, by false representations, induce another to make a contract by which the latter will lose money; or may make false statements about the character of his neighbor by which the neighbor will lose the esteem and good will of the community; or may, by carelessly driving an automobile, run over and injure another person. In each of these cases, a common law action of tort may be brought to recover for the damage suffered.

In the case of *Wartman v. Empire Loan Co.*,[1] decided in 1907 by the Texas Court of Civil Appeals, Justice Talbot defined the phrase *action of tort* as follows:

An action of tort, strictly speaking and as it is commonly understood, is one in which the complainant seeks to recover damages for defamation of character, the wrongful and forcible taking of his property or injury to it, or for unlawful violence inflicted upon his person.

Actions of Replevin.

When one person has in his possession property that another has a right to have, a common law action of replevin may be brought to gain its possession from the wrongful holder.

In the case of *Maclary v. Turner*,[2] decided in 1891 by the Superior Court of Errors and Appeals of Delaware, Justice Cullin said:

Replevin lies for all goods and chattels unlawfully taken or detained, and may be brought whenever one person claims personal property in the possession of another, and this whether the claimant has ever had possession or not, and whether his property in the goods be absolute or qualified, provided he has the right to the possession.

Actions in Rem.

An action *in rem* is one by which a person seeks to assert a claim against property by reason of some interest in it which he has acquired or one between plaintiffs and defendants in which the right of ownership of certain property is to be determined. For example, a

[1] 45 Texas Civil Appeals Rep., 467, 471.
[2] 9 Houston (Del.) Rep. 281, 284.

ship builder that repairs a vessel acquires by his work an interest or right of ownership in it. In order to assert that right, he may bring his action against the thing (*res*) itself—the vessel—instead of against the owners. Also a person who has an interest in a trust fund created by a will can bring an action *in rem* against the trustee in order to obtain an accounting.

In the case of *Holcomb v. Kelly*,[1] decided in 1907 by the New York Supreme Court, Justice Benton said:

A proceeding *in rem* is one to determine the state or condition of the thing itself. In a strict sense, it is a term applied to a proceeding taken directly against the property, without reference to the title of the individual claimants; but in a true and more general sense a term applied to actions between parties where the direct object is to reach and dispose of property owned by them or of some interest therein.

In the case of *Gorham Co. v. United E. & C. Co.*,[2] decided in 1911 by the New York Court of Appeals, Judge Hiscock said:

It would be difficult . . . to define with accurate completeness such a proceeding [*in rem*], but there are certain essential features thereof which we may bring to mind. . . . Such a proceeding, as its name implies, is prosecuted against a "thing" instead of a person. The court acquires jurisdiction by possession of this subject-matter rather than by a recognized and effective service of process on some person. By virtue of this possession it determines facts whereon it pronounces judgment which operating upon and through the thing in its possession is conclusive

[1] 114 New York Supplement, 1048, 1051.
[2] 202 N. Y. Rep., 342, 348.

upon all persons having an interest therein though not served with process.

"It is a distinguishing feature of a proceeding *in rem* that the jurisdiction of the court, in a particular case, rests merely upon the seizure or attachment of the property. No personal notice to any individual is required. The *res* [thing], being brought within the jurisdiction of the court, becomes subject to its adjudication, and all parties interested are supposed to be duly apprised of the proceedings, by the mere taking of the property, or by the usual proclamation or published notice. This jurisdiction empowers the Court to adjudicate upon the status of the *res*, or to order it to be disposed of in a given way, according to the object of the action." (Black on Judgments, Section 794.)

Real Actions.

When one person is in possession of real estate such as lands or houses, and another person has a better right to that real estate, a common law real action may be brought to settle the dispute and determine who is the real owner.

In the case of *Hall v. Decker*,[1] decided in 1860 by the Supreme Judicial Court of Maine, Justice Kent defined real actions in the following words:

Real actions are those brought for the *specific recovery* of lands, tenements or hereditaments.[2]   The essential and distinguishing fact that gives an action the character of a *real* action is, that it seeks to recover *specifically* the land and its possession.   Stevens on Pl., p. 3.

[1] 48 Maine Rep., 255.
[2] Tenements are rights in land or its use such as rights of way or of homestead. Hereditaments are a species of property rights annexed to land like the possession of heirlooms.

CHAPTER XIII

Writs.

In the trial of a common law action, the parties present evidence in support of their contentions; the judge determines the rules of law that the jury is to follow in its consideration of the questions at issue; the jury render a decision called a verdict in favor of one of the contestants; and the judge directs that a judgment in accordance with the verdict be entered by the clerk. The plaintiff, if successful, is then entitled to a remedy at the common law, which is given in the form of a writ. A writ is "a precept in writing, couched in the form of a letter, running in the name of the king, president, or state, issuing from a court of justice, and sealed with its seal, addressed to a sheriff or other officer of the law, or directly to the person whose action the court desires to command, either as the commencement of a suit or other proceeding, or as incidental to its progress, and requiring the performance of a specified act, or giving authority and commission to have it done."[1]

Writs of Execution.

A writ of execution is a written command issued by a court to a sheriff or other officer of the executive de-

[1] Black, Law Dictionary.

partment of the government directing him to enforce a judgment.

In the case of *Southern California Land Co. v. Hotel Co.*,[1] decided in 1892 by the Supreme Court of California, Justice Harrison said:

A writ of execution is defined to be "process authorizing the seizure and appropriation of the property of a defendant for the satisfaction of a judgment against him." (Anderson's Law Dict.) When issued upon a judgment running generally against the property of the defendant, it is an authority to the sheriff to seize of the property of the defendant a sufficient amount to satisfy the judgment.

Writs of Mandamus.

A writ of mandamus is a written command addressed to an officer of a government, directing him to perform the duties of the office he holds.

In the case of *People v. Hallett*,[2] decided in 1871 by the Supreme Court of Colorado Territory, Justice Belford said:

It has been well said that, in order to maintain a system of government which will be able to secure to the citizen his rights, it is necessary to have persons appointed or chosen to administer the law. And, when persons are thus clothed with the power and have assumed the duties of a public officer, they have taken upon themselves the obligation to perform those duties, and if they neglect or refuse to do so, any one whose rights are thereby injuriously affected is entitled to demand relief. The remedy provided by our system of law, as well as that of England, is a process, issuing from the judicial branch of the government, which seeks to compel the officer to go forward and to do that which is enjoined upon him by the position he holds.

[1] 94 California Rep., 217, 221.   [2] 1 Colorado Rep., 352, 354.

176 THE REASONABLENESS OF THE LAW

This process is denominated a writ of mandamus, and when there is a right to execute an office, perform a service, or exercise a function, more especially if it be a matter of public concern or attended with profit, and a person having such right is wrongfully kept out of possession or dispossessed of such right, and has no other specific legal remedy, the court will interfere by mandamus upon reasons of justice and of public policy to preserve peace, order and good government.

Writs of Prohibition.

A writ of prohibition is a written command issued by a court prohibiting an inferior court from proceeding with the trial of an action with which it is not authorized to deal.

In the case of *People v. Judge Superior Court*,[1] decided in 1879 by the Supreme Court of Michigan, Justice Marston said:

The writ of prohibition is a remedy provided by the common law to prevent the encroachment of jurisdiction. It is a proper remedy in cases where the court exceeds the bounds of its jurisdiction, or takes cognizance of matters not arising within its jurisdiction. It can only be interposed in a clear case of excess of jurisdiction, and may lie to a part and not to the whole. . . . It can only be resorted to where other remedies are ineffectual to meet the exigencies of the case. It is a preventive, rather than a remedial process.

Writs of Quo Warranto.

A writ of *quo warranto* (by what right) is a process by which a State or the United States may determine the authority or warrant upon which any person is exercising the powers and duties of a public office. It also

[1] 3 Northwestern Reporter 850, 853.

issues in cases where individual citizens wish to ascertain the authority of an officer of a corporation or other body.

In the case of *State v. Perpetual etc. Insurance Co.*,[1] decided by the Supreme Court of Missouri in 1843, Justice Scott said:

> A writ of *quo warranto* is in the nature of a writ of right for the State against any person who claims or exercises any office, to inquire by what authority he supports his claim, in order to determine the right. 3 Blacks. Com. 262 (a). . . . It issues on demand of the proper officer of the State, as a matter of course, and there is no more necessity for an application . . . for this writ than there would be for a summons.

Writs of Certiorari.

A writ of *certiorari* is a process by which supreme courts at the request of petitioners obtain from lower courts and officers the records of proceedings that are to be reviewed on appeal. It "is a common-law prerogative writ issued from a superior court directed to one of inferior jurisdiction, commanding the latter to certify and return to the former the record in a particular case. The writ is also used, in some jurisdictions, to review not only proceedings of inferior courts but also proceedings of inferior officers, boards, and tribunals."[2]

Writs of Habeas Corpus.

"The writ of habeas corpus is defined as a writ directed to a person detaining another and commanding him to produce the body of the prisoner at a certain

[1] 8 Missouri Rep., 330, 331.   [2] 11 Corpus Juris, 87, 88.

time and place, with the day and cause of his caption
[seizure] and detention, and to do, submit to, and receive whatsoever the court or judge awarding the writ
shall determine in that behalf."[1]   It is a remedy especially designed to test the legality of the proceedings
by which a person has been imprisoned.   A person arrested upon a charge of crime, who has been refused
the right to go free upon giving bail, may by its means
test the right of the magistrate thus to order his detention.   A person confined in a prison under a sentence
pronounced by a court can thus obtain his liberty if
that court had no power to order his imprisonment.
An alleged insane person can be freed from a lunatic
asylum by habeas corpus if his sanity can be proved in
court.   A person confined in a prison, if needed as a witness in the trial of a case, can by this writ be brought to
the court to testify.

In the case of *People ex rel Pruyne v. Walts*,[2] decided
in 1890 by the N. Y. Court of Appeals, Justice Brown
said:

The common-law writ of habeas corpus was a writ in
behalf of liberty, and its purpose was to deliver a prisoner
from unjust imprisonment and illegal and improper restraint.

[1] 15 Am. & Eng. Ency. Law (2nd Ed.), 128.
[2] 122 N. Y. Rep., 238, 241.

PART IV

Equity: A Law of Prevention

CHAPTER XIV

Nature of Equity.

In modern society people have with one another relations which involve duties on each side. A husband is in duty bound to support and protect his wife; she is equally bound to safeguard and care for the home. Parents ought to support their children; children ought to obey their fathers and mothers. Persons who have the right to occupy real estate only during their lives ought not to tear down buildings or cut down timber or otherwise injure the property of those who will succeed them; the ultimate owners ought not to interfere with the use of the real estate by the life occupants. Buyers and sellers, mortgagors and mortgagees, trustees and beneficiaries of trusts, partners and copartners, principals and agents, employers and employees, landlords and tenants,—each and all owe to one another duties that the law ought to safeguard.

The common law provides remedies in the form of damages, which the courts assess against individuals who have failed to perform their legal duties; but the common law does not give any remedies, until after the failures have wrought injury. It does not interfere to prevent the injury from being inflicted. Cases are constantly arising in which the damages caused by such wrongful acts cannot be sufficiently adjusted by money awards. Consequently, there must be another form of law that will prevent those wrongful acts from being committed. That form of law is equity.

In cases in which the common law does not provide a sufficient remedy, the injured party may have recourse to a court of equity. In these cases the equity courts compel persons to perform acts essential to justice and to refrain from acts contrary to justice. A court of equity may command a person to perform a contract or may prohibit him from committing an injurious act. If the seller of a farm refuses to deliver a deed, an equity court will direct him to do so, so that the buyer may be able to take possession and earn his living by cultivating the soil; the common law would give the buyer only the profit he might make by selling the land to someone else and would give no compensation for the inconvenience and loss through being deprived of his means of livelihood. Likewise, a court of equity will prohibit a person from carrying on a slaughtering business in the residence district of a city; whereas the common law would only award damages for the loss of value of the houses in the neighborhood but would not compensate the owners for having been forced either to live in a bad smelling neighborhood or to move.

In the case of *Watson v. Sutherland*,[1] decided in 1866, the U. S. Supreme Court applied the rule that equity jurisdiction exists only when there is no sufficient remedy at law. That case was a proceeding in equity by which the petitioner had asked the U. S. Circuit Court of Maryland to forbid the sale of the stock in trade of a business concern under judgments that had

[1] 5 Wallace (U. S.) Rep., 74, 78.

been obtained by its creditors. The petitioner contended that he had purchased this stock in trade from the insolvents, and that, if the creditors were not prevented from selling it, he would be ruined. The creditors answered by alleging that the sale to the petitioner was fraudulent and had been made in order to cheat them, and that, even if the sale was not fraudulent, the petitioner had a plain, complete, and adequate remedy at law, and had no right to relief in equity. The circuit court ruled in favor of the petitioner and granted him the restraining order he had asked for. The creditors then took the case to the U. S. Supreme Court by a writ of error. In deciding that the case was one in which the petitioner had a right to sue in equity, Justice Davis said:

It is contended that the injunction should have been refused, because there was a complete remedy at law. If the remedy at law is sufficient, equity cannot give relief, "but it is not enough that there is a remedy at law; it must be plain and adequate, or in other words, as practical and efficient to the ends of justice, and its prompt administration, as the remedy in equity" [Citing *Boyce's Exor. v. Grundy*, 3 Peters 210]. How could Sutherland [the petitioner] be compensated at law, for the injuries he would suffer, should the grievances of which he complains be consummated?

If the appellants made the levy, and prosecuted it in good faith, without circumstances of aggravation, in the honest belief that Wroth & Fullerton [the insolvent firm] owned the stock of goods (which they swear to in their answer), and it should turn out, in an action at law instituted by Sutherland for trepass, that the merchandise belonged exclusively to him, it is well settled that the measure of damages, if the property were not sold, could not extend beyond the injury done to it, or, if sold, to the value of it, when taken, with interest from the time of the taking down to the trial.

And this is an equal rule, whether the suit is against the marshal or the attaching creditors, if the proceedings have been fairly conducted, and there has been no abuse of authority. . . . "Legal compensation refers solely to the injury to *the property taken*, and not to any collateral or consequential damages, *resulting to the owner*, by the trespass" [citing *Pacific Ins. Co. v Conard*, 1 Baldwin, 142]. Loss of trade, destruction of credit, and failure of business prospects, are collateral or consequential damages, which it is claimed would result from the trespass, but for which compensation cannot be awarded in a trial at law.

Commercial ruin to Sutherland [the petitioner] might, therefore, be the effect of closing his store and selling his goods, and yet the common law fail to reach the mischief. To prevent a consequence like this, a court of equity steps in, arrests the proceedings *in limine* [at the beginning, or before they go further]; brings the parties before it; hears their allegations and proofs, and decrees, either that the proceedings shall be unrestrained, or else perpetually enjoined. The absence of a plain and adequate remedy at law affords the only test of equity jurisdiction, and the application of the principle to a particular case, must depend altogether upon the character of the case, as disclosed in the pleadings. In the case we are considering, it is very clear that the remedy in equity could alone furnish relief, and that the ends of justice require the injunction to be issued.

English Origin of Equity.

Equity had its origin in England during the fourteenth century. The common law had then taken form as a system of administering justice by awarding damages to those who had been injured by wrongful acts. It was felt that some improvement in legal process was necessary to enable the courts to prevent injuries, the only remedy then available in such cases being by petition to the king. The common law lawyers and courts were unwilling to change the established procedure, partly because they clung to old ideals of law, partly because they were jealous of the Lord Chancellor to whom the king as the fountain of justice, often referred these petitions for relief.   In time the custom of presenting petitions to the king gave way to the plan of presenting them directly to the chancellor, and the courts of the chancellor became courts of chancery or of equity. The story of the origin and growth of equity in England is given as follows by competent authority:[1]

English equity as a system administered by a tribunal apart from the established courts made its first appearance in the reign of Edward I, its origin being due wholly to the inability, and to a limited extent the unwillingness, of the common-law courts to entertain and give relief in every case, and thus meet all the requirements of justice. The separate administration of equity began in the practice of referring causes to the chancellor. That office was a very ancient one, but up to that period its functions had been ministerial rather than judicial.   In the reign of Edward I it became not uncommon to refer to the chancellor petitions which had been presented to the king and council. Such petitions had long constituted a means of obtaining relief either against, or independently of, the ordinary courts of law.   In time the custom of sending them to the chancellor led to the addressing of such petitions to that official directly, and in this way chancery became a recognized form for the relief of litigants and the correction of legal abuses. . . .   During the reign of Edward III . . . the court came to sit regularly at Westminster for hearing causes.   By the end of the reign of Henry V (1413–1422)

[1] Corpus Juris, *Equity*.

the purely formative period was over, and chancery was one of the established courts of the realm. The period following the establishment of chancery was marked by a struggle for supremacy between it and the other courts. While this extended to other matters, the center of the conflict was the right of chancery to interfere by injunction with the proceedings of the common-law courts. From the reign of Henry VI (1422–1461), and even earlier, the chancellor had granted the extraordinary writ to enjoin the enforcement of judgments, and even to prevent the commencement of actions; but this was always against the protests of the common-law judges who lost no opportunity to make those writs ineffectual. After a controversy lasting for nearly two centuries, the prerogatives of the court of chancery were finally confirmed by a royal decree in 1616. Within a short time chancery jurisdiction became extended to nearly its modern scope. The doctrine of *stare decisis* [what has been decided stands and may not be changed] became an established part of equity jurisprudence. Thenceforth equity ceased to be a mere corrective agency and became a definite system of jurisprudence occupying the field side by side with the common law, each with a distinct jurisdiction, and therefore necessarily there grew up, not only two distinct systems of practice in these courts, but also two distinct systems of substantive jurisprudence, that in the courts of chancery being the system which we call "equity."

Establishment of Equity in the United States.

Courts of Equity were a late growth in the United States, although beginnings were made in some of the colonies. In the case of *Wells v. Pierce*,[1] decided in 1853 by the Superior Court of Judicature of New Hampshire, Justice Bell said:

[1] 27 N. H. Rep., 503, 512.

This court has a broad jurisdiction, as a court of equity, in all cases of trust, fraud, accidents or mistakes, *Rev. Sts.*, Ch., 171, Sec. 6. The limits of their jurisdiction in these cases are coextensive with those of the court of chancery, and other courts of equity in England. Equity, as a great branch of the law of their native country, was brought over by the colonists, and has always existed as a part of the common law, in its broadest sense, in New Hampshire. While our territory was under the colonial government of Massachusetts, there is reason to believe that the general court exercised original chancery jurisdiction. *Wash. Jud. His. of Mass.*, 34; *An. Charters of Mass.*, 94. Under the first royal governor of this province, Robert Mason was appointed chancellor of the province, and among the early records are to be found bills in equity, which were heard and decided before him. 1 *Belk. His.*, 198 and 200. In 1692, by "an act for establishing courts of judicature," it was provided, that "there shall be a court of chancery within this province, which said court shall have power to hear and determine all matters of equity, and shall be esteemed and accounted the high court of chancery of this province, that the governor and council be the said high court of chancery," etc. It is not known that this law was ever repealed, and it is supposed that the governor and council, who composed the court of appeals, continued to exercise chancery powers till the revolution.

Although equity was a part of the law which the first colonists brought to America, it did not flourish during the colonial era. The Americans of that day were a nation of farmers. Land was cheap and easily obtainable. There was very little commerce and almost no manufacturing. Hence few cases arose in which the interference of a court of equity was at all needed. Equity procedure was also unpopular because in many of the colonies, equity cases were decided by the governor and council instead of by judges and juries. Justice Story in his *Commentaries on Equity Jurisprudence*,[1] says:

Equity jurisprudence scarcely had an existence, in any large and appropriate sense of the terms, in any part of New England during its colonial state (1 *Dane Abridg.*, Ch. 1, Art. 7, Sec. 51; 7 *Dane Abridg.*, Ch. 225, Arts. 1, 2). In Massachusetts and Rhode Island, it still has but a very limited extent. In Maine and New Hampshire more general equity powers have been, within a few years, given to their highest Courts of Law. In Vermont and Connecticut it had an earlier establishment, in the former State since the Revolution and in the latter a short time before the Revolution. 2 *Swift. Dig.*, P. 15, Ed. 1823. In Virginia there does not seem to have been any court having chancery powers earlier than the Act of 1700, Ch. 4. 3 *Tucker's Black*, 7. In New York the first Court of Chancery was established in 1701; but it was so unpopular, from its powers being vested in the Governor and Council, that it had very little business until it was reorganized in 1778 (1 *Johns. Ch. Rep. Preface; Campb. and Camb. American Chancery Digest, Preface*, 6; *Blake's Chan.*, Introduct. VIII). In New Jersey it was established in 1705 (1 *Fonbl. Eq.* by Laussat. Edit. 1831, p. 14, note). Mr. Laussat, in his *Essay on Equity in Pennsylvania* (1826), has given an account of its origin and present state in that Commonwealth. From this account we learn that the permanent establishment of a Court of Equity was successfully resisted by the people during the whole of its colonial existence; and that the year 1790 is the true point at which we must fix the establishment of Equity in the Jurisprudence of Pennsylvania.

Origin of Equity Jurisdiction of the Federal Courts.

The equity powers of the courts of the United States, like their other powers, are derived from the U. S. Con-

[1] Sect. 56 Note.

stitution and from Acts of Congress. The judicial department of the national government, like the other departments, has no powers except those conferred by the fundamental law.

In the case of *Noonan v. Lee*,[1] decided in 1862 by the U. S. Supreme Court, Justice Swayne said:

> The equity jurisdiction of the courts of the United States is derived from the constitution and laws of the United States.

Equity Procedure in State Courts.

The States of the Union may be divided into three groups or classes: those in which distinct courts of equity exist; those in which equity powers are exercised by the ordinary law courts; and those in which the distinction between law and equity has been abolished by statute. In the States belonging to the first two groups, cases in equity are heard and determined by courts in which the judges decide all questions of fact without the aid of juries. In the third group, cases in equity are heard and decided in the same way as questions at law, that is, by judges and juries. By far the greater number of the States belong in the second and third groups, and the modern tendency seems to be toward abolishing the distinction between trials at law and in equity, but retaining the remedies given by equity.

Equity Procedure in the Federal Courts.

The courts of the United States, though exercising jurisdiction in cases which arise in the States, follow their own rules of practice without regard to the procedure in equity in the State courts.

[1] 2 Black (U. S.) Rep., 499, 509.

In the case of *Boyle v. Zacharie*,[1] decided in 1832 by the U. S. Supreme Court, Justice Story said:

The chancery jurisdiction given by the Constitution and laws of the United States is the same in all the States of the Union and the rule of decision is the same in all. In the exercise of that jurisdiction the courts of the United States are not governed by the State practice; but the Act of Congress of 1792 (Ch. 26) provided that the modes of proceeding in equity suits shall be according to the principles, rules and usages which belong to courts of equity as contradistinguished from courts of law. And the settled doctrine of this court is, that the remedies in equity are to be administered, not according to the State practice but according to the practice of courts of equity in the parent country, as contradistinguished from that of courts of law; subject, of course, to the provisions of the acts of Congress, and to such alterations and rules as in the exercise of the power delegated by those acts, the courts of the United States may, from time to time, prescribe.

[1] 6 Peters (U. S.) Rep., 648, 658.

CHAPTER XV

Principles of Equity.

The substance of equity jurisprudence is found in a number of maxims. "A great authority (Sir James Mackintosh) has described maxims as 'the condensed good sense of nations.' In the English law, these modes of expression were once more highly valued than now. It was declared that 'maxims are the foundation of the law, and the conclusions of reason' (Motto of Broom's *Legal Maxims*), and the earlier commentators and judges were especially fond of stating the law in the form of maxims. . . . It is still recognized by good authority that legal maxims have not wholly lost their importance, and that, when used with proper discrimination, they form a not unimportant part of the literature of our jurisprudence. 'The maxims of equity possess a peculiar value not attaching to those of law because the former are the fruitful germs from which these doctrines and rules [of equity] have grown by a process of natural evolution' (Pomeroy's *Equitable Jurisprudence*, sec. 360). Around these maxims, too, there have accumulated a vast number of decisions which construe them."[1]

[1] 11 *Am. & Eng. Ency. Law & Eq.*, 156.

The following maxims illustrate the scope and nature of equity jurisprudence.

Equity will not suffer a Wrong to be without a Remedy.

This maxim includes the fundamental theory of equity that it gives relief wherever a right exists and there is no adequate remedy at law.[1]

The case of *Joy v. St. Louis*,[2] decided in 1891 by the U. S. Supreme Court, grew out of a number of contracts entered into by certain railroads for the joint use of a right of way through Forest Park, St. Louis, under permits given by the park commissioners of the city. One of the questions was whether the court would enforce the specific performance of a contract which would involve its constant supervision of a business requiring skill, personal labor, cultivated judgment, and constant expenditure of money in seeing to it that the railroads performed continuously and for all time any obligations which might accrue from time to time. Justice Blatchford, dealing with this point in the decision, said:

It is one of the most useful functions of a court of equity that its methods of procedure are capable of being made such as to accommodate themselves to the development of the interests of the public, in the progress of trade and traffic, by new methods of intercourse and transportation. The present case is a striking illustration. Here is a great public park, one of the lungs of an important city, which, in order to maintain its usefulness as a park, must be as free as possible from being serrated by railroads; and yet the interests of the public demand that it shall be crossed

[1] See above p. 182.
[2] 138 U. S. Rep., 1, 50.

by a railroad.   But the evil consequences of such crossing are to be reduced to a minimum by having a single right of way, and a single set of tracks, to be used by all the railroads which desire to cross the park.   These two antagonisms must be reconciled, and that can be done only by the interposition of a court of equity, which thus will be exercising one of its most beneficial functions.

He who seeks Equity, must do Equity.

In order to obtain relief in a court of equity, the petitioner must himself have acted honestly and in good faith.   Equity will not help those who try to overreach others.

The case of *Otis v. Gregory*,[1] decided in 1887 by the Supreme Court of Indiana, was a proceeding in equity by which one Mrs. Mary E. Gregory asked for a judicial determination of her right of ownership to a tract of land in Indiana to which she said Amos Otis, the defendant, had set up a claim that prevented her from selling it.   In 1873, Mrs. Gregory, then living in Michigan, had become indebted to Otis in the sum of $460.00, which was secured by a mortgage on land in Michigan made by her but not signed by her husband, because by the Michigan laws a married woman could make the same contracts concerning real estate as an unmarried woman.   In 1874, she sold the Michigan land, and paid the mortgage held by Otis by giving him a mortgage on the Indiana land which was not signed by her husband, though by the Indiana law a husband had legal rights in his wife's real estate not subject to her control.   Both parties seem to have acted in good faith, believing that the law was the same in Indiana as in Michigan.   When this bill in equity came up in court, Mr. Otis contended

[1] 111 Indiana Rep., 504, 507, 512, 515.

that it would be inequitable to cancel his mortgage, though it was defective because not signed by the husband of the petitioner, without payment of the debt it was intended to secure. His position was that since Mrs. Gregory had come into a court of equity asking its aid to cancel an alleged invalid mortgage, which had been made and received in good faith, she ought to accept the aid of the court in subordination to the maxim, "He who seeks equity, must do equity." In sustaining this contention, Justice Mitchell said:

That this maxim, in its true spirit and purpose, expresses the principle which lies at the foundation of all equity proceedings, guiding and governing courts of equity at every stage in the administration of justice, is one of the distinguishing excellencies underlying all chancery jurisdiction. Pomeroy Eq. Jur. Sections 120, 363. In a court of equity the principle thus expressed is as authoritative as though it were enacted into positive law. In its proper sense it is a universal rule, binding upon parties and courts in all controversies in which complete justice can only be accomplished by its application, within reasonable and recognized rules.

Plowden, speaking of the quality of maxims, in *Colthirst v. Bejushin*, 1 Plow. 21, 27, says: "Further, there are two principal things from whence arguments may be drawn, that is to say, our maxims, and reason, which is the mother of all laws. But maxims are the foundations of the law, and the conclusions of reason, and therefore they ought not to be impugned, but always to be admitted; yet these maxims may by the help of reason, be compared together, and set one against another (although they do not vary), where it may be distinguished by reason that a thing is nearer to one maxim than to another, or placed between two maxims; nevertheless they ought never to be impeached or impugned, but always be observed and held as firm principles and authorities of themselves."

Accepting the maxim above referred to as in the highest degree authoritative, it becomes proper to inquire concerning the manner of its application in the practical adjustment of controversies between parties.

What is the "equity" which a party appealing to a court of chancery must do before he is entitled to relief? Can a party who becomes a plaintiff in a court of equity be compelled, as the price of the relief demanded, to surrender to the defendant something which the latter could not have compelled by some proceeding, either at law or in equity, in case the former had not appealed to the court? If he can, then the rule that he who would have equity must do equity depends for its application in each case upon the arbitrary notions of the chancellor concerning the equities between the parties. The effect of such an application of the rule would inevitably, in many cases, be to refuse aid to which a plaintiff would be entitled, except upon condition that the latter should concede to the defendant some supposed equitable right which was not enforceable at law or cognizable in a court of equity, and, hence, not within any description of legal or equitable right.

So far as any general rule on the subject can be laid down, it may, with assurance, be stated that a plaintiff, who shows himself otherwise entitled to the aid of a court of equity, will not be denied relief, unless the defendant brings forward some corresponding equity, growing out of the subject matter then in suit, which would at some time subsequent to the transaction, in some form of proceeding, entitle him to a remedy against the other party in respect to the subject-matter involved. It can not be maintained in reason that a defendant, to whom the plaintiff is under some imperfect obligation of a merely moral character, which never had ripened, and never could ripen into an enforceable legal or equitable right, may nevertheless, for some merely sinister purpose, defeat an equity to which a plaintiff is entitled. . . . As was said by the learned vice-chancellor, in *Hanson v. Keatry,* 4 *Hare,* (Eng.) 1; "The court can never lawfully impose merely arbitrary conditions upon a plaintiff, only because he stands in that position upon the record, but can only require him to give the defendant that which by the law of the court, independently of the mere position of the parties on the record, is the right of the defendant in respect of the subject of the suit." . . .

Has the appellant [Mr. Otis] any equity within the principles already laid down which the court may require the appellee [Mrs. Gregory] to recognize, as a condition upon which it will afford her the relief to which she . . . is entitled? Has the appellant an equitable right . . . to maintain a bill to declare and enforce a lien against the appellee's La Porte County [Indiana] property? If he has, the maxim "He who seeks equity must do equity" imperatively requires that relief be denied the plaintiff, except upon condition that she consent that the decree shall also adjust the corresponding equities of the appellant. . . . Before the appellee can have the relief which she demands, she must recognize the corresponding equity of the appellant.

He who Comes into Equity, must do so with Clean Hands.

Relief in equity is for those who deserve it. Those who claim relief from fraud must in the case before the court themselves have clean hands and honest consciences.

In the case of *Fetridge v. Wells,*[1] decided in 1857 by the New York Superior Court at special term, the plaintiff, who manufactured and sold as a cosmetic a preparation that he called "The Balm of a Thousand Flowers," had obtained a temporary injunction restrain-

[1] 4 Abbott's (N. Y.) Practice Rep., 144, 148.

ing the defendants from manufacturing a preparation called "The Balm of Ten Thousand Flowers." The injunction had been granted on the ground that the name used by the defendants was calculated to mislead people into buying the defendant's preparation when they thought they were buying the article made by the plaintiff. The defendants asked the court to set aside the injunction on the ground that the preparation made by the plaintiff was neither a balm nor a cosmetic, but was a soap, and that, as he had not come into equity with clean hands, he ought not to have the benefit of an equitable remedy. The court said it was evident that the name of the plaintiff's preparation was used to deceive the public, to attract and impose upon customers; that no representation could be more material than that of the ingredients of a compound recommended and sold as a medicine; that there was none so likely to induce confidence in its use, and none, when false, that would more probably be injurious to the public. The court therefore decided that the plaintiff had been guilty of such fraudulent practices in the matter that he could not have relief in equity. Justice Duer, in the course of the decision, said:

Those who come into a court of equity seeking equity, must come with pure hands and a pure conscience. If they claim relief against the fraud of others, they must be free themselves from the imputation. If the sales made by the plaintiff and his firm are effected, or sought to be, by misrepresentation and falsehood, they cannot be listened to when they complain that by the fraudulent rivalry of others their own fraudulent profits are diminished. An exclusive privilege for deceiving the public is assuredly not one that a court of equity can be required to aid or sanction. To do so would be to forfeit its name and character.

Equity Aids the Vigilant; not Those who Sleep on their Rights.

It is no part of the province of equity to enforce stale claims, the supposition being that a person who does not enforce his rights has consented to be deprived of them.

The case of *Speidel v. Henrici*,[1] decided in 1887 by the U. S. Supreme Court, grew out of the dealings of the Harmony Society with its members. This Society was one of the remarkable communistic-religious communities that were established in the United States in the early part of the nineteenth century. Speidel's parents were German farmers, who had been followers while still living in Germany of a religious fanatic named Rapp, who preached the doctrine that the millenium was at hand and that the only persons who would be saved were those who should form a settlement by themselves under his guidance and control. In 1804 and 1805, he came to our country with about one hundred and twenty-five families, and formed a settlement at Harmony in Butler County, Pennsylvania. The members gave all their property to him and lived together as one household, wholly abandoning marriage and ordinary family life. Speidel had been born in 1807, while his father and mother still lived together. He remained a member of the community until he was twenty-four years old, and during the last twelve years of his membership worked for it without any compensation except the necessities of life. He had been forced to leave the Harmonists in 1831 because he was about to be married. Rapp died in 1847 possessed of a great amount of property that had been given to him in trust by the members of the community.

[1] 120 U. S. Rep., 377, 387, 389.

Cornelius L. Baker and Jacob Henrici succeeded him as trustees of the property, which in 1882 was said to amount to more than eight million dollars. On June 7, 1882, Speidel brought this action in equity in the U. S. Circuit Court of Western Pennsylvania by means of a bill or complaint in which he asked that the trust be set aside and annulled "as resting upon fraud and iniquity and being contrary to public policy and the law of the land"; that the assets be divided up among the persons interested; and that he have his share of such assets together with compensation for his work for the community. The circuit court dismissed the complaint upon the ground that, by waiting from 1831 to 1882 before taking action, he had allowed his claim to become stale. He then took the case to the U. S. Supreme Court, where the decision of the circuit court was affirmed. In the opinion of the court, Justice Gray said:

Courts of equity uniformly decline to assist a person who has slept upon his rights and shows no excuse for his laches [negligence or dilatoriness] in asserting them. "A court of equity," says Lord Camden, "has always refused its aid to stale demands, where the party has slept upon his rights, and acquiesced for a great length of time. Nothing can call forth this court into activity, but conscience, good faith and reasonable diligence; where these are wanting, the court is passive, and does nothing. Laches and neglect are always discountenanced, and therefore, from the beginning of this jurisdiction, there was always a limitation to suits in this court." . . . The plaintiff, upon his own showing, withdrew from the community in 1831, and never returned to it, and for more than fifty years, took no step to demand an account of the trustees, or to follow up the rights which he claimed in this bill. If he ever had any rights, he could not assert them after such a delay. . . .

200 THE REASONABLENESS OF THE LAW

In any aspect of the case, therefore, if it was not strictly within the statute of limitations, yet the plaintiff showed so little vigilance, and so great laches, that the Circuit Court rightly held that he was not entitled to relief in equity.

Equity Acts Specifically; not by Way of Compensation.

The most significant distinction between a case at law and a case in equity is that the law gives an injured person damages for a loss sustained by the wrongful act of another while equity in a proper case directs a specific act that will prevent the injury.

The case of *Brighton v. White*,[1] decided in 1890 by the Supreme Court of Indiana, was an action to foreclose a mortgage, in which the defense presented was that the mortgage in question did not really belong to the plaintiff because it had been assigned to him by a bank which at the time was insolvent and had no right to dispose of its property. In the decision of this case, Justice Elliott said:

It is settled that where a lien upon real estate is to be foreclosed, the equity power of the court is called into exercise, and the entire issue is for trial by the court [without a jury]. . . . It is not meant, of course, that the necessity for applying general principles of equity requires that the case be treated as one for the chancellor, but it is meant that where the relief that must be awarded is essentially equitable, the case is one for the court. The distinction between the two classes of cases [at law and in equity] is, as a general rule, to be determined by ascertaining whether the decree is one operating specifically, as, for instance, in the foreclosure of liens, or one operating generally, as, for instance, in an ordinary money judgment. The maxim is that "Equity acts specifically," and where a specific decree is

[1] 128 Indiana Rep., 320, 323.

required, there is an exercise of equity jurisdiction, and, necessarily, the main feature of the case is equitable, and as such controls the incidents.

Equity Acts in Personam.

The meaning of this maxim is that equity deals with the persons that are concerned in a controversy and only incidentally with the rights or property that may be at stake.

In the case of *Great Falls Manufacturing Company v. Worster*,[1] decided in 1851 by the Supreme Court of Judicature of New Hampshire, the petitioners asked the court to order the respondent, a citizen of New Hampshire, to desist from destroying a dam located in the State of Maine. The petitioners were a New Hampshire corporation owning in that State five cotton mills operated by water power from ponds that were partly in Maine. The respondent had partly destroyed a dam in Maine and had threatened to remove the whole of it. His answer to this suit in equity was that a New Hampshire court had no power to restrain a New Hampshire man from committing in Maine an act injurious to a citizen of New Hampshire. The court overruled this contention in a decision, in which Chief Justice Gilchrist said:

The courts are not asked to assume any jurisdiction, or exercise any control over the land in Maine, or to interfere with the laws of that State. Nothing more is asked than that the respondent, a citizen of New Hampshire, and residing within her limits, shall be subject to her laws, and that, being within reach of the process of this court, he shall be forbidden to go elsewhere and commit an injury

[1] 23 New Hampshire Rep., 462, 465, 470.

to the property of other citizens, situated here, and entitled to the protection of our laws.

In the case of *Penn v. Lord Baltimore*, 1 Ves., 444, *Lord Hardwicke* recognized and acted upon the principle, that equity, as it acts primarily *in personam*, and not merely *in rem*, may make a decree, where the person against whom relief is sought, is within the jurisdiction upon the ground of a contract, or any equity subsisting between the parties respecting property situated out of the jurisdiction. A decree was made for the specific performance of a contract relating to the boundary between the colonies of Pennsylvania and Maryland. . . . He . . . said, "The conscience of the party was bound by this agreement, and being within the jurisdiction of this court, which acts *in personam*, the court may properly decree it as an agreement." This case decides, that although the subject matter of a contract be land out of the jurisdiction, the boundary of the land may be settled by a decree for the specific performance of the contract. In this way a party within the jurisdiction may be compelled to do an act of justice, in relation to land out of the jurisdiction. The case is a leading one. . . .

It would be a great defect in the administration of the law, if the mere fact, that the property was out of the State could deprive the court of the power to act. As much injustice may be perpetrated in a given case, against the citizens of this State, by going out of the jurisdiction and committing a wrong, as by staying here and doing it. . . . As the principle which is sought to be applied here, has been recognized for nearly two hundred years, we have no hesitation in holding that the court has jurisdiction to issue the injunction prayed for.

Equity Follows the Law.

When the law stops short of securing the rights of the parties to a controversy, equity continues the remedies that may be needed in order to give justice.

The case of *Isgrigg, executor, v. Schooley*,[1] decided in 1890 by the Supreme Court of Indiana, grew out of an action brought by the widow of one W. H. Schooley, who had died in 1886, against a lodge of the Knights of Honor to recover the amount of a beneficiary certificate payable to her upon his death. Edward G. Isgrigg, executor of W. H. Schooley's will, filed a cross complaint in which he claimed that Mrs. Schooley had abandoned her husband more than two years before his death when he was an invalid needing her care; that Schooley had endeavored to change the beneficiary named in the certificate from his wife to an uncle who had cared for him, and had complied with all the by-laws of the order relating to such changing of beneficiaries; but that he had been unable to surrender the certificate because his wife had it in her possession and refused to give it up; and that Schooley had then made his will giving the fund to his uncle. The court ruled that, on these facts, the uncle was entitled to the money. Justice Olds said:

"For the purpose of determining the rights between these defendants, the proceeding is governed by equitable principles. The fund is held in trust by the order for the person to whom it belongs; and it is true in this, as in every other case, equity follows the law, so far as the law goes in securing the rights of the parties, and no further; and when the law stops short of securing this object, equity continues the remedy until complete justice is done. In other words, equity is the perfection of the law, and is always open to those who have just rights to enforce where the law is inadequate. Any other conclusion would show our system of jurisprudence not only a failure, but a delusion and a snare. Justice alone can be considered in a court of chancery,

[1] 125 Indiana Rep., 94, 100.

and technicalities never be tolerated except to obtain and not destroy it." See Bacon, *Ben. Soc.*, etc., Sec. 310.

What we have quoted is decisive of the question in this case. The right of the assured to make a change of the beneficiary existed as soon as the certificate was issued; by the conditions in the by-laws a mode of making such change was prescribed, which it was the duty of the member to follow while it was within his power to do so. . . .

The facts stated in each paragraph of the cross-complaint show such compliance with the by-laws in changing the beneficiary as entitles the new beneficiary . . . to recover the funds.

Equity Delights to do Justice and not by Halves.

The aim of equity is to have in court all persons whose rights or property are involved in any particular litigation and to render a complete decree adjusting all the rights and protecting all the parties against future litigations.

The following facts were presented in the case of *Decker v. Caskey*,[1] decided in 1831 by the Court of Chancery of New Jersey: In 1816, John Caskey conveyed his farm at Wantage, New Jersey, to his son, William Caskey. The son, in 1819, mortgaged the farm to Joseph and David D. Chandler to secure the payment of a sum of money. This mortgage had been transferred to Bowdoin Decker, the complainant, who found out that the deed from John to William Caskey had never been recorded. The heirs of John Caskey claimed that he never had deeded the farm to William Caskey and asserted that it was their property by inheritance. The complainant then brought this action in equity against the heirs of William Caskey, who was dead, his claim being that John Caskey's heirs had

[1] 1 New Jersey Equity Rep., 427, 433.

fraudently possessed themselves of the deed to William Caskey and had either concealed or destroyed it. He, therefore, asked for an order of court for a discovery or investigation of the facts, for the production of the deed in question, and for the foreclosure of the mortgage. The main question in the case was whether the heirs of John Caskey, who were thus charged with misconduct, ought to have been made defendants. The court ruled that they must be made parties in a decision, in which Justice Ewing said:

I am unwilling to recommend to the chancellor . . . to make a decree for the relief of the complainant as against the heirs of William Caskey only; because it is the desire as well as the duty of this court, never to do justice by halves—never merely to beget business for another court— and never, when a case is fairly within its jurisdiction, to leave open the door for litigation farther or in any other place, if it can possibly be here closed. . . . If a decree against the heirs of William, as to the whole premises, or as to William's share as an heir of his father only, were now to be made, and the bill be dismissed without prejudice as to the rest of the defendants, the complainant would be left to seek his claims as to the rest of the premises [covered by the mortgage], or as to the other parties [heirs of John Caskey], in another suit or in another court, and they would be exposed to further litigation.

Equity Regards as Done that which Ought to be Done.

Equity will compel a person to do any act that he is under a legal obligation to do.

The case of *Goodell v. Monroe*,[1] decided in 1916 by the Court of Errors and Appeals of New Jersey, was a decision upon a bill in equity by which an administra-

[1] 87 New Jersey Equity Rep., 328, 334, 337.

tor of an estate sought to compel a bank to surrender a bond and mortgage which an executor who had been removed for misconduct had previously used in obtaining a loan from the institution. The executor had previously demanded payment of the mortgage from the president of the bank who owned the mortgaged premises. Instead of making payment, the bank president had made a loan of the amount of the mortgage to the executor individually, and the executor had first assigned the mortgage to himself personally and had used it as collateral security for the loan. Then the executor had used the proceeds of the loan mostly for his own purposes and had not paid the money over to the estate. After he had been removed as executor, Mr. Goodell, who took over the estate as administrator, brought this action upon the ground that the whole transaction was illegal and void. The court ruled in his favor in a decision, in which Justice Trenchard said:

The bank knew, from the very face of the proceeding, and otherwise, that Taylor [the Executor] was pledging securities of the estate to secure his individual note; it knew that the securities had been transferred from Taylor, executor, to Taylor, individually, without consideration, and for the express purpose of preventing the transaction from speaking as a loan to the executor for the purposes of the estate. . . . This arrangement was more than a mere matter of form. It amounted, substantially, to an arrangement between Taylor and the bank by which the bank agreed with Taylor that Taylor should convert the bond and mortgage belonging to the estate to his own use for the purpose of obtaining a loan from the bank as an individual, trusting to Taylor to pay the estate the money he owed it for the conversion of the bond and mortgage. . . .

The transaction is deemed to have given rise to a species of equitable guaranty by the bank that its participation in that irregular dealing with the assets of the estate should not result in loss to the latter, and to that extent, the bank was bound to see to the application of the money loaned. How this guaranty should be worked out was at the will of the bank, provided the equitable results be obtained. It might have been by making its check to the executor as such, or by otherwise assuming the responsibility for the application of the money to the purposes of the estate—but however done, the duty that was controlling is that expressed in the maxim "Equity regards as done that which ought to have been done," which means that where an obligation rests upon a person to perform an act, equity will treat the person in whose favor the act should be performed as clothed with the same interest and entitled to the same rights as if the act were actually performed. . . .

The record [will be] remitted to the court of chancery, to the end that it be decreed that the bond and mortgage be assigned by the bank to the complainant.

Equity Regards Substance Rather than Form.

A court of equity looks beyond the terms of an instrument or writing to the real transaction between the parties.

The case of *Peugh v. Davis*,[1] decided in 1877 by the U. S. Supreme Court, was a suit in equity to redeem certain real estate in the City of Washington, which had been conveyed by a deed absolute in form but given as security for money loaned. In March, 1857, Samuel A. Peugh had borrowed $2000 on a sixty day note from Henry S. Davis and had given him as security a deed of the land in question. This loan had been paid at maturity and the deed had been returned. In May, 1857,

[1] 96 U. S. Rep., 332, 336.

Peugh borrowed $1500 of Davis for sixty days and re-delivered the deed. Upon this sum, interest was paid up to the following September; but the principal sum not being paid, Davis recorded the deed. In January, 1858, Peugh borrowed $600 more from Davis and gave him a further written agreement reciting that he had previously sold the premises to him, and also gave him a receipt for $2000 purporting to be in full payment for the purchase of the land. The question before the court was whether the whole transaction was an absolute conveyance of land or only a mortgage to secure the payment of money. The Court ruled that it was a mortgage in a decision, in which Justice Field said:

> It is an established doctrine that a court of equity will treat a deed, absolute in form, as a mortgage, when it is executed as security for a loan of money. That court looks beyond the terms of the instrument to the real transaction; and when that is shown to be one of security, and not of sale, it will give effect to the actual contract of the parties.

Equity Imputes an Intention to Fulfil an Obligation.

Equity assumes that a man intends to do what he is legally bound to do.

The Supreme Court of Arkansas, in the case of *Lee v. Foushee*,[1] decided in 1909, ruled that a man who had taken part in a sale of land made by his mother but had not signed the deed, would be held in equity himself to have sold the land, if it afterward appeared that he was the real owner. One John Lee had made a contract with Mary Foushee and her son Mack Foushee for the purchase of the land. The mother signed the deed, but the son did not because he supposed that he had no

[1] 91 Arkansas Rep., 468, 474.

title. It was shown that he really was the owner under a clause of his grandfather's will. In declaring that the transaction amounted to a sale by the son, Justice Wood said:

The proof shows that the appellee [Mack Foushee] fully intended to sign the deed and thereby convey all the interest he might have. "Equity looks on that as done, which ought to have been done." "Equity imputes an intention to fulfil an obligation." These familiar maxims of equity are sufficient authority for denying to the appellee under the evidence in this record the relief which he seeks, and for granting to the appellant the relief sought by his cross-complaint.

Equality is Equity.

Equity will treat all members of a class as upon an equal footing.

In the case of *Matter of Empire State Surety Company*,[1] decided in 1915 by the New York Court of Appeals, in which the issue was the proper distribution of the assets of an insolvent surety company, the court ruled that each of the creditors was entitled to his proportionate share of the property realized. Judge Seabury, giving the decision of the court, said:

The principle that equality is equity is especially applicable to the settlement of insolvent estates. Where equity acquires jurisdiction to distribute the assets of an insolvent fiduciary, distribution is made proportionately to all those having claims against the fund. . . . The principle that equality is equity is to be given effect only by adhering to a uniform rule by which the rights of all creditors are to be determined.

[1] 214 New York Rep., 553, 568.

Between Equal Equities the Law will Prevail.

He who seeks the aid of equity must show that his rights are superior to those of the persons against whom he asks a remedy.

In the case of *Forman v. Executors of Brewer*,[1] decided in 1900 by the Court of Errors and Appeals of New Jersey, the holders of two judgments against Henry C. Forman, obtained in 1872 and 1873, asked the court to rule that their claims were superior to the lien of a mortgage in the form of a deed of conveyance, made by Forman in 1871 to secure payment of loans to one Bulson, which in 1879 had been conveyed by Bulson to Edmund Brewer, deceased, who made loans to Forman after he took the conveyance. The legal title to the property had thus been held by Bulson from 1871 to 1879 and by Brewer since 1879, while the equitable title was held by Forman, and the two judgments were only equitable liens against it. The court decided that inasmuch as the legal title vested in Brewer he had a right, as against the holders of equal equitable titles, to whatever protection it afforded. Justice Dixon said:

The appellants [the judgment holders] contend that their judgments should be decreed to have been liens upon the land from the dates thereof, and should have priority over all advances made by Brewer after those dates [of the judgments]. . . . This contention might prevail if the legal title to the land had been in Forman, so that the judgments against him constituted a legal lien. But as Forman has never had legal title since the judgments were entered, the appellants must rest solely on their equitable claims, and we think that the relations of Forman and Brewer were such as to make the latter's claim for his advances as good in equity as those of the judgment creditors, in view of their

[1] 62 New Jersey Equity Rep., 748, 750.

knowledge and acquiescence in the situation. Hence the legal title vested in Brewer should not be taken away without conceding to him whatever protection it may afford for the payment of his iust debts.

Between Equal Equities the First in Order of Time will Prevail.

As between persons having only equitable interests, the first in order of time has the better right.

In the case of *State Bank of Mayville v. Jennings*,[1] decided at the Equity Term of the New York Supreme Court for Cattaraugus County in 1912, the question at issue was whether a pledge of a leasehold estate in a lot of the Chatauqua Assembly which had not been completed by delivery of the lease, was entitled to a priority claim as against a subsequent assignment and delivery of the same lease. In deciding this case, Justice Brown said:

The general rule undoubtedly is that in equity between conflicting equitable interests or liens, other things being equal, the one that is prior in time is superior in right.

[1] 78 Miscellaneous (New York) Rep., 524, 526.

CHAPTER XVI

Applications for Relief.

An application for relief in equity is made either by a "petition," or by a "bill," or by a "complaint," each of those words having the same meaning and being used interchangeably. Such a petition, bill, or complaint is presented to a court of equity, which thereupon issues a subpœna commanding the person against whom relief is sought to appear in court and answer the matters alleged by the petitioner. When an answer has been filed in which the allegations of the petitioner or plaintiff are denied or contradicted, an issue is established upon which the court will take evidence, decide upon the truth or falsity of the contentions of both petitioner and defendant, will apply to its decision of matters of fact the rules of equity and will award an appropriate remedy.

The important distinction between this procedure and that which is followed in a case at law is that the judge of a court of equity decides upon the truth of the contentions between the parties, while in a court of law such questions of fact are decided by a jury. The only exception to this rule is that a judge of a court of equity has a right to refer questions of fact to a jury if he so desires, but such reference is wholly optional.

He is not obliged, as in a law case, to let the jury pass upon the facts while he decides questions of law.

The more important cases which courts of equity decide are as follow: actions for the specific performance of contracts; petitions for the re-execution, reformation, rescission and cancellation of contracts; petitions for the partition of real estate; bills for the establishment of boundary lines; complaints for the dissolution of partnerships; creditors bills; bills of discovery; bills of *quia timet*; petitions for the foreclosure of liens and mortgages.

Actions for Specific Performance of Contracts.

A bill for specific performance is a petition in which a court is asked to command a person to perform an agreement or contract according to its precise terms.[1] For example, a court in equity will compel a person who has made a contract to sell and convey real estate, to execute and deliver to the owner a deed of the property. It would be unjust to leave the purchaser to his right at law to have damages for the injuries caused by the refusal to convey real estate, because damages incident to not having a home to live in or farming land to raise food on cannot be estimated in money. The remedy at law being insufficient, resort must be had to equity.

The suit of *Rison v. Newberry*,[2] decided in 1894 by the Supreme Court of Appeals of Virginia, was an action in equity in which the plaintiff asked the court to compel the performance of a contract to purchase certain land in Wythe County, Virginia. The defendants had agreed to buy 700 out of 706 acres of the plaintiff's

[1] 22 *Am. & Eng. Ency. of Law*, 909.
[2] 90 Virginia Rep., 513, 521.

farm, the remaining six acres being land on which the
plaintiff's house was situated. The plaintiff did not
act wholly in good faith and in the end was unable to
give a perfect title because one of the owners was a
minor. Nevertheless, he demanded specific performance of the contract by the purchasers. The circuit
court in which the case was first tried decided that he
was entitled to such performance if a portion of the
purchase money should be left in the hands of the court
to indemnify the purchasers for any defect in the title
arising from the infancy of one of the owners. This
decree was reversed by the Supreme Court of Appeals
upon the ground that equity would not interfere except to compel the performance of the original contract according to its exact terms, which was impossible
under the circumstances. In the opinion of the court
Justice Lacy said:

Specific performance is an equitable remedy, which com-
pels the performance of a contract in the precise terms
agreed upon, or such a substantial performance as will do
justice between the parties under the circumstances of
the case. 22 Am. & Eng. Enc. Law, p. 909. Bouvier
defines it as the "actual accomplishment of a contract by a
party bound to fulfill it." Burrill defines it: "The performance of a contract in the precise terms agreed upon; strict
performance." Mr. Justice Washington, speaking for the
Supreme Court of the United States in *Hunt v. Rousmanier*,
1 Pet. 14, says: "Equity may compel parties to perform
their agreements, when fairly entered into, according to
their terms; but it has no power to make agreements for
parties, and then compel them to execute the same. The
former is a legitimate branch of its jurisdiction, and in its
exercise highly beneficial to society. The latter is without
its authority, and the exercise of it would not only be a
usurpation of power, but would be highly mischievous in

its consequences." . . . Under the circumstances of this case, we think Newberry [the plaintiff in the lower court] is not entitled to the aid of a court of equity to have his contract specifically executed.

Re-execution of Contracts.

It sometimes happens that documents of great value, such as deeds of real estate or contracts involving large sums of money, have been lost, destroyed, or so mislaid that they cannot be found after diligent search. In such cases, equity has special jurisdiction to decree the re-execution of such instruments on the ground that otherwise rights would be lost for which no compensation could be obtained by an action under the rules of the common law.

The case of *Cummings v. Coe*,[1] decided in 1858 by the Supreme Court of California, was a proceeding in equity in which it was shown to the court that a deed made by the defendant to the plaintiff had been accidentally destroyed by fire while in the possession of the notary public who had taken the acknowledgment of the defendant but had not attached to the deed his certificate that he had done so. The plaintiff had asked the defendant to make a new deed, and the defendant had refused. The court decided that the defendant must make the new deed as requested. In the opinion of the court, Justice Field said:

The proof of the execution of the deed and of its accidental destruction, is full and satisfactory, and the jurisdiction of a Court of Equity to decree a re-execution of the deed is unquestionable. The jurisdiction is maintained in such cases where the destruction would create a defect in the deraignment [chain of continuity] of the plaintiff's title,

[1] 10 California Rep., 529, 531.

and thus embarrass the assertion of his rights to the property. "If a conveyance to a purchaser," observed Sugden, "have accidentally been burned, the seller will be compelled, upon a re-sale, to join in a conveyance to the new purchaser, or, of course, if the estate is not re-sold, to again convey to the purchaser. (*On Vendors*, Chap. IX, Sec. 4, 27; Adams' *Equity*, 167.)

Reformation of Contracts.

"When an agreement is made and reduced to writing, but, through mistake, inadvertence, or fraud, the writing fails to express correctly the contract really made, a court of equity will reform the instrument in conformity with the real intention of the parties."[1] The court, in such cases, makes a decree declaring how the instrument is to be read and understood.

The case of *Adams v. Stevens*,[2] decided in 1861 by the Supreme Court of Maine, was a bill in equity to reform a deed which the parties intended to be a mortgage, but by mistake did not make it in legal form. In 1828, Jonathan Stevens deeded his farm to his son Elisha, who thereupon gave back a deed which provided that he should support his father and mother as long as they lived. This latter deed, however, did not contain words indicating that, if the provision for support was fulfilled, this deed should be null and void. Technically it was an absolute deed and not a mortgage. Until 1852 all the parties treated the transaction as a mortgage given as a guaranty that the son would support the father; then the father made another deed to Trueman A. Stevens. The latter thereupon insisted that he owned the premises and that Elisha

[1] 22 Am. & Eng. Ency. Law, 713.
[2] 49 Maine Rep., 362, 366.

had parted with all his rights by his deed to his father. In the meantime, Elisha had deeded the farm to a Mr. Adams, who was willing to carry out the agreement to support Elisha's father and mother. Mr. Adams' title under the circumstances was not valid, unless he could obtain a decree by a court of equity so reforming the deed of Elisha to Jonathan that it should operate as a mortgage and not as a full conveyance. In deciding the issue raised by Mr. Adams' petition for this relief, Justice Rice said:

From the pleadings and evidence in the case, we are entirely satisfied that Trueman A. [Stevens], at the time he took his deed from Jonathan, not only had knowledge of the existence of the deed from Elisha to Jonathan, dated March 10, 1828, but that he also well knew the purposes for which such deed was given, and that it was originally designed by the parties thereto to be a mortgage, and that such had been understood to be its character by all the intermediate parties through whom the plaintiff claims title from Elisha, and that the said Jonathan had always understood said deed to be a mortgage, and so treated it.

The complainant now prays for a decree by which said deed from Elisha to Jonathan may be reformed by the addition of those words which it is alleged were omitted by mistake, and which are necessary to constitute said deed a mortgage, so as to effectuate what is affirmed to have been the original intention of the parties thereto, and for general relief. . . .

To reform an instrument in equity, is to make a decree, that a deed, or other agreement, shall be made or construed as it was originally intended by the parties, when an error as to a fact has been committed. *Lumbert v. Hill*, 41 Maine, 475.

The complainant is entitled to a decree to have the mistake corrected.

Rescission and Cancellation of Contracts.

A court of equity will also rescind or cancel a deed or contract which is apparently legal, but is voidable because one of the parties has been deceived or cheated into making it, or has made it without knowing the facts, or has made it under a mistaken idea of its terms. In these cases, equity interferes on the principle that the party who appeals for relief has reason to fear that the instrument may be wrongfully used against him and that, if so used, he will have no sufficient remedy at law.

In the case of *De Voin v. De Voin*,[1] decided in 1890 by the Supreme Court of Wisconsin, the issue was upon a contract which had been made upon the basis of a computation of certain debts which the defendant in the case had agreed to assume. It was afterward found that these debts were greater than the parties had supposed. In commenting upon these facts, Justice Lyon said:

The alleged mistake in the written agreement is not that the instrument does not express the terms of the contract just as the parties directed it to be written, but that there was a mistake in one subject matter of the contract, to wit, the amount of the firm liabilities, but for which mistake no contract would have been made, or, if made, its terms would have been different. . . . We strongly incline to the opinion that, whether the mistake was or was not mutual, the only remedy of the plaintiff was promptly to rescind the contract, or institute appropriate proceedings to that end. If the mistake was not mutual—that is, if the plaintiff entered into the contract on the basis of the actual indebtedness of the firm, and the defendant entered into it without any reference thereto,—the minds of the parties did not meet as respects that important element in their contract. This is also a valid ground for the cancella-

[1] 76 Wisconsin Rep., 66, 70.

tion of the contract in equity. 2 Pom. *Eq. Jur.*, Sect. 870, and cases cited; 1 Story *Eq. Jur.*, Sect. 144.

The rule on the subject is thus stated by Mr. Pomeroy: "Cancellation is appropriate when there is an apparently valid written agreement or transaction embodied in writing, while in fact, by reason of a mistake of both or one of the parties, either no agreement at all has really been made, since the minds of both parties have failed to meet upon the same matters, or else the agreement or transaction is different, with respect to its subject matter or terms, from that which was intended." Pages 343, 344.

Partition of Real Estate.

Whenever by inheritance or by deed two or more persons own undivided shares of real estate, a court of equity, upon the petition of one or more of such owners, either will subdivide the property so that each of the parties shall have his fair share or will order it sold and the proceeds shared by such parties. In each case, the court makes a decree commanding the owners to make and execute such deeds or conveyances as will accomplish the partition which is desired.

In the case of *Gay v. Parpart*,[1] decided in 1882 by the U. S. Supreme Court, the petition was for the partition of certain real estate in Chicago among the children of one Charles D. Flagler. The defense set up was that the case should have been brought in the Circuit Court of Cook County, Illinois. In deciding upon this point, the court reviewed the principles of equity or chancery jurisdiction in partition proceedings. In the course of the decision, Justice Miller said:

The first thing which suggests itself as proper to be considered in the solution of this question is to ascertain what

[1] 106 U. S. Rep., 679, 689.

was the law of the State of Illinois on the subject of partition at the date of that decree. Looking at the statutes of
the State as we find them in the revision of 1880, with
reference to the sources from which this revision is taken,
we find that they made provision distinctly for two modes
of effecting a partition, one of which . . . was by bill of
chancery . . . and the other by petition to the Circuit
Court of the proper County. . . . The proceeding which
we are now to consider declares itself in its force to be in
chancery. . . . We take it for granted that the statute of
Illinois, in making this provision and in leaving the parties
to proceed by bill of chancery, intended that such a proceeding should have the force and effect of a partition in the
High Court of Chancery of England, and in the main conform to the established chancery practice. . . . Its purpose
is to make a division among the parties before the court, of
real estate in which they had interests or estates that were
not in controversy among themselves.

It is another principle of the chancery jurisdiction in
partition that a decree does not itself transfer or convey
title even after the allotment of the respective shares of
each of the parties to the proceedings, but that the legal
title remains as it was before.

In this respect a decree is unlike a writ of partition at
the common law, which in such cases operates on the title
only by way of estoppel [by preventing the parties from
contesting the title]. In chancery, however, this difficulty
is remedied by a decree that the parties shall make the necessary conveyances to each other, and that they may be
compelled to do so by attachment, imprisonment, and other
powers of the court over them in person.

Dissolution of Partnerships.

Courts of equity have power to hear and decide cases
in which one or more persons carrying on business together as partners wish to dissolve the partnership,

either because the business cannot be carried on except at a loss, or because of misconduct or fraud on the part of members of the firm. Under the rules of the common law, one partner could sue his associates for an accounting after the term for which the partnership was created had expired, but the remedy was seldom used because the law courts could only give judgments for sums of money and could not compel the parties to do justice to one another. A court of equity, on the other hand, could in proper cases before a partnership came to an end, issue decrees directing the sale of all the assets of a firm and the division of those assets among its members in proportion to their respective interests under their contract to carry on business together; and if such decrees were disobeyed, could send to jail the persons who disregarded them. At common law, a partner could sue his partners for his share of the firms' property after the agreement to do business together had expired. At equity, a partner could have the contract set aside, either because the business was not profitable or because his partners were cheating him, and could have its property sold and divided up before the partnership contract had expired. Obviously the equitable remedy was by far the better and was consequently most frequently used, while the remedy at law became obsolete.

In the case of *Seighortner v. Weissenborn*,[1] decided in 1869 by the Court of Errors and Appeals of New Jersey, Chancellor Zabriskie said:

Courts of equity will, for sufficient cause, dissolve a partnership before the expiration of the term for which it was entered into. And it is a sufficient cause for dissolu-

[1] 20 New Jersey Equity Rep., 172, 177.

tion, that it clearly appears that the business for which the partnership was formed is impracticable, or cannot be carried on except at a loss. The object of all commercial partnerships is *profit*, and when that cannot be obtained, the object fails, and the partnership should be terminated. *Baring v. Dix*, 1 Cox 213; *Jennings v. Baddeley*, 3 Kay & Johns 78; *Bailey v. Ford*, 13 Sim. 495. And this doctrine is adopted and approved by elementary writers of learning, *Collyer on Part.*, Sec. 291; *Story on Part.*, Sec. 290.

The partnership will also be dissolved where all confidence between the parties has been destroyed, so that they cannot proceed together in prosecuting the business for which it was formed. And this result follows not only when such want of confidence is occasioned by the misconduct or gross mismanagement of the partner against whom the dissolution is sought, but when such want of confidence and distrust has arisen from other circumstances, provided it has become such as cannot probably be overcome.

In the case of *Bracken v. Kennedy*,[1] decided in 1842 by the Supreme Court of Illinois, Justice Caton said:

In matters of controversy . . . between partners, it is now most usual and by far the most convenient, to resort to a court of equity for their final adjudication and settlement. The practice of this court is much better adapted to unravel, and definitely settle such complicated questions as frequently arise among partners than a court of law; and it is now one of the most usual proceedings to be met with in courts of equity. It is not unusual that almost the entire proof of the merits of a case between partners is locked up in the bosoms of the parties themselves, or is contained in books and papers in the possession of one or the other party, and this court can afford the only key to the disclosure of the one, or the production of the

[1] 4 Illinois Rep., 558, 562.

other. Here, either party may compel the other to purge his conscience, on oath, and declare the truth; and the court will compel the production of all such papers and books, as may be necessary to elucidate the rights or liabilities of the parties. . . . It is true that courts of law still pretend to afford a remedy in case of difficulty between partners, by the action of account, but it is so incomplete and unsatisfactory, that it is now nearly obsolete; and the complaining partner almost universally lays his complaint before a court of chancery, where he finds a prompt and efficient remedy, from the superior facilities which it possesses of doing complete justice between the parties.

Settlement of Boundary Lines.

Whenever the boundaries between different tracts of land have become uncertain because the original landmarks have been forgotten, the owners can have the boundaries re-established by courts either of law or of equity. Ordinarily, when only a few land owners are interested in the case, one of them will bring against the others a suit at law in which he will ask for damages for trespass committed by his neighbors by going upon his property. The court, in deciding whether any such trespass has been committed, will find out by the testimony of witnesses and by reference to deeds just where the true boundary lines run, and will thus establish new boundaries on which the parties can afterward set up new land-marks. In some cases, however, especially where there are a large number of adjacent tracts, a remedy may be had in a court of equity, which will act in order to avoid the necessity of having a great number of law suits to settle disputes which can be adjudicated in one action.

In the case of *Beatty v. Dixon*,[1] decided in 1880 by

[1] 56 California Rep., 619, 622.

the Supreme Court of California, the court, passing upon an appeal from the decision of a district court which had decided an action in equity brought to fix the boundary lines of a number of mining claims, declared the rule of equity in such cases. Justice Sharpstein said:

This action was commenced against nineteen defendants. It is alleged, among other things in the complaint, that the plaintiff and the defendants are the owners in severalty [ownership of undivided portions] of a certain tract of land, the boundaries of which, through the lapse of time, the carelessness of occupants, and the absence of natural monuments, have become confused and uncertain. The external lines of the entire tract, and those describing the several subdivisions of it, have been obliterated, so that no one of the defendants is occupying according to the original boundaries of his claim, which causes those occupying tracts contiguous to plaintiff's to encroach upon his land. All of the parties are equally interested in having said boundaries determined in one action, in order to avoid a multiplicity of suits at law, which would necessarily have to be resorted to if the relief prayed for in this action be denied. The appellants in their answers do not deny any of these allegations, except that which charges them with encroaching upon the lands of others, and they pray that the true lines of their several tracts may be fixed and established.

One of the grounds upon which it is insisted that the judgment in this case should be reversed is, that the facts alleged do not constitute a sufficient ground for the interference of a court of equity. This raises the question whether the case is one within the exclusive jurisdiction of a court of law, or of which a court of equity has concurrent jurisdiction. The circumstance that the plaintiff might obtain all the relief to which he is entitled in a court of law would not necessarily oust a court of equity of jurisdiction of the case. There might, nevertheless, be some equitable ground upon which that jurisdiction could be upheld; "such as fraud, or some relation between the parties which makes it the duty of one of them to protect and preserve the boundaries; or the prevention of a multiplicity of suits; or that the question affects a large number of persons, and the boundaries have become confused by the lapse of time, accident, or mistake." (*Wetherbee v. Dunn*, 36 Cal. 255.) One writer on equity jurisprudence says: "The relief which equity affords in the case of confusion of boundaries is referable to the head of accident. When *lands* have become mixed or confounded without the fault of the plaintiff, equity will appoint a commission to settle the boundaries." (*Willard Eq. Jur.* 56.) The prevailing doctrine upon the subject is well expressed, we think, by Mr. Tyler who says: "From the cases examined, it is very clear that, both in England and in this country, courts of equity will always take cognizance of controversies in respect to boundaries of land whenever the parties cannot obtain substantial justice in a court of law, or where equitable circumstances are shown, calling for the interference of a court of equity; although, as a rule, unless some statute exists upon the subject, the existence of a controverted boundary is not of itself alone a ground for relief in equity. Other circumstances must be shown which seem to require the interference of the Court." (Tyler's *Law of Boundaries*, 266. . . .)

After a careful consideration of the points presented by the appellants, we are satisfied that the order and judgment of the Court below ought not to be disturbed.

Creditors Bills.

It sometimes happens that persons who are in debt have rights of property such as the income of trust funds which cannot be seized by their creditors to satisfy judgments obtained in court. Sometimes also persons who are in debt transfer their property to their wives or otherwise so dispose of it that their creditors cannot, by the remedies open in law actions, seize and apply it to the payment of debts due. In each case, a petition can be filed in a court of equity, asking that the persons who hold the trust funds or have possession of property so conveyed be directed to use it in payment of the debtor's obligations. Such petitions are called creditor's bills.

In the case of *Miller v. Davidson*,[1] decided in 1846 by the Supreme Court of Illinois, Justice Caton said:

> Where a creditor seeks to satisfy his debt out of some equitable estate of the defendant, which is not liable to a levy and sale under an execution at law, then he must exhaust his remedy at law by obtaining judgment and getting an execution returned *nulla bona* [that the debtor has no property that can be seized], before he can come into a court of equity for the purpose of reaching the equitable estate of the defendant; and this is necessary to give the court jurisdiction, for otherwise it does not appear but that the party has a complete remedy at law. This is what may be strictly termed a creditor's bill. There is another sort of creditor's bill very nearly allied to this, yet where the plaintiff is not bound to go quite so far before he comes into this court, and that is where he seeks to remove a fraudulent incumbrance out of the way of his execution. There he may file his bill as soon as he obtains his judgment.

In order to sustain a creditor's bill in equity, the petitioner must first of all show the court that he has no sufficient remedy at law.

[1] 8 Illinois Rep., 518, 522.

In the case of *Huening v. Buckley*,[1] decided in 1899 by the Appellate Court of Illinois, the creditors alleged that the defendant Buckley, against whom they had obtained a judgment, had told the sheriff that she had a homestead right[2] in property which he sought to attach and sell to pay the judgment. The statement was false; but the sheriff refused to proceed with the execution on the judgment, and sent it back to the court with his certificate that it had not been satisfied. The creditors then brought a creditors action against Mrs. Buckley, who set up as a defense that they had a complete remedy at law and had no right to proceed in equity. The court in which the case was first heard, decided in her favor; and the plaintiffs then appealed to the Appellate Court, which upheld the ruling in a decision, in which Justice Windes said:

The only question necessary to be considered is whether the appellants [the creditors] have a complete, adequate and sufficient remedy at law to enforce their judgment against the appellee Buckley. If they have, then the decree dismissing the bill was proper. . . .

It is claimed that because Buckley fraudulently represented to the sheriff that she had a claim or right of homestead in said real estate, . . . appellants have the right because of such fraudulent claim and representations to come into equity for relief. . . .

The sheriff was directed by the writ of execution in his hands and by the appellants to sell this real estate. It was his duty to serve the writ and to inquire whether or not the claim of the appellee was true that the property levied upon

[1] 87 Illinois Appellate Court Decisions, 648.

[2] A "homestead" is a house and land set apart as a home for the family, which is exempt from attachment except for debts incurred in repairing or improving it.

by him was exempt, and for failure so to do is liable to an action [authorities cited].

But it is not necessary that appellants have resort to their action against the sheriff for his failure to execute the writ [of execution]. They may proceed in the County Court by motion or petition for a rule on the sheriff to show cause for not making the sale, or for contempt in disobeying the writ [authorities cited]. . . .

Appellants made no basis by their bill to sustain it as a creditors bill solely because there was no return of the execution *nulla bona*, and besides, its allegations show that the real estate in question was subject to their judgment, the title thereto being of record in the name of the debtor, and no reason why it should not have been sold by the sheriff for their claims. The decree of the Circuit Court is therefore affirmed.

Foreclosure of Liens and Mortgages.

A lien is a claim upon property based upon some work performed or service rendered. A shoemaker has a lien upon shoes for his charges for repairs. A hotel keeper has a lien upon the baggage of his guests for the value of the food and lodging he supplies. A railroad has a lien upon merchandise which it carries from place to place to the extent of its freight charges. A carpenter has for his wages a lien upon a house which he builds or repairs. A dealer in building supplies has a lien upon a house for the value of lumber or bricks used in its erection. A person who lends money to the owner of a house, receiving as security a deed or mortgage, has a lien upon the property for the amount of the loan.

All of these liens or claims are founded upon some contract either implied by law from the circumstances or made in writing. For the law supposes that a contract is made when one person does work or performs a service for another. A deed or mortgage may be a contract by which property is given as security for a loan.

These liens are either liens on personal property, or articles which can be taken from place to place; or liens upon real property which consists of land, buildings on land, and rights to use land.

Obviously the value to the holder of any of these liens is that he can apply the property upon which he has the claim to the payment of the debt due him. This is accomplished by foreclosure or exercising full ownership rights. The shoemaker, for example, will not give to the owner the shoes he has repaired until his bill is paid. If his bill is not paid, he forcloses the lien by selling the shoes to some other person. The holder of a mortgage upon real property which remains in the possession of the owner until the debt is due, takes possession of the property pledged in case the debt is not paid at maturity, and either holds it for his own or sells it to satisfy the debt, any balance remaining after the sale being the property of the owner. The first procedure is called "strict foreclosure"; the second, "foreclosure by sale."

In the case of *Ansonia Bank's Appeal from Commissioners*,[1] decided in 1890 by the Supreme Court of Errors of Connecticut, Chief Justice Andrews said:

Any proceeding which cuts off the mortgagor's equity of redemption in the mortgaged property beyond recall would be a foreclosure in the sense of this statute [prescribing procedure for the foreclosure of mortages]. That a decree for the sale of mortgaged property, such as was had in this case, does so cut off the mortgagor's equity of re-

[1] 58 Connecticut Rep., 257, 260.

demption in it beyond possibility of recall, is not open to question. . . . The only equitable remedies of the mortgagee for enforcing the lien of the mortgage when it has become due, are "strict foreclosure" [in which the mortgagee obtains ownership of the property] and "foreclosure by judicial sale" [in which the property mortgaged is sold and the proceeds applied to the payment of the debt]; the latter of which is by far the most common in this country.

Bills of Discovery.

A person who has a claim against another sometimes is unable to prove in court the facts on which his rights are based without the testimony of his opponent or the production of books and documents in his adversary's possession. In such cases, a bill of discovery may be brought in a court of equity to obtain such evidence before the claimant brings his action at law.

In the case of *State v. Security Savings Co.*,[1] decided in 1896 by the Supreme Court of Oregon, Chief Justice Bean said:

A bill of discovery . . . is a mere instrument of procedure in aid of the relief sought by the party in some other judicial controversy, filed for the sole purpose of proving the plaintiff's case from the defendant's own mouth, or from documents in his possession, and asking no relief in the suit except it may be a temporary stay of the proceedings in another suit to which the discovery relates. Pomeroy's *Equity Jurisprudence*, Sec. 191.

Bills of Peace and Quia Timet.

Courts of equity will hear and determine bills of peace, which are brought to prevent vexatious suits and to restrain evil disposed persons from unlawful acts, and

[1] 28 Oregon Rep., 410, 420.

bills of *quia timet* (because there is reason for fear) to prevent anticipated injuries to property.

In the case of *Bailey v. Southwick*,[1] decided in 1872 by the General Term of the Supreme Court of New York, Presiding Justice Potter said:

> It is . . . claimed by the plaintiff that the complaint can be sustained as a *bill of peace* or of *quia timet*. A bill of peace is most generally brought after suit instituted, and generally to try a right that has been tried at law and seeks an injunction, though there are a few cases where they may be brought before the party is actually prosecuted. . . . The cases where bills of peace can be maintained are principally limited to cases of injunctions to stay proceedings at law, to restrain vexatious suits, to restrain the alienation of property, to restrain waste, to restrain trespasses, and to prevent irreparable mischiefs. The object generally is to establish and perpetuate a right which the party claims, and which, from its nature, may be controverted by different persons at different times, and by different actions, or it may lie where separate attempts have been unsuccessfully made to overthrow the same right, and where justice requires that the party should be quieted in the right. Its obvious design is to procure repose from perpetual litigation, and it is therefore justly called a bill of peace. . . .
>
> Bills of *quia timet* are also known in the practice of equity as bills of prevention, and are used to accomplish the ends of precautionary justice. The name of the bill is taken from the expression of the party's fears in the application. He fears some future probable injury to his rights or interests, and not because an injury has already occurred which requires relief. Its object is to secure the preservation of property to its appropriate uses where there is future or contingent danger of its being diminished or converted to other uses, or lost by gross neglect, without the inter-

[1] 6 Lansing (N. Y.) Rep., 356, 363.

position of the court. It generally relates to personal property, and is applicable as against executors and administrators, trustees and corporations, where there is danger of devastation, waste or collusion, by which estates may be diminished, and where the appointment of a receiver is necessary.

CHAPTER XVII

Injunction.

The object of a case in equity is to obtain an order called an injunction, by which the court commands to be done some act which is essential to justice or forbids to be done some act which is contrary to justice. The one is a mandatory injunction; the other is a prohibitory injunction.

In the case of *Parsons v. Marye*,[1] decided in 1885 by the U. S. Circuit Court for the Eastern District of Virginia, Circuit Judge Hughes said:

> Jeremy, in his *Equity Jurisdiction*, says: "An injunction is a writ framed *according to the circumstances of the case, commanding* an act which the court regards as essential to justice, or *restraining* an act which it considers contrary to equity and good conscience." The mandatory injunction may be in the direct form of a command, or in the direct form of prohibiting the refusal to do an act to which another has a right.

Contempt of Court.

Courts of equity inflict punishments in the form of fines or imprisonments or both upon persons who by disregarding or disobeying injunctions are guilty of

[1] 23 Federal Reporter, 113, 121.

contempt of court, which has been defined in the following words:

> In its broad sense a contempt is a disregard of, or disobedience to, the commands of a public authority, legislative or judicial, or an interruption of its proceedings by disorderly behavior or insolent language, in its presence, or so near thereto as to disturb its proceedings or impair the respect due to its authority.[1]

The power of a court of equity to punish contempts committed by disregard or disobedience of injunctions was described as follows by Justice Brewer in the case of *In re Debs*,[2] decided in 1895 by the U. S. Supreme Court:

> The power of the court to make an order carries with it the equal power to punish for a disobedience of that order, and the inquiry as to the question of disobedience has been, from time immemorial, the special function of the court. And this is no technical rule. In order that a court may compel obedience to its orders it must have the right to inquire whether there has been any disobedience thereof. To submit the question of disobedience to another tribunal, be it a jury or another court, would operate to deprive the proceeding of half its efficiency. . . . A court, enforcing obedience to its orders by proceedings for contempt, is not executing the criminal laws of the land, but only securing to suitors the rights which it has adjudged them entitled to.

[1] Am. & Eng. Ency. of Law—Contempt.
[2] 158 U. S. Rep., 564, 594, 596.

PART V
International Law

CHAPTER XVIII

Nature of International Law.

Many American citizens carry on the business of selling American products in foreign countries just as citizens of foreign countries sell their products here. In carrying on this kind of business these merchants extend credits to one another. In each case, the creditors are entitled to the benefit of the laws for the collection of debts of the nations where the debtors reside.

Merchants who sell goods and merchandise to citizens of other countries must in many cases send the articles in which they deal across oceans over which no one nation has dominion. Such merchants have the right to have their property while in transit protected from pirates.

In time of war, merchants of the nations which are at peace have the right to continue their business dealings with one another without interruption by the naval or military forces of the warring nations.

In time of war, merchants of nations that are at peace sell their wares to merchants of the nations that are at war; and the nations that are at war try to deprive their enemies of the benefits of that commerce. Hence, there must be rules to determine the rights of citizens of neutral nations in their dealings with citizens of warring nations.

Citizens of one country frequently go to other countries and sometimes reside in those countries for long periods. Such persons are entitled not only to the protection of the laws of the country in which they happen to be, but also to the protection of their own government.

Persons who live permanently away from their own countries sometimes claim the protection of their own governments, which they no longer support. The extent of the protection which they have the right to claim must be determined.

Great numbers of emigrants are constantly leaving the countries of their birth. The countries to which they go are naturally unwilling to add to their existing populations aliens who by reason of age or disease may become public charges, or who by reason of their political opinions may be troublesome, or who by competing with native-born laborers may reduce the rate of wages and lower the standard of living. Therefore nations regulate the admission of foreigners and provide for their expulsion if undesirable.

Persons who have committed crimes in one country often try to escape punishment by going to other countries. It is for the interest of a country where a criminal has taken refuge, as well as of the country in which he has committed an offense, to send him back to suffer punishment.

In time of war, there is a tendency to use cruel and morally indefensible methods, which inflict unnecessary injuries upon both combatants and non-combatants. Therefore the severities of warfare ought to be mitigated.

A nation has no authority outside of its own territory.

Its government cannot apprehend in another country and hold for trial in its courts a person accused of violating its laws. Neither can its government compel persons living outside of its borders to answer in its courts the complaints of its citizens. Its laws are not binding upon other nations and their citizens. Its courts have no right to judge disputes about the rights of its citizens residing or owning property in other countries. Its government cannot protect against warring nations its rights as a neutral except by the use of force.

For these reasons, the civilized nations of the world accept and recognize a number of principles regulating their relations with one another, safeguarding the rights of citizens of one country in another, and mitigating the severities of warfare. These principles form a body of law which is just as real as any other law though it depends for enforcement upon good faith in the first instance and upon force in the last resort. This body of law is international law.

"The law of nations," says Blackstone,[1] "is a system of rules, deducible by natural reason and established by universal consent among the civilized inhabitants of the world; in order to decide all disputes, to regulate all ceremonies and civilities, and to insure the observance of justice and good faith in the intercourse which must frequently occur between two or more independent states and the individuals belonging to each. This general law is founded upon this principle, that different nations ought in time of peace to do one another all the good they can, and in time of war as little harm as possible, without prejudice to their own real interests."

[1] *Commentaries*, Book IV., Ch. IV., 1765.

In the case of *Regina v. Keyn*,[1] Lord Coleridge said:

Strictly speaking, "international law" is an inexact expression, and is apt to mislead if its inexactness is not kept in mind. Law implies a law-giver and a tribunal capable of enforcing it and coercing its transgressors. But there is no common law-giver to sovereign states; and no tribunal has power to bind them by decrees or coerce them if they transgress. The law of nations is that collection of usages which civilized states have agreed to observe in their dealings with one another. What these usages are, whether a particular one has or has not been agreed to, must be matter of evidence. Treaties and acts of state are but evidence of the agreement of nations, and do not in this country [Great Britain], at least, *per se* bind the tribunals. Neither, certainly, does a consensus of jurists; but it is evidence of the agreement of nations on international points; and on such points, when they arise, the English courts give effect, as part of English law, to such agreement.

On the other hand, Lord Russell of Killowen, in his speech to the American Bar Association in 1896,[2] said that the view expressed by Lord Coleridge is based on too narrow a definition of law, a definition which "relies too much on force as the governing idea." He said further:

If the development of law is historically considered, it will be found to exclude that body of customary law which in early stages of society precedes law, which assumes definitely the character of positive command coupled with primitive sanctions. . . . As government becomes more

[1] 2 Exchequer Decisions (English) 153; Quoted in 16 *Am. & Eng. Ency. of Law*, 1124.

[2] 30 American Law Review, 643; quoted in 16 *Am. & Eng. Ency. of Law*, 1125.

frankly democratic . . . laws bear less and less the character of commands imposed by a coercive authority, and acquire more and more the character of customary law founded on consent. . . . I claim then that the aggregate of the rules to which nations have agreed to conform in their conduct toward one another are properly to be designated "international law."

Beginnings of International Law; Ancient Empires.

In the earliest times of which we have any knowledge, some efforts were made to protect the rights of persons who lived or owned property outside of the countries in which they had their homes. For the most part these efforts were confined to the policing of the great trade routes between Asia and Europe which every conqueror wanted to control. These conquerors stationed at strategic points along the caravan routes military contingents that protected the traders from robbery and violence and collected tolls and customs duties. They also enforced laws regulating the dealings of the traders with the inhabitants of the communities along the trade routes in order to prevent attacks of either on the other. These laws taken together formed a body of rudimentary international law.

Beginnings of International Law; The Law of the Seas.

The first codes of international law were framed by the maritime nations of ancient Greece whose governments, in order to prevent their mariners when on voyages to distant places from committing crimes that might result in war, made laws regulating the conduct of shipmasters and seamen. The earliest of these codes of which we have any real knowledge is the Code of Rhodes, which is said to have been adopted afterward by the Roman emperors. The only sentence of the Rhodian code that has been preserved in its original form states the doctrine of jettison:—that when goods are thrown overboard to lighten a ship in a storm, the owners of goods saved must share the losses by which they benefit.[1] During the Middle Ages and at a later period, a number of marine codes designed to safeguard the rights of maritime states as the ultimate owners of the ships and cargoes of their subjects, were made by the city state of Amalfi, Italy, by the Hanseatic League, and by Louis XIV of France.

The history of the law of the sea is given in the case of *The Scotia*,[2] decided by the U. S. Supreme Court in 1871. About midnight on April 8, 1867, the *Scotia*, a Cunard steamship, was sailing westward near the middle of the Atlantic ocean, on her way from Liverpool to New York. Her lookouts were properly set and her lights burning and rightly placed, according to certain regulations for preventing collisions at sea, made by British orders in council in 1863 in pursuance of an act of Parliament. These rules and regulations were the same as those established by an act of Congress in 1864 for the same purpose, which applied to American ships just as the British regulations applied to British ships. At the same time and about one or two miles west of the *Scotia*, the *Berkshire*, an American sailing ship, was sailing eastward on her voyage from New Orleans to Havre and was not exhibiting colored lights as required by the act of Congress which has been referred to. When the vessels neared one another, each tried to avoid the other, but was unable to do so; and the *Scotia* ran into

---

[1] Hershey, *Essentials of International Public Law*, p. 40.
[2] 14 Wallace (U. S.) Rep., 170, 187.

the *Berkshire* and sunk her. The owners of the *Berkshire* then brought an action against the *Scotia* to recover for the loss they had sustained, basing their demand upon the argument that, being a steamer, it was the duty of the *Scotia*, by a rule of the sea, to keep clear of sailing vessels; and that if she had changed her course or slowed up, the collision would not have occurred. On behalf of the *Scotia*, it was argued that the *Berkshire* did not carry the side lights prescribed by the regulations of both nations; and therefore damages could not be awarded to the owners of the *Berkshire*. The question before the court, therefore, was whether its decision should be governed by the law of the sea (where the collision took place), that steamers should keep clear of sailing vessels, or by the law of the United States (where the action was brought), that vessels at sea should carry certain lights. In passing upon this question Justice Strong said:

It must be conceded . . . that the rights and merits of a case may be governed by a different law from that which controls a court in which a remedy may be sought. The question still remains, what was the law of the place where the collision occurred, and at the time when it occurred. Conceding that it was not the law of the United States, nor that of Great Britain, nor the concurrent regulations of the two governments, but that it was the law of the sea, was it the ancient maritime law, that which existed before the commercial nations of the world adopted the regulations [respecting lights at sea], . . . or the law changed after those regulations were adopted? Undoubtedly, no single nation can change the law of the sea. That law is of universal obligation, and no statute of one or two nations can create obligations for the world. Like all the laws of nations, it rests upon the common consent of civilized communities. It is of force, not because it was prescribed by any superior power, but because it has been generally accepted as a rule of conduct. Whatever may have been its origin, whether in the usages of navigation or in the ordinances of maritime states, or in both, it has become the law of the sea only by the concurrent sanction of those nations who may be said to constitute the commercial world. Many of the usages which prevail, and which have the force of law, doubtless originated in the positive prescriptions of some single state, which were at first of limited effect, but which when generally accepted became of universal obligation. The Rhodian law is supposed to have been the earliest system of marine rules. It was a code for Rhodians only, but it soon became of general authority because accepted and assented to as a wise and desirable system by other maritime nations. The same may be said of the Amalphitan table, of the ordinances of the Hanseatic League, and of parts of the marine ordinances of Louis XIV. They all became the law of the sea, not on account of their origin, but by reason of their acceptance as such. And it is evident that unless general consent is efficacious to give sanction to international law, there never can be that growth and development of maritime rules which the constant changes in the instruments and necessities of navigation require. Changes in nautical rules have taken place. How have they been accomplished if not by the concurrent assent, express or implied, of maritime nations? When, therefore, we find such rules of navigation as are mentioned in the British orders in council of January 9th, 1863, and in our act of Congress of 1864, accepted as obligatory rules by more than thirty of the principal commercial states of the world, including almost all which have any shipping on the Atlantic Ocean, we are constrained to regard them as in part at least, and so far as relates to these vessels, the laws of the sea, and as having been the law at the time when the collision . . . took place.

The Discovery of America, a Background of Modern International Law.

Up to the time of the discovery of the American continents, international law was almost exclusively a law of the sea rather than of the land. During the Middle Ages, the rulers of the civilized world had regarded the portions of the surface of the earth under their control as private property which God had given to them. Each of them guarded his domains as well as he could from the encroachments of neighboring enemies without reference to any law except the law of force. When the new world was discovered, each of them wished to seize and hold for himself as much of its territory as might be possible. Ferdinand and Isabella at once set up the claim that inasmuch as their officer, Christopher Columbus, had discovered it, the whole belonged to them; and the Portuguese who had discovered the route to the East Indies made similar claims to their discoveries. In the early days of discovery, it was supposed that the new world was a part of Asia and that Spain and Portugal were claiming the same territory under different discoveries. Pope Alexander VI in 1493 attempted to settle the dispute by drawing, from the North to the South Pole in what he thought was the middle of the Atlantic ocean, an arbitrary Line of Demarcation, and assigning all new lands east of it to Portugal and all west of it to Spain. A little later, by a treaty between Spain and Portugal, the line was fixed at a point 370 leagues west of the Cape Verde Islands, so that the greater part of Brazil fell to Portugal. The kings of France and England refused to accept the Pope's decree. Indeed, Francis I of France declared that, if Father Adam had given America to Spain, he would like to see the title deeds. The French planted colonies in Canada and at the mouth of the Mississippi, and claimed by right of discovery nearly all of North America northward of Mexico and Florida and west of the Allegheny mountains. The English, on similar grounds, claimed a great strip of territory along the Atlantic coast from Maine to Florida and westward to the Pacific ocean. At first each insisted upon the rights gained by discovery and disputed the claims set up by the others. But all of them finally agreed upon one principle: the discovery of unoccupied territory gave title, which might be made valid by possession, to the government by whose subjects or by whose' authority the discovery had been made. Thus was established a new principle or rule of international law.

This rule was described by the U. S. Supreme Court in 1823 in the case of *Johnson v. McIntosh*,[1] in which the plaintiff claimed certain lands under a purchase and conveyance made in 1773 by the chiefs of the Illinois and the Piankeshaw Indians, and the defendants claimed the same lands under a patent, granted by the United States. In disposing of this question, the court decided that the United States had adopted the principle of international law that discovery gives to the government by whose citizens or subjects it is made, the right to appropriate the lands discovered. The lands in question were situated in the territory that had been ceded by Great Britain to the United States. The court ruled that, inasmuch as the United States had derived its title from Great Britain, which had held the lands under treaties of cession from France, the government whose subjects had discovered the Mississippi valley in which the disputed lands were situated, our government by its patent had given a perfect title to

[1] 8 Wheaton (U. S.) Rep., 543, 572.

the defendant. In reaching this conclusion, Chief Justice Marshall explained as follows the rule of international law concerning discovery and occupation:

On the discovery of this immense continent, the great nations of Europe were eager to appropriate to themselves so much of it as they could respectively acquire. Its vast extent afforded an ample field to the ambition and enterprise of all; and the character and religion of its inhabitants afforded an apology for considering them as a people over whom the superior genius of Europe might claim an ascendency. The potentates of the old world found no difficulty in convincing themselves that they made ample compensation to the inhabitants of the new, by bestowing on them civilization and Christianity, in exchange for unlimited independence. But, as they were all in pursuit of nearly the same object, it was necessary, in order to avoid conflicting settlements, and consequent war with each other, to establish a principle, which all should acknowledge as the law by which the right of acquisition, which they all asserted, should be regulated as between themselves. This principle was, that discovery gave title to the government by whose subjects, or by whose authority, it was made, against all other European governments, which title might be consummated by possession. The exclusion of all other Europeans, necessarily gave to the nation making the discovery the sole right of acquiring the soil from the natives, and establishing settlements upon it. It was a right with which no Europeans could interfere. It was a right which all asserted for themselves, and to the assertion of which, by others, all assented.

Modern International Law.

International law as a body of rules regulating the rights and duties of nations began to take on its present form during the 17th century. In 1625, Hugo Grotius, one of the greatest jurists that ever lived, gave to the world his work entitled *De Jure Belli ac Pacis*, in which he promulgated the principle that each of the civilized nations of the world ought to have laws regulating its dealings with other nations based upon the same ideals of right and wrong as the laws which regulate the dealings with one another of the members of a community. Since the Peace of Westphalia (1648) which recognized the equality of the Catholic and Lutheran Confessions in Germany, and the independence and legal equality of the states of Western Christendom, whether Catholic or Protestant, the theories of Grotius have been regarded as the basis of international law. Those theories have been elaborated by Vattel, Puffendorf, and other students of international economics, and have been adopted by the governments of the world as rules of international conduct. They have been followed by the judicial tribunals of all civilized nations and thus have in each nation the same force and effect as rules of law established by statutes and declared by courts of justice.

Another form of international law is found in the political policies of a number of the more important nations, such as the American Monroe Doctrine, that forbids further European expansion in the continents of this hemisphere; the Drago Doctrine, that opposes the collection of national debts by military measures; and the Calvo Doctrine, that a nation ought not to interfere with the affairs of another nation in order to enforce the claims of its citizens.

Still another form of international law consists of stipulations or conventions made by international conferences, such as the agreement for the disuse of privateers in warfare made by the Congress of Paris in 1856, the regulations for naval warfare made by the London Conference of 1909, the rules framed by the Hague Conferences of 1899 and 1907, and the Convention for the establishment of a League of Nations and a World Court of Arbitration made by the Paris Conference of 1919.

Lastly international law has been most firmly established by the provisions of international treaties by which two or more nations have agreed to be governed in their dealings with one another by clearly defined rules.

In the case of *Hilton v. Guyot*,[1] decided in 1894 by the U. S. Supreme Court, Justice Gray said:

International law, in its widest and most comprehensive sense . . . including not only questions of right between nations, governed by what has been appropriately called the law of nations; but also questions arising under what is usually called private international law, or the conflict of law, and concerning the rights of persons within the territory and dominion of one nation by reason of acts, private or public, done within the dominion of another nation . . . is part of our law and must be ascertained and administered by courts of justice as often as such questions are presented in litigation between man and man, duly submitted to their determination.

The most certain guide, no doubt, for the decision of such cases, is a treaty or a statute of this country. But when . . . there is no written law upon the subject, the duty still rests upon the judicial tribunals of ascertaining and declaring what the law is, whenever it becomes necessary to do so, in order to determine the rights of parties to suits regularly brought before them. In doing this, the courts must obtain such aid as they can from judicial decisions,

[1] 159 U. S. Rep., 113, 163.

from the works of jurists and commentators, and from the acts and usages of civilized nations.

Treaties as Formal Statements of International Law.

Customs and usages, opinions of eminent writers and judges, political policies, and conventions are more or less informal expressions of international law. Treaties are formal declarations of international law contained in written instruments.

In the *Head Money Cases*,[1] decided in 1884 by the U. S. Supreme Court, Justice Miller said:

A treaty is primarily a compact between independent nations. It depends for the enforcement of its provisions on the interest and the honor of the governments which are parties to it. If these fail, its infraction becomes the subject of international negotiations and reclamations, so far as the injured party chooses to seek redress, which may in the end be enforced by actual war. It is obvious that with all this the judicial courts have nothing to do and can give no redress. But a treaty may also contain provisions which confer certain rights upon the citizens or subjects of one of the nations residing in the territorial limits of the other, which partake of the nature of municipal law, and which are capable of enforcement as between private parties in the courts of the country. An illustration of this character is found in treaties, which regulate the mutual rights of citizens and subjects of the contracting nations in regard to rights of property by descent or inheritance, when the individuals concerned are aliens.

Modification of Treaties by Statutes.

In the *Chinese Exclusion Case*,[2] decided in 1888 by the U. S. Supreme Court, it was distinctly ruled that a

[1] 112 U. S. Rep., 580, 598.   [2] 130 U. S. Rep., 581, 600,

treaty, like any other part of the supreme law of the land, can be modified or repealed by a subsequent act of legislation. Justice Field said:

The objection made is, that the act of 1888 impairs a right vested under the treaty of 1880 [with China] as a law of the United States, and the statutes of 1882 and 1884 passed in execution of it. It must be conceded that the act of 1888 is in contravention of express treaty stipulations of the treaty of . . . 1880, but it is not on that account invalid or to be restricted in its enforcement. The treaties were of no greater legal obligation than the act of Congress. By the Constitution, laws made in pursuance thereof and treaties made under the authority of the United States are both declared to be the supreme law of the land, and no paramount authority is given to one over the other. A treaty, it is true, is in its nature a contract between nations and is often merely promissory in its character, requiring legislation to carry its stipulations into effect. Such legislation will be open to future repeal or amendment. If the treaty operates by its own force, and relates to a subject within the power of Congress, it can be deemed in that particular only the equivalent of a legislative act, to be repealed or modified at the pleasure of Congress. In either case, the last expression of the sovereign will must control.

National Policies in International Law: The Monroe Doctrine.

After the fall of Napoleon Bonaparte in 1815, the Emperors of Austria and Russia and the King of Prussia formed the Holy Alliance, to preserve the rights and interests of European dynasties—an alliance of monarchs that was intended to suppress the rising spirit of republicanism. The United States paid no attention to this alliance until 1823, when the allied monarchs undertook to assist the king of Spain to recover his former dependencies in America. President Monroe in his message to Congress of December 2, 1823, took the position that the United States would regard any meddling by European powers with the new Spanish-American republics "as a manifestation of an unfriendly disposition toward the United States" and "any attempt to extend their system to any portion of this hemisphere as dangerous to our peace and safety."

The Monroe Doctrine has since been expanded by the United States into a general policy of dealing with controversies between European and American governments. In 1895, for example, President Cleveland insisted upon and obtained the consent of Great Britain to the arbitration of a boundary dispute between British Guiana and Venezuela which was afterward carried to a successful conclusion.

It has also been construed by the United States as imposing a duty upon the United States to see to it that the American governments which look to the United States for protection from European governments shall themselves fulfill their international obligations. In 1905, President Roosevelt negotiated with San Domingo a treaty by which the United States undertook to deal with the bonded debts of that republic so that European governments to which the debts were due, should have no just cause to take measures to collect them. Mr. Frederick R. Coudert, an American lawyer who is an authority on international law, says:[1]

I am aware that in some respects the Monroe Doctrine is vague. . . . Its strongest adherents do not always define it in the same fashion. Yet I think we are safe in saying that it cannot be considered altogether from the stand-

[1] 9 Bench and Bar, 18.

point of American rights, but that it also comports corresponding duty. This duty was tersely expressed in
President Roosevelt's Message of 1905, referring to the proposed Treaty with San Domingo [for the settlement of the
financial obligations of that republic]:

"Either we must abandon our duty under our traditional
policy toward the Dominican people, who aspire to a republican form of government while they are actually
drifting into a condition of permanent anarchy, in which
case we must permit some other government to adopt its
own measures in order to safeguard its own interests, or else
we must ourselves take seasonable and appropriate action." . . .

The Venezuela boundary controversy of 1895 involved
perhaps the greatest extent to which we have carried the
Monroe Doctrine. When we insisted that Great Britain
should arbitrate a boundary dispute with Venezuela we
went to an extent which many persons thought unjustifiable. However that may be, Great Britain has acquiesced
in our interpretation of the Monroe Doctrine and as far
as she is concerned, the controversy seems to be moot.
Germany assented to it in connection with the Venezuela
blockade question.

International Practice.

International law is like other forms of law in that it
consists of customs, principles, and rules that have only
an academic interest except when they are used to promote the safety and welfare of man. The government
and courts of each nation use it as a rule of action in
safe-guarding the rights of that nation and in performing the duties of that nation to other nations and their
citizens. Hence we have to ascertain how each nation
practices international law in order to know how it effects the objects for which it exists. For example, dur-

ing the latter part of June, 1923, the United States, as a means of enforcing the National Prohibition Law, seized on board a British vessel a quantity of intoxicating liquor that had been stored under British customs seals. Technically the vessel was part of the territory of Great Britain and subject to the laws of that country, but our government took the position that a foreign ship while in American waters is subject to American laws and therefore that the liquor was subject to seizure. The British Government accepted our ruling on the question involved as an exercise by the government of the United States of its right to put in practice in its own way the principles of international law.

The United States has put in practice the principles of international law on many occasions. Its first international act was the making in 1778 of the treaty with France by which our independence was recognized. It made with Great Britain in 1783, the treaty which definitely declared the separation of the two nations. In 1784, it entered into a treaty of commerce and neutrality with Prussia. In 1794, it made a commercial treaty with Great Britain. Since then, it has made with other nations conventions and treaties for the security of trade and commerce, for the abolition of privateering in war, for the suppression of piracy and the slave trade, for the protection of our citizens in foreign countries and of citizens of other nations in our country, for the settlement of international boundaries, for the ascertainment of the rights of neutrals in time of war, for the extradition of fugitives from justice, for the arbitration of international disputes that might otherwise have to be settled by war, and for other objects in which it has a common interest with other nations. It has settled by diplomatic negotiations a number of controversies with other nations. It has protested in due form against the acts of other nations that have violated its rights of neutrality, resenting the interference with its commerce occasioned by the orders in council of Great Britain and the Berlin and Milan Decrees of Napoleon Bonaparte, and insisting at the outset of the World War that Great Britain "refrain from all unnecessary interference with the freedom of trade between [neutral] nations,"[1] and holding the Imperial German Government "to a strict accountability for such acts of their naval authorities"[2] as would by the use of submarines within a "war zone" jeopardize American lives or property. It has promulgated in the Monroe Doctrine the principle that the American continents are not subject to further European colonization or expansion. It has taken part in the settlement by arbitration of many international questions like the fishing rights of Americans in Canadian waters. It has carried on against other nations wars for the assertion of its rights; for example, the War of 1812, which grew in part out of the impressment of American seamen by British ships of war; the Spanish-American War of 1898, which put an end in Cuba to a state of anarchy that interfered with the rights of American citizens; and the World War, in which the Germans compelled us to take part by carrying on a submarine warfare that was destructive to our commerce. It has regulated by law the immigration of foreigners and has enacted and enforced laws extending to citizens of other countries residing here the rights that it claims for our citizens residing in other countries. It has enacted and enforced laws to prevent and punish acts in violation of the duties of

[1] Communication of the U. S. Secretary of State, Dec. 26, 1914.
[2] Communication of the U. S. Secretary of State, Feb. 10, 1915.

neutrality that our nation while at peace owes to other nations that are at war.

International Law, A Rudimentary World Government.

The United States and the nations with which it has had these dealings are bodies politic or associations each composed of all the persons who live in its territory under the protection of its government. Each is a sovereign body, having supreme unlimited control over the persons that are its members and over all the land and other property that it owns. Each has a government or organization of public officers to carry on its business. Each, like its citizens, has the rights of life, liberty and property; the right of life to a nation is its right to continue to exist unless by misconduct it interferes with the right of life of another nation; its right of liberty is its right to have its own independent government so long as it so conducts that government as not to interfere with the rights of other nations to have their independent governments; its right of property is its right to possess the territory and other property within its boundaries and to exercise any rights it may have in the territory of another nation,[1] so long as it does not permit the use of such property to the injury of other nations.

The United States and the other nations, as sovereign bodies politic possessed of these rights, carry on an imperfect world government by means of international law, just as each of them carries on its organized government according to its own laws. These nations realize that a better world government ought to be established. Many of the citizens of these nations not

[1] The fishing rights of the United States in the waters of the Canadian coast are a part of our national property situated outside of our territory.

only criticize their own systems of national government, but even condemn the very idea of nationality. Some of them, believing in the brotherhood of man, wish to eliminate national boundary lines and to establish a single world government. Others even more radical wish to create a world government based on economic rather than on political relations. More conservative people, believing that all progress is an orderly evolution, advocate a League of Nations with a definite constitution and a permanent court. They believe that existing international law can be made into a more perfect system of world government.

CHAPTER XIX

The following are among the more important principles of international law.

·A Nation has Powers of Sovereignty over its Land Areas and over a Part of the Seas along its Coast Lines.

The territory over which a nation has the right to exercise sovereign powers includes all of the land within its borders; all ports, harbors, bays, and enclosed arms of the sea along its coast, and a marginal belt of the sea extending outward three geographic miles. This territorial jurisdiction over parts of the seas was originally established in recognition of the fact that by means of cannon with a range of one marine league, nations could and did exercise real dominion over the seas adjacent to their coasts. Beyond that distance, no nation could claim jurisdiction because it could not enforce any such claims. It is true that England has at times claimed that the channel waters and the North Sea were parts of the English dominions, but that claim was never admitted by other nations or made good by the English.

The nature and extent of this territorial sovereignty as it affects merchant ships was considered in a group of cases under the general title of *Cunard Steamship Co. Ltd. et al. v. Mellon et al.*,[1] decided April 3, 1923, by the U. S. Supreme Court. In the decision which covered all these cases, the court dealt with the application to merchant ships of the provision of the Volstead law prohibiting "the . . . transportation of intoxicating liquors within, the importation thereof into, or the exportation thereof from the United States and all territory subject to the jurisdiction thereof for beverage purposes." Two questions arose: (1) Whether the prohibition of the law extended to American merchant ships outside the waters of the United States, whether on the high seas or in foreign ports, and (2) whether it covered foreign merchant ships, when, within the territorial waters of the United States. The court thus had to determine whether or not an American merchant ship was a part of the territory of the United States and subject to its government and laws wherever such ship may be, and whether or not a foreign merchant ship is a part of the territory of the nation by whose citizens it is owned, and as such a part of the territory of that nation and subject solely to its government and laws; even when within the territory of the United States. The court ruled that the law is not intended to apply to American ships outside of the territorial waters of the United States, except to a limited extent in the Panama Canal Zone, and is intended to apply to all merchant vessels, foreign and domestic alike when within those waters. Therefore an American ship is not, according to this decision, prohibited by the Volstead law from carrying intoxicating liquors outside of the territorial waters of the United States, and both foreign and American merchant ships are prohibited from so doing while

[1] 262 U. S. Rep., 100.

within such territorial waters. In the course of the de-
cison,[1] Justice Van Devanter said:

It is now settled in the United States and recognized elsewhere that the territory subject to its jurisdiction includes
the land areas under its dominion and control, the ports,
harbors, bays and other enclosed arms of the sea along
its coast and a marginal belt of the sea extending from the
coast line outward a marine league, or three geographic
miles [citations]. This, we hold, is the territory which the
[Eighteenth] Amendment designates as its field of operation; and the designation is not of a part of this territory
but of "all" of it.

The defendants [the Secretary of the Treasury and other
officers of the United States] contend that the Amendment
also covers domestic merchant ships outside the waters of
the United States, whether on the high seas or in foreign
waters. But it does not say so, and what it does say . . .
shows, that it is confined to the physical territory of the
United States. In support of their contention, the defendants refer to the statement sometimes made that a merchant ship is a part of the territory of the country whose
flag she flies. But this, as has been aptly observed, is a
figure of speech, or metaphor [citations]. The jurisdiction
which it is intended to describe arises out of the nationality
of the ship, as established by her domicile, registry and the
use of the flag, and partakes more of the characteristics of
personal than of territorial sovereignty [citations]. It is
chiefly applicable to ships on the high seas, where there is
no territorial sovereign; and as respects ships in foreign
territorial waters it has little application beyond what
is affirmatively or tacitly permitted by the local sovereign
[citations].

The defendants further contend that the Amendment

[1] Justices McReynolds and Brandeis dissented from the decision of
the Court

covers foreign merchant ships when within the territorial waters of the United States. Of course, if it were true that a ship is a part of the territory of the country whose flag she carries, the contention would fail. But, as that is a fiction, we think the contention is right.

A merchant ship of one country voluntarily entering the territorial limits of another subjects itself to the jurisdiction of the latter. The jurisdiction attaches in virtue of her presence, just as with other objects within those limits. During her stay she is entitled to the protection of the laws of that place and correlatively is bound to yield obedience to them. Of course, the local sovereign may out of considerations of public policy choose to forego the exertion of its juridiction, or exert the same only in a limited way, but this is a matter resting solely in its discretion. . . .

Examining the Act as a whole, we think it shows very plainly, first, that it is intended to be operative throughout the territorial limits of the United States, with one single exception, stated in the Canal Zone provision; second, that it is not intended to apply to domestic vessels, when outside the territorial waters of the United States, and, thirdly, that it is intended to apply to all merchant vessels, whether foreign or domestic, when within those waters, save as the Panama Canal Zone exception provides otherwise.

Possibly the rule may be modified in the near future because heavy ordnance now has a range of twelve miles or more and nations having sea coasts are able to exercise force over a greater distance from their shores. The Soviet government of Russia has suggested such a change, and a treaty is being negotiated between Great Britain and the United States to extend the maritime jurisdiction of the United States to twelve miles off shore for the enforcement of the 18th Amendment. Secretary of State Hughes, in a statement under date of December 8, 1923, discusses as follows the proposed treaty in the light of international law:

At the present time, in the absence of treaty, the United States is, in many instances, not permitted under international law to use its forces on the high seas to check the operation of foreign vessels from foreign ports engaged in the transportation and sale of liquor. Authority in such cases, with respect to the high seas, cannot be effectively conferred by Acts of Congress, if these are in contravention of international law, even though such legislative acts as municipal law would govern the decisions of our own courts. Where international rights and obligations are involved, questions of this sort would naturally come before an international tribunal whose decisions would be governed by international law and would not be controlled by municipal law. . . .

It is apparent that this Government should welcome aid for the enforcement of the Eighteenth Amendment with respect to foreign vessels outside the three mile limit, and that appropriate agreement with interested foreign States is important.

A Nation has the Right of Independence.

Each nation has the right to have the kind of government it likes best, to have diplomatic relations with other governments, to make and enforce its own laws, to regulate the commerce of its citizens, to prescribe rules concerning immigration, to govern its own citizens and all who live in its territory, and to frame its own policies.

In 1865, just before the Civil War ended, Napoleon III, the French emperor, sent a military expedition to Mexico, ostensibly to compel the Mexican Republic to pay its bonds owned by French citizens but really to establish an empire under Maximilian, an Austrian prince.

The United States at once intervened on the ground that the French government had violated the principle of the Monroe Doctrine prohibiting European expansion in the American continents, and had infringed the right of the Mexican nation to independence by interfering with its government. The French government yielded to our protests and withdrew its forces, whereupon Maximilian's empire fell, and he himself was executed.

In 1868, the United States made a treaty with China which gave to the inhabitants of each country the right to live in the other. Under the protection of this treaty, great numbers of Chinese laborers came to the United States where their competition with American labor produced much irritation and caused many disturbances of the peace. Hence, in 1880, a supplementary treaty was made, which gave our government the right to regulate, limit, and suspend the immigration of such Chinese laborers. In 1882, Congress enacted a law prohibiting the immigration of Chinese laborers for a period of ten years, but permitting those already here to go and come from China as they might choose, and in 1888 passed another law forbidding the readmission to the United States of Chinese laborers who had had the right to live here and had gone back to China for visits expecting to be allowed to return as provided by the first law. The validity of the latter law was challenged in *The Chinese Exclusion Case*,[1] decided in 1888 by the U. S. Supreme Court, in which Justice Field, passing upon the right of a nation to regulate immigration, said:

To preserve its independence, and give security against foreign aggression and encroachment, is the highest duty

[1] 130 U. S. Rep., 581, 606.

of every nation, and to attain these ends, nearly all other considerations are to be subordinated. It matters not in what form such aggression and encroachment come, whether from the foreign nation acting in its national character, or from vast hordes of its people crowding in upon us. The government, possessing the powers which are to be exercised for protection and security, is clothed with authority to determine the occasion on which the powers shall be called forth. . . . If, therefore, the government of the United States, through its legislative department, considers the presence of foreigners of a different race in this country, who will not assimilate with us, to be dangerous to its peace and security, their exclusion is not to be stayed because at the time there are no actual hostilities with the nation of which the foreigners are subjects.

That the government of the United States, through the action of its legislative departments, can exclude aliens from its territory, is a proposition which we do not think open to controversy. Jurisdiction over its own territory to that extent is an incident of every independent nation. It is a part of its independence. If it could not exclude aliens, it would be to that extent subject to the control of another power.

In the *Passenger Cases*,[1] decided in 1868, the United States Supreme Court held that under international law and by the Constitution of the United States, Congress had power generally to regulate immigration. The States of New York and Massachusetts had asserted that each of the States had exclusive power to regulate the immigration of aliens within its borders and that the United States had no power to interfere with the execution of their laws upon the subject. The laws of these States had imposed taxes upon incoming

[1] 7 Howard (U. S.) Rep., 287, 415.

immigrants, really in order to prevent paupers and diseased persons from becoming members of their communities, but ostensibly to provide a fund for the support and care of such unfortunate persons. The enforcement of these laws was resisted in the courts upon the ground that they were in conflict with the treaties between the United States and Great Britain and upon the further ground that immigration is a part of that foreign commerce over which, under the Constitution of the United States, Congress has exclusive power of regulation. The Supreme Court held that these State statutes were unconstitutional as regulations of foreign commerce over which the national government has jurisdiction. Justice Wayne said:

All commerce between nations is permissive or conventional. The first includes every allowance of it, under what is termed by writers upon international law the liberty or freedom of commerce, its allowance by statutes, or by the orders of any magistracy having the power to exercise the sovereignty of a nation in respect to commerce. Conventional commerce is, of course, that which nations carry on with each other under treaty stipulations. . . . Commerce between nations or among States has several branches. Martens, in his *Summary of the Law of Nations*, says: "It consists in selling the superfluity; in purchasing articles of necessity, as well productions, as manufactures; in buying from one nation and selling to another, or in transporting the merchandise from the buyer to the seller to gain the freight. Generally speaking, the commerce in Europe is so far free, that no nation refuses positively and entirely to permit the subjects of another nation, when even there is no treaty between them, to trade with its possessions in or out of Europe, or to establish themselves in its territory for that purpose. A state of war forms here a natural exception. However, as long as there is no treaty existing, every state retains its natural right to lay on such commerce whatever restriction it pleases. A nation is then fully authorized to prohibit the entry or exportation of certain merchandise, to institute customs and to augment them at pleasure, to prescribe the manner in which the commerce with its dominions shall be carried on, to point out the places where it shall be carried on, or to exempt it from certain parts of its dominions, to exercise freely its sovereign power over the foreigners living in its territories, to make whatever distinctions between the nations with whom it trades it may find conducive to its interests." . . . Applying the foregoing reasoning to the acts of Massachusetts and New York, and whatever may be the motive for such enactments or their legislative denomination, if they practically operate as regulations of commerce, or as restraints upon navigation, they are unconstitutional. When they are considered in connection with the existing legislation of Congress in respect to trade and navigation, and with treaty stipulations, they are certainly found to be in conflict with the supreme law of the land.

Nations have Equal Rights.

Under the law, nations like individuals are equals. A strong and rich nation may be able to crush a weaker nation by force, but so far as the law is concerned its strength is of no advantage.

The case of *The Antelope*,[1] decided in 1825 by the U. S. Supreme Court, grew out of the capture by a Venezuelan privateer of a number of Spanish and Portuguese vessels engaged in the slave trade and carrying cargoes of negroes. The privateer had been wrecked off the coast of Brazil and had transferred the negroes to one of the captured vessels, the *Antelope*, which in turn had been captured at sea by a U. S. revenue cutter on

[1] 10 Wheaton (U. S.) Rep., 66, 122.

the ground that she was engaged in the slave trade in violation of the laws of the United States. In the proceedings in the U. S. Court at Savannah for the condemnation of the *Antelope* and her cargo, the Spanish and Portuguese vice-consuls interposed the claim that a number of the negroes were the property of Spanish and Portuguese subjects lawfully engaged in the slave trade; that Spain and Portugal, having equal rights with other nations either to legalize or to prohibit the slave trade, had legalized it; that the United States could not make its laws prohibiting the traffic superior to the laws of the nations legalizing it; and, therefore, that the negroes claimed by them should be surrendered to the Spanish and Portuguese owners. In sustaining this contention, Chief Justice Marshall said:

No principle of law is more universally acknowledged than the perfect equality of nations. It results from this equality, that no one can rightfully impose a rule on another. Each legislates for itself, but its legislation can operate on itself alone. A right, then, which is vested in all by the consent of all, can be devested only by consent; and this [slave] trade, in which all [the nations] have participated, must remain lawful to those who cannot be induced to relinquish it.

A Nation Ought Neither to Do nor Permit to Be Done Acts Inconsistent with the Welfare of Other Nations.

The World War, in all its stages, was based upon acts which the nations concerned regarded or said they regarded as dangerous to their safety. Austria-Hungary regarded the assassination at Sarajevo in July, 1914, of Grand Duke Ferdinand, the heir to the throne, as an act of aggression by Serbia upon the Austrian Empire.

THE REASONABLENESS OF THE LAW

The Russian Imperial Government resented as an in-
fringement of the sovereignty of a sister Slav state the
demands of the Austrians on Serbia growing out of the
assassination. The German Empire declared war
against Russia on the ground that the Russian inter-
vention in the quarrel was dangerous to the welfare of the
German Imperial Goverment. The French Republic
refused the demand of the German Empire for the
temporary possession of French forts as a guaranty
that France would not take part with Russia in the war,
and opposed by force the military occupation of Belgium by the Germans. The British Empire entered
the war on the ground that the violation by Germany
of the international neutrality of Belgium was dangerous to the British government. The United States, in
1917, declared war against the German Imperial Government on the ground that the destruction of American
merchant ships by German submarines engaged in
blockading the British Islands was an act of war against
a neutral nation.

A Nation has the Right of Self-Defense.

Self-preservation is the first law of nature. A nation, as well as an individual, has the right to take such
measures as are necessary for its own safety and defense, to preserve the integrity and inviolability of its
own territory, and to safeguard its independent government. This right was the subject of diplomatic negotiations between the United States and Great Britain
in the case of *The Caroline*, described as follows:[1]

During the Canadian insurrection in the winter of 1837-
1838, the American steamboat *Caroline* was being used

[1] Hershey, *Essentials of International Public Law*, 145 n.

by Canadian insurgents and their American sympathizers to transport recruits and military supplies from Schlosser, N. Y., on the American side of Niagara River, to Navy Island, the headquarters 'of the insurgents. This island, through which ran the boundary line between Canada and the United States, was located in the midst of the Niagara River. It was believed that the *Caroline* would also be used to transport the expedition from Navy Island to the Canadian shore. In the night of Dec. 29, 1837, she was seized by Canadian forces at Schlosser, N. Y., and set adrift over the Niagara Falls. . . . In the course of the correspondence between the American and British governments, . . . Daniel Webster, then Secretary of State, laid down the rule which Lord Ashburton [acting for Great Britain] admitted was applicable to the case. Webster contended that to justify the conduct of the Canadian authorities [for violating American territory], England must show "a necessity of self-defense, instant, overwhelming, and leaving no choice of means, and no moment for deliberation." . . . as also that the "local authorities of Canada did nothing unreasonable or excessive, since the act justified by the necessity of self-defense must be limited by that necessity."

A Nation Ought to Protect its Citizens Living or Owning Property in Other Countries.

Citizenship is the right of a person to membership in a nation. According to American law, a citizen of the United States is a person born or naturalized in the United States and living under the protection of its laws. An American-born citizen can lose his citizenship only by becoming a citizen of another nation. A naturalized American citizen can abandon his citizenship by going back to his own country and living there two years or by living in a third country five years. This rule is not universal. Some nations hold that, while their citizens may become citizens of other nations, they are not thereby relieved of their duties to their own governments, which are still bound to protect them. In either case, the nation is equally bound to protect its citizens wherever they may be.

In 1898, after the sinking of the *Maine* in the harbor of Havana, our government declared war upon Spain, partly on account of that outrage, partly on the ground of humanity to prevent the cruelties perpetrated by General Weyler's government in Cuba, but chiefly because the Spanish government had not protected the sugar plantations and other property owned by American citizens in Cuba.

In 1895, the right of American citizens to be protected in the possession of their property situated in another country was passed upon by the U. S. Supreme Court in the case of *Hilton v. Guyot*,[1] in which the Court held that our government would not enforce decisions of the courts of foreign nations concerning American property rights, if the courts of those nations refused to enforce decisions of American courts concerning property rights of their citizens in this country. In that case, a French business house sued in the U. S. Court in New York the firm of A. T. Stewart & Co. of New York and Paris upon two judgments that had been issued by the French courts. One of the defenses presented was that, as the French courts would not recognize the judgments of American courts, their judgments ought not to be recognized by the tribunals of the United States. In the decision sustaining this defense, Justice Gray said:

[1] 159 U. S. Rep., 580, 598.

When an action is brought in a court of this country, by a citizen of a foreign country against one of our own citizens, to recover a sum of money adjudged by the courts of that country to be due from the defendant to the plaintiff, and the foreign judgment appears to have been rendered by a competent court, having jurisdiction of the cause and of the parties, and upon due allegations and proofs, and opportunity to defend against them, and its proceedings are according to the course of a civilized jurisprudence, and are stated in a clear and formal record, the judgment is *prima facie* evidence, at least, of the truth of the matter adjudged; and it should be held conclusive upon the merits tried in the foreign court, unless some special ground is shown for impeaching the judgment, as by showing that it was effected by fraud or prejudice, or that, by the principles of international law, and by the comity of our own country, it should not be given full faith and credit. . . .   The defendants, in their answer, cited the . . . provisions of the statutes of France, and alleged, and at trial offered to prove, that, by the construction given to these statutes by the judicial tribunals of France, when the judgments of tribunals of foreign countries against the citizens of France are sued upon in the courts of France, the merits of the controversies upon which those judgments are based are examined anew, unless a treaty to the contrary effect exists between the Republic of France and the country in which such judgment is obtained (which is not the case between the Republic of France and the United States) and that the tribunals of the Republic of France give no force and effect, within the jurisdiction of that country, to the judgments duly rendered by courts of competent jurisdiction of the United States against citizens of France after proper personal service of the process of those courts has been made therein in this country. We are of opinion that this evidence should have been admitted. . . .   The reasonable, if not the necessary, conclusion appears to us to be that judgments rendered in France, or in any other foreign country, by the laws of which our judgments are reviewable upon the merits, are not entitled to full faith and conclusive effect when sued upon in this country, but are *prima facie* evidence only of the justice of the plaintiff's claim. In holding such a judgment, for want of reciprocity, not to be conclusive evidence of the merits of the claim, we do not proceed upon any theory of retaliation upon one person by reason of injustice done to another, but upon the broad ground that international law is founded upon mutuality and reciprocity, and that by the principles of international law recognized in most civilized countries, and by the comity of our own country, which it is our judicial duty to know and to declare, the judgment is not entitled to be considered conclusive.

A Nation Ought to Fulfil its Treaty Obligations.

In the case of *Tucker v. Alexandroff*,[1] decided in 1901 by the U. S. Supreme Court, the issue before the Court hinged upon the right of the commander of a Russian warship to apprehend a seaman who had deserted the vessel at Philadelphia, had renounced his allegiance to the Czar, had declared his intention to become an American citizen, and had obtained employment here. Alexandroff, the deserter, had entered the Russian naval service as a conscript in 1896, had been assigned to duty as an assistant physician, and in 1899 had been sent with an officer and a detail of fifty-three men to Philadelphia to take possession of a cruiser under construction at Cramp's shipyard. He left Philadelphia without leave and went to New York, where he took the first steps toward becoming an American citizen. He was afterward arrested upon request of the Russian vice consul, and was committed

[1] 183 U. S. Rep., 424, 437, 439, 445, 449.

upon a *mittimus*[1] which stated that he had been charged by the captain of the cruiser with being a deserter, and as such a person who under the terms of our treaty with Russia ought to be delivered up to Russian consular agents here to be put back upon the vessel to which he belonged. Our treaty with Russia made in 1832 provided that consular officers should be authorized to require the assistance of the local authorities to arrest, detain, and imprison deserters from ships of war and merchant vessels, and that such deserters when arrested should be placed at the disposal of those officers to be restored to the vessels to which they belonged. The case came up in the U. S. District Court under a writ of habeas corpus sued out by Alexandroff. This court decided in his favor and ordered his discharge from custody. The Russian vice consul then took the case to the U. S. Supreme Court by a writ of *certiorari*. This court reversed the decision on the ground that the case was within the treaty providing for the arrest and restoration to their vessels of deserting seamen. In the course of the opinion of the court, Justice Brown interpreted the provisions of the commercial treaty between the United States and Russia, saying:

We think . . . that the rights of the parties must be determined by the treaty, but that this particular convention being operative upon both powers, and intended for their mutual protection, should be interpreted in a spirit of *uberrima fides* [extreme good faith], and in a manner to carry out its manifest purpose. . . . As treaties are solemn engagements entered into between independent

[1] A *mittimus* is a warrant issued by a magistrate directing the keeper of a prison to keep confined pending trial or the giving of bail a person charged with crime.

nations for the common advancement of their interests and the interests of civilization, and as their main object is, not only to avoid war and secure a lasting and perpetual peace, but to promote a friendly feeling between the people of the two countries, they should be interpreted in that broad and liberal spirit which is calculated to make for the existence of a perpetual amity, so far as it can be done without the sacrifice of individual rights or those principles of personal liberty which lie at the foundation of our jurisprudence. . . . What, then, are the stipulations to which we must look for a solution of the question involved in this case? They are found in the 9th article of the treaty, which authorizes the arrest and surrender of "deserters from the ships of war and merchant vessels of their country." It is insisted, however, that this article is no proper foundation for the arrest of Alexandroff for three reasons: First, that the Variag was not a Russian ship of war; second, that Alexandroff was not a deserter from such ship; third, that his membership of such crew was not proved by the exhibition of registers of vessels, the rolls of the crew, or by other official documents. The case depends upon the answer to these questions. 1. At the time Alexandroff arrived in Philadelphia, the Variag was still upon the stocks. Whatever be the proper construction of the word under the treaty, she was not then a *ship* in the ordinary sense of the term, but shortly thereafter and long before Alexandroff deserted, she was launched and thereby became a ship in its legal sense. A ship is born when she is launched, and lives so long as her identity is preserved. . . . Inasmuch as the Variag had been launched and was lying in the stream at the time of Alexandroff's desertion, we think she was a ship within the meaning of the treaty. . . . We are also of opinion that she was a Russian ship of war within the meaning of the treaty. The contract under which she was built not only provided that she was to be built for the imperial Russian government, but should be constantly, during the continuance of the contract, inspected by a board of inspection appointed by the Russian Ministry of Marine, who should have full liberty to enter the premises of the contractors for such purpose; and that speed trials should be made by the contractors in the presence of such board of inspection. . . . 2. Was Alexandroff a deserter from a Russian ship of war within the meaning of the treaty, or was he merely a deserter from the Russian naval service, a fact which of itself would not be sufficient to authorize his arrest under Article IX of the treaty? To be a deserter from a particular ship he must have been a member of the crew of such ship, and bound to remain in its service until discharged. It is earnestly insisted that, although he had been detailed to serve thereafter as a member of the crew of the Variag, her crew had never been organized as such, that the detail was merely preliminary to such organization, and that Alexandroff had never set foot upon the vessel. This argument necessarily presupposes that seamen do not become a "crew" until they have actually gone on board the vessel, and entered upon the performance of their duties. We cannot acquiesce in this position. The more reasonable view is that seamen become obligated to merchant vessels from the time they sign the shipping articles, and that from that time they may incur the penalities of desertion. . . . The Variag being a ship of war, there was no signing of shipping articles, as required in the merchant service, since the seamen were enlisted or conscribed to serve where ordered. But there was a practical equivalent for the shipping articles in the detail of Alexandroff to this vessel. He entered the Russian naval service in 1896, and his term of service had not expired. He was, of course, subject to the orders of his officers, and was sent as a member of the force of one officer and fifty-three men ordered to take possession of the Variag, as soon as she was completed. From the moment of such assignment and until relieved therefrom, he was as much bound to the service of the Variag, and a member of her crew, as if he had signed shipping articles. . . . We are of opinion that his case is within the treaty.

A Nation ought to Surrender Fugitives from Justice.

In the case of *Fong Yue Ting v. U. S.*,[1] decided in 1893 by the U. S. Supreme Court, Justice Gray defined the term "extradition" as follows:

"Extradition" is the surrender to another country of one accused of an offence against its laws, there to be tried, and, if found guilty, punished.

The extradition of criminals is an American contribution to international law. In the early days of New England, the colonies of Massachusetts Bay, Plymouth, Connecticut, and New Haven entered into a confederation, which was in effect a treaty for mutual support and protection. This treaty contained among other provisions, a stipulation for the mutual surrender of fugitives from justice. In the case of *Kentucky v. Dennison*,[2] decided in 1860 by the U. S. Supreme Court, Chief Justice Taney said:

The necessity of this policy of mutual support, in bringing offenders to justice, . . . seems to have been first recognized and acted on in the American colonies; for we find by Winthrop's "History of Massachusetts," Vol. 2, pages 121 and 126, that as early as 1643, by "articles of confederation between the plantations under the government of Massachusetts, the plantation under the government of New Plymouth, the plantations under the government of Connecticut and the government of New Haven, with the plantations in combination therewith," these

[1] 149 U. S. Rep., 698, 709.
[2] 24 Howard (U. S.) Rep., 66, 100.

plantations pledged themselves to each other that, "upon the escape of any prisoner or fugitive for any criminal cause, whether by breaking prison, or getting from the officer, or otherwise escaping, upon the certificate of two magistrates of the jurisdiction out of which the escape was made that he was a prisoner or such an offender at the time of the escape, the magistrate, or some of them, of the jurisdiction where, for the present, the said prisoner or fugitive abideth, shall forthwith grant such a warrant as the case will bear, for the apprehending of any such person, and the delivery of him into the hands of the officer or other person who pursueth him; and if there be help required for the safe returning of any such offender, then it shall be granted unto him that craves the same, he paying the charges thereof."

Extradition is not an international duty. In the case of *U. S. v. Rauscher*,[1] decided in 1886 by the U. S. Supreme Court, Justice Miller said:

It is only in modern times that the nations of the earth have imposed upon themselves the obligation of delivering up these fugitives from justice to the States where their crimes were committed, for trial and punishment. This has been done generally by treaties made by one independent nation with another. Prior to these treaties and apart from them, it may be stated as the general result of the writers upon international law, that there was no well-defined obligation on one country to deliver up such fugitives to another, and though such delivery was often made, it was upon the principle of comity, and within the discretion of the government whose action was invoked; and it has never been recognized as among those obligations of one country towards another which rest upon established principles of international law.

[1] 119 U. S. Rep., 407, 411.

In Time of a War, a Neutral Nation is under an Obligation not to Take the Part of Either Belligerent.

In the case of *The Three Friends*,[1] decided in 1897 by the U. S. Supreme Court, the facts were: A steamboat loaded with military supplies which were to be sent to the revolutionists who were then carrying on in Cuba a civil war against the Spanish government with which the United States was at peace, had been seized and detained by our government for violation of a section of our neutrality law, which prohibited such acts. In passing upon the questions raised in this case, Chief Justice Fuller defined the word "neutrality" as follows:

Neutrality, strictly speaking, consists in abstinence from any participation in a public, private or civil war, and in impartiality of conduct toward both parties, but the maintenance unbroken of peaceful relations between two powers when the domestic peace of one of them is disturbed is not neutrality in the sense in which the word is used when the disturbance has acquired such head as to have demanded the recognition of belligerency. And, as mere matter of municipal administration, no nation can permit unauthorized acts of war within its territory in infraction of its sovereignty, while good faith towards friendly nations requires their prevention.

In the case of *Wiborg v. U. S.*,[2] decided in 1896 by the U. S. Supreme Court, Chief Justice Fuller summarized the neutrality statutes of the United States in the following words:

Title LXVII of the Revised Statutes, headed "Neutrality," embraces eleven sections, from 5281 to 5291 inclusive. Section 5281 prohibits the acceptance of com-

---

[1] 166 U. S. Rep., 1, 52.　　　　[2] 163 U. S. Rep., 632, 646.

missions from a foreign power by citizens of the United States within our territory to serve against any sovereign with whom we are at peace. Section 5282 prohibits any person from enlisting in this country in the service of any foreign power and from hiring or retaining any other person to enlist or to go abroad for the purpose of enlisting. Section 5283 deals with fitting out and arming vessels in this country in favor of one foreign power as against another foreign power with which we are at peace. Section 5284 prohibits citizens from the fitting out or arming, without the United States, of vessels to cruise against citizens of the United States; and Section 5285, the augmenting of the force of a foreign vessel of war serving against a friendly sovereign. Sections 5287 to 5290 provide for the enforcement of the preceding sections, and Section 5291, that the provisions set forth shall not be construed to prevent the enlistment of certain foreign citizens in the United States. Section 5286 is as follows: "Every person who, within the jurisdiction of the United States, begins, or sets on foot, or provides or prepares the means for, any military expedition or enterprise, to be carried on from thence against the territory of any foreign prince or state, or of any colony, district or people, with whom the United States are at peace, shall be deemed guilty of a high misdemeanor, and shall be fined not exceeding three thousand dollars, and imprisoned not more than three years."

At the beginning of the World War, President Wilson issued a proclamation of the neutrality of the United States, and afterward, on August 21, 1914, published an appeal to the American nation "to act and speak in the true spirit of neutrality which is the spirit of impartiality and fairness and friendliness to all concerned," saying that "The United States must be neutral in fact as well as in name in these times that are to try men's souls. We must be impartial in thought as well as in action, must put a curb upon our sentiments as well as upon every transaction that might be construed as a preference of one party to the struggle before another."[1]

Before entering the World War, the United States enforced its statutes prohibiting and punishing acts of hostility committed on its soil by adherents of any of the combatant nations. It prosecuted one Capt. Robert Fay, who attempted to destroy the merchant ships of the Allied Nations by means of bombs timed to explode when the vessels were at sea, and procured the recall of Ambassador Dumba of Austria-Hungry, who had promoted strikes in industrial plants in the United States engaged in the manufacture of munitions. It did not attempt to prevent the sale by American manufacturers of munitions of war to any of the combatants, because combatants have the right to deal in the markets of neutral nations, which are open upon equal terms to all the world. The fact that the naval power of the Allies was so much greater than that of the Central Powers that they could transport from this country to the seat of war articles of use in warfare while the Germans and Austrians could not do so, did not impose upon the United States, as a neutral nation, the obligation of preventing the British from buying munitions in our markets.[2] The German Government protested against our attitude in this matter, but without giving any reason why the United States should not follow the rule laid down by the Hague Conference of 1907 that "a neutral power is not bound to prevent the ex-

[1] Diplomatic Correspondence, Department of State, European War Series, No. 2, p. 17.

[2] State Department, Diplomatic Correspondence, European War Series, No. 2, p. 58.

port or transit, for the use of either belligerent, of arms, ammunitions, or, in general, of anything which could be of use to an army or fleet."

On the other hand, the right of a neutral nation to open its markets to all the participants in a war does not extend to attempts to violate a blockade by which one of the belligerents is carrying on war against another. If the citizens of a neutral nation attempt to send munitions of war to one of the combatants by shipping them to a neutral port, there to be trans-shipped to a blockaded port, they cannot complain if the cargoes are seized and condemned as contraband of war. The case of *The Springbok*,[1] decided in 1866 by the U. S. Supreme Court, grew out of the blockade of the Confederate States enforced by the U. S. Navy as one of the operations of the Civil War. The *Springbok*, a British vessel chartered by a London mercantile firm, was captured by the U. S. gunboat *Sonora* while going from London to Nassau, New Providence, a British possession near the southern coast of the United States. Her cargo consisted of uniforms, cavalry sabres, and other articles for the use of the Confederacy. The ship and cargo were brought to New York as a prize. The British owners claimed the vessel as their property, seized in violation of international law, and the owners of the cargo put in a similar claim. In the decision that the cargo had been lawfully seized, Chief Justice Chase said:

Upon the whole case, we cannot doubt, that the cargo was orginally shipped with intent to violate the blockade; that the owners of the cargo intended that it should be transshipped at Nassau into some vessel more likely to

[1] 5 Wallace (U. S.) Rep., 1.

succeed in reaching safely a blockaded port than the *Springbok;* that the voyage from London to the blockaded port was, as to cargo, both in law and in the intent of the parties, one voyage; and that the liability to condemnation, if captured during any part of that voyage, attached to the cargo from the time of sailing.

In the case of *The Nereide*,[1] decided in 1815, the U. S. Supreme Court ruled that goods belonging to a citizen of a neutral nation are not forfeited because they happen to form part of the cargo of an armed belligerent vessel.

On December 19, 1813, during the War of 1812, the *Nereide*, a British-owned armed vessel chartered by a citizen of Buenos Aires, was captured at sea by the American privateer, the *Governor Tompkins*, and brought to the port of New York where the vessel and cargo were libelled. The part of the cargo that belonged to British subjects was condemned without opposition, but the part that belonged to the Spanish subject residing at Buenos Aires was claimed on the ground that, the United States being at peace with Spain, the property of Spanish subjects was exempt from capture and forfeiture, though found on a captured enemy vessel. In the decision in favor of the claimants, Chief Justice Marshall said:

The . . . point to be considered is the right of a neutral to place his goods on board an armed belligerent merchantman.

That a neutral may lawfully put his goods on board a belligerant ship for conveyance on the ocean, is universally recognized as the original rule of the law of nations.

[1] 9 Cranch (U. S.) Rep., 389.

It is . . . founded on the plain and simple principle that the property of a friend remains his property wherever it is found. "Since it is not," says Vattel, B. 3, c. 5, s. 75, "the place where a thing is that determines the nature of that thing, but the character of the person to whom it belongs, things belonging to a neutral person which happen to be in an enemy's country, or on board an enemy's ships, are to be distinguished from those which belong to the enemy."
. .. .

It is deemed of much importance that the rule is universally laid down in terms which comprehend an armed as well as an unarmed vessel; and that armed vessels have never been excepted from it. . . .

In point of fact, it is believed that a belligerent vessel rarely sails unarmed; so that this exception from the rule would be greater than the rule itself. . . . It would be strange if a rule laid down, with a view to war, in such broad terms as to have universal application, should be so construed as to exclude from its operation almost every case for which it purports to provide; and yet that not a dictum should be found in the books pointing to such a construction.

The antiquity of the rule is certainly not unworthy of consideration. It is to be traced back to the time when almost every merchantman was in a condition for self-defence, and the implements of war were so light, and so cheap, that scarcely any would sail without them.

A belligerent has a perfect right to arm in his own defence; and a neutral has a perfect right to transport his goods in a belligerent vessel. These rights do not interfere with each other. The neutral has no control over the belligerent's right to arm—ought he to be accountable for the exercise of it?

By placing neutral property in a belligerent ship, that property, according to the positive rules of law, does not cease to be neutral. Why should it be changed by the exercise of a belligerent right, universally acknowledged and in common use when the rule was laid down, and over which the neutral had no control?

The belligerent answers that by arming, his rights are impaired. By placing his goods under the guns of an enemy, the neutral has taken part with the enemy, and assumed the hostile character.

Previous to that examination which the court has been able to make of the reasoning by which this proposition is sustained, one remark will be made which applies to a great part of it. The argument which, taken in its fair sense, would prove that it is unlawful to deposit goods for transportation in the vessel of an enemy generally, however imposing its form, must be unsound, because it is a contradiction of acknowledged law. . . .

The *Nereide* . . . is an open and declared belligerent, claiming all the rights, and subject to all the dangers, of the belligerent character. She conveys neutral property, which does not engage in her warlike equipments, or in any employment she may make of them; which is put on board solely for the purpose of transportation, and which encounters the hazard incident to its situation; the hazard of being taken into port, and obliged to seek another conveyance, should its carrier be captured.

Nations that are at War Ought to Refrain from Unnecessary Severities in Military Operations.

The sinking of the *Lusitania* by a German submarine in 1915, with the loss of the lives of more than a hundred American citizens, the execution by Germans in 1915 of Edith Cavell, an English nurse, on a charge of having assisted French and Belgian soldiers to cross the Belgian frontier and go to England; the execution in 1916 of Capt. Fryatt, an English sea captain for attempting to run down a German submarine that was attacking his ship; the cruelties perpetrated by the

German army of occupation in Belgium throughout the World War; the use by the Germans of poison gases and liquid fire in their military operations; the transportation of civilian workmen from Belgium to Germany; and numerous other atrocious deeds of the Central Powers, resulting in reprisals of extreme severity by the Allies, have all demonstrated that civilization has not yet advanced to a point where unnecessary and useless severities are not to be expected as incidents of warfare. The prevention of such cruelties and the confinement of warfare to the operations of armies and navies is one of the ideals of international law, toward which some progress has been made.

In the case of *The Paquete Habaña*,[1] decided in 1899 by the U. S. Supreme Court, two fishing smacks, owned by Spanish subjects and running in and out of Havana, were captured in 1898 by the United States blockading squadron, which was then carrying on a part of our naval operations of the Spanish War. The vessels were taken to Key West, Florida, and there condemned by the U. S. courts as prizes of war. The owners appealed to the U. S. Supreme Court upon the ground that coast fishing vessels, unarmed and honestly pursuing their peaceful calling, are, by an established rule of international law, exempt from capture as prizes of war. In sustaining this contention, Justice Gray said:

By an ancient usage among civilized nations, beginning centuries ago, and gradually ripening into a rule of international law, coast fishing vessels, pursuing their vocation of catching and bringing in fresh fish, have been recognized as exempt, with their cargoes, and crews, from capture as prize of war. . . . At the present day, by the general

[1] 175 U. S. Rep., 677, 686, 708.

consent of the civilized nations of the world, and independently of any express treaty or other public act, it is an established rule of international law, founded on considerations of humanity to a poor and industrious order of men, and of the mutual convenience of belligerent states, that coast fishing vessels, with their implements and supplies, cargoes and crews, unarmed, and honestly pursuing their peaceful calling of catching and bringing in fresh fish, are exempt from capture as prizes of war.

CHAPTER XX

ENFORCEMENT OF INTERNATIONAL LAW

Methods of Enforcement.

International cases or disputes between nations about rights of sovereignty and independence and about the rights of citizens of one nation under the laws of another must be decided either by diplomatic negotiations, or by arbitrations, or by appeals to force. The dispute between the United States and Great Britain about the great territory of Oregon, which originally included all of what is now British Columbia, was decided in 1846 by diplomatic negotiations. The controversies between the United States and Great Britain over the northeastern boundary line that now separates Maine from Canada and over the fishing rights of American citizens in Canadian waters were determined by arbitrating tribunals. The international disputes which caused the World War were brought to an end by an appeal to force.

International cases have not been decided like disputes between individuals living under a government because there has been no international tribunal having jurisdiction over a sovereign independent nation; nor has there been an international government having power to compel the government of a nation to submit to its judgments and obey its decrees. Such a tribunal and such a government are at present impossible because a sovereign nation has equal authority and power with all other nations; otherwise it would not be a sovereign. An independent government is not and cannot be controlled by any other government; otherwise it would not be independent. International government, such as it is, rests upon public opinion and the good faith which nations ought to observe in their dealings with one another and in their observance of the rules of international law accepted by them as the basis of their mutual relations. It has no power to deal with international questions except by mutual agreements arrived at by diplomatic negotiations, or by accepting the adjudications of arbitration courts established by mutual consent, or by taking up arms against one another and settling the issues by fighting till one of the combatants is compelled to submit.

Diplomatic Negotiations.

Each of the civilized nations has diplomatic agents called ambassadors or envoys or ministers, who reside "near"[1] the seats of government of other nations, and commercial agents called consuls, who have their posts of duty in the principal cities of the world. Whenever a nation believes that its rights of sovereignty or of independence have been violated in any way, it can, and usually does, instruct its diplomatic agent to the government of the nation against which it has a grievance to present its complaint to the officers of that government in charge of the department of foreign affairs. The questions at issue are then discussed and in some cases a decision satisfactory to both nations is reached.

---

[1] By a fiction of international law, the residence of a diplomatic agent is regarded as a portion of the territory of the nation he represents.

The complaints of the Japanese government that the laws of California excluding Japanese subjects from the privileges of land ownership in that State are inconsistent with the treaty between the United States and Japan, have been the subject of discussions and negotiations between the Japanese ambassador at Washington and the Secretary of State of the United States. In the course of these negotiations, the United States has pointed out that its treaty with Japan did not contain any provisions giving Japanese citizens residing in America the privilege claimed for them, and that under our system of national and State governments the nation had no power to dictate the economic policy of a State. The Secretary of State also took pains to assure the Japanese ambassador that "the California statute [regulating alien land ownership in that State], far from being indicative of any national discriminatory policy, was not even to be regarded as an expression of political or racial antagonism, but was rather to be considered as the emanation of economic conditions, which were in this instance of a local character."[1]

The position taken by the Secretary of State has been confirmed by the U. S. Supreme Court in two decisions, one of which referred to the California alien land law and the other to a similar law of the State of Washington. The latter case, *Terrace and Nakatsuka* v. *Thompson*,[2] decided November 12, 1923, was an action in equity to enjoin the attorney general of the State from prosecuting a landowner who wished to make a lease to a Japanese alien, who under the laws of the United States could not become a naturalized citi-

[1] American-Japanese Discussions Relating to Land Tenure Law of California, Department of State, p. 15.

[2] Advance Opinions.

zen, in violation of a Washington law that forbade the owning or leasing of land in that State by aliens that had not in good faith declared their intention to become citizens. In the decision that the law was constitutional, Justice Butler said:

We think that the treaty [between the United States and Japan] not only contains no provision giving Japanese the right to own or lease land for agricultural purposes, but, when viewed in the light of the negotiations leading up to its consummation, the language shows that the high contracting parties respectively intended to withhold a treaty grant of that right to the citizens or subjects of either in the territories of the other. The right "to carry on trade" or "to own or lease and occupy houses, manufactories, warehouses and shops," or "to lease land for residential and manufacturing purposes," or "to do anything incident to or necessary for trade" cannot be said to include the right to own or lease or to have any title to or interest in land for agricultural purposes. The enumeration of rights to own or lease for other specified purposes impliedly negatives the right to own or lease land for these purposes.

During the first part of President Wilson's first term of office, the deplorable condition of affairs in Mexico was a source of peril and anxiety to the government of the United States. After the abdication and flight of President Diaz, Madero had become President of Mexico only to be overthrown and murdered by General Huerta. Huerta's government was challenged by a number of revolutionary leaders like Zapata and Villa, who were little better than bandits. "War and disorder, devastation and confusion, seemed to threaten to become the settled fortune of the distracted coun-

[1] President Wilson's address to Congress, Aug. 27, 1913.

try."[1] In the hope of putting an end to this distressing condition, President Wilson sent to Mexico as his personal representative, John Lind, former governor of Minnesota, with instructions to bring about if possible a cessation of the guerilla war then going on, a national election in which all the contending parties should take part, and the consent of Gen. Huerta to refrain from being a candidate for the presidency. "Mr. Lind executed his delicate and difficult mission with singular tact, firmness, and good judgment, and made clear to the authorities at the City of Mexico not only the purpose of his visit, but also the spirit in which it had been undertaken. But the proposals he submitted were rejected."[1]

Arbitrations.

International disputes which the nations concerned are unable to determine by means of diplomatic negotiations are often referred to boards of arbitration. One of the most difficult questions between the United States and Great Britain at the close of the War for Independence was the nature and extent of the fishing rights of the United States along the coasts of Newfoundland. Throughout the colonial era the people of New England had had unlimited fishing rights in these waters, and had also been accustomed to land at convenient places and dry the fish they had caught. During the negotiation of the Peace of Paris in 1782–1783, our representatives insisted that the rights of the colonies in the fishing grounds were a part of the territorial dominions of those colonies and continued to be their property when they became independent States. The British took the position that, when the colonies ceased to be a part of the British Empire, they lost all privileges in the territorial

[1] President Wilson's address to Congress, Aug. 27, 1913.

292 THE REASONABLENESS OF THE LAW

dominions of Great Britain. The question was adjusted temporarily by an article of the treaty giving the people of the United States the *right* to continue the deep sea fisheries, which indeed could not be disputed, and the *liberty* to participate in the in-shore[1] fisheries, which was more questionable, together with the *liberty* to land and dry and cure their fish in uninhabited places along the shore. After the War of 1812, the British set up the claim that the *liberties* provided for in the Treaty of Paris had been abrogated by the event of war and would not be renewed. The negotiators of the Treaty of Ghent, which ended our second war with Great Britain, could not agree on this matter and our rights were left undefined. In 1818, diplomatic commissioners of both nations met at London and made a commercial convention which limited the fishing rights of the United States to the southern coasts of Newfoundland and Labrador, and included a renunciation of our fishing rights in waters within three marine miles of the coasts of other parts of the British dominions in America. Between 1836 and 1839, the government of Nova Scotia violated the Convention of London by imposing duties on American fishing vessels going through the Strait of Canso, and by seizing vessels that did not pay the duties. The international questions growing out of these seizures were settled in favor of the United States, and in 1853 a treaty of reciprocity was made reestablishing American fishing rights as provided by the Convention of 1818. From time to time afterward there were controversies over American fishing rights, growing out of seizures of American fishing vessels for the offense

[1] One of the rules of international law is that the territory of a nation includes all gulfs, bays, inlets, and a space of three nautical miles from its shore into the ocean.

of purchasing bait in Canadian waters in violation of the laws of Canada. These controversies, by a treaty made at Washington in 1871, were referred to a commission that granted to Great Britain an award of $5,500,000 for reciprocal concessions. The Treaty of Washington did not put an end to the disputes. In January, 1878, at Fortune Bay in Newfoundland, American fishermen were attacked by the inhabitants and prevented from taking fish on the ground of violation of Newfoundland laws against fishing on Sunday and the use of seines at that season of the year. This incident was the subject of diplomatic negotiations which ended in the payment of damages by Great Britain, but without any decision concerning the right of the Newfoundland government to legislate concerning American fishermen. The Treaty of Washington was terminated by the United States in 1885, by the United States giving notice to that effect to the British government, and our fishing rights again became subject to the convention of 1818. From time to time afterward, Newfoundland enforced regulations which made difficult the exercise of American fishing rights, until 1907, when the whole question was submitted to a tribunal chosen from the Permanent Court of Arbitration at The Hague. This tribunal rendered a comprehensive decision of the fisheries rights of the United States in Canadian waters, thus ending by peaceful arbitration, a dispute that had begun more than a century before and might have been the cause of great wars, if the two nations had not preferred rational methods to appeals to force.

Appeals to Force.

International cases that cannot be settled by negotiation or by arbitration must necessarily be decided by warfare; that is, by conflicts of armed forces. At the beginning of the World War efforts were made in vain by diplomats to prevent the spread of the war. During its progress, the United States repeatedly offered to act as arbitrator and mediator between the combatants, but without success. In the end, the United States was compelled to take part in the strife, partly to punish the lawless submarine warfare on our commerce carried on by the Germans, but chiefly to bring to an end a contest in arms that threatened the very life of modern civilization. The World War, like other wars, was thus a resort to force in a case in which negotiation had failed and arbitration had been refused.

In the case of *Foster v. Neilson*,[1] decided in 1829 by the U. S. Supreme Court, Chief Justice Marshall said:

There being no tribunal to decide [controversies between nations], . . . each determines for itself on its own rights, and if they cannot adjust their differences peaceably, the right remains with the strongest.

[1] 2 Peters, U. S. Rep., 253.

PART VI
Statute Law

CHAPTER XXI

Nature of Statute Law.

The law has been variously conceived either as the ideal of right and justice or as the body of rules that have been found useful in regulating the dealings of persons with one another or as the command of the supreme governing power of a society. It consists of constitutions; the rules of the common law, of equity, and of international law; and statutes. It is never an arbitrary, unchangeable system of rules. The basic principles of government embodied in constitutions must be amended from time to time in order to conform to the changing ideals of the people. The rules of the common law and the procedure in equity must be modified or expanded at intervals in order to be applicable to the varying conditions of society. Statutes which usually accurately reflect the will of the people at a given time frequently need subsequent amendment or repeal.

In old times in England when only the few knew how to read and write, the people in their mutual dealings changed their customs and usages of conduct and dealing by adopting new customs and usages whenever new circumstances made such new customs and usages desirable. Courts of justice, whenever cases involving new customs and usages came before them, made new rules of law and of equity, which displaced the old.

In course of time, the great council of England, the Parliament, which originally was a body that decided how much money was needed to carry on the government and advised the king concerning the ways and means by which the money should be collected, began to make acts or statutes that *declared* the rules of law which should be applied in given cases in which it was desirable to modify old rules or adopt new ones. This method of making or declaring the law by legislative act had become a part of the English constitution at the beginning of the English colonization of America, and was brought to this country by the founders of English Colonial America.

The people of the original thirteen States, following the forms of the colonial governments, adopted constitutions, each of which gave to legislatures the power to make the laws—the legislative power, prescribed the rules which those legislatures should follow in exercising that power, and limited its exercise by bills of rights. The People of the United States, in like manner and for the same reason, adopted the Constitution of the United States which vested the legislative power in the Congress, made rules to be followed in the making of laws, and enumerated the objects for which laws might or might not be made.

The constitutions of the States and the Constitution of the United States, as fundamental laws, thus give to legislatures the power to make from time to time such laws as are needed. Constitutions are the sources of the legislative power; legislatures are the instruments of that power. Constitutions create the legislatures

through which the people declare their will in matters
of governmental policy.

Legislatures.

The legislatures of the States and the Congress of the
United States are political bodies composed of representatives and senators who are elected by the people.
In a few States that have initiative and referendum
provisions in their constitutions, the people share the
law-making power with the legislature.

In the case of *State ex rel Schrader v. Polley*,[1] decided
in 1910 by the Supreme Court of South Dakota, Justice
McCoy said:

We are of the opinion that the word "Legislature," as
used in Section 4, Art. I, of the federal constitution does
not mean simply the members who compose the Legislature,
acting in some ministerial capacity, but refers to and means
the law-making body and power of the State, as established by the State Constitution, and which includes the
whole constitutional law-making machinery of the State.
State governments are divided into executive, legislative
and judicial departments, and the federal Constitution
refers to the "Legislature" in the same sense of its being
the legislative department of the State, whether it is
denominated a Legislature, General Assembly or by some
other name. Under Sec. 1, Art. 3 of the State Constitution, . . . the people of this State [South Dakota] have
reserved to themselves, as a part of the law-making power,
the right to vote by referendum upon any law passed by
the Legislature, with certain specified exceptions, prior to the
going into effect of such law. . . . Under the Constitution of the State, the people, by means of the initiative

[1] 26 So. Dakota Rep., 5.

and referendum, are a part and parcel of the law-making power of this State.

Powers of Legislatures.

Subject to the supreme power of the people, our State and national legislatures have supreme powers of government. State legislatures can enact statutes imposing taxes to any amount they see fit and of any kind they like except as forbidden by our national constitution. They can direct as they think best the expenditure of money raised by taxes. They can, on the other hand, refuse to levy taxes or can levy taxes only to raise limited amounts of money so that, in the one case, they can bring the work of government to a standstill for want of funds or, in the other, can hamper its operations and render it ineffective. By appropriating money according to their own ideas of public needs, they can control the governmental policy of their States. Except as controlled by bills of rights and the provisions of the Constitution of the United States, they can enact statutes prescribing for the people any laws regulating conduct and business relations which in their opinion are advisable.

In the case of *Cincinnati v. Railroad Commissioners*,[1] decided in 1852 by the Supreme Court of Ohio, Justice Ranney said:

One of the principles lying at the very foundation of these [American] systems [of government] . . . is that all political power resides with the people—that government is founded "on their sole authority, and organized for the great purpose of protecting their rights and liberties and securing their independence" and that "they have at all

[1] 1 Ohio State Rep., 77.

times a complete power to alter, reform, or abolish their governments, whenever they may deem it necessary" (Constitution of Ohio, 1802, Art. VIII, Sec. 1.). They have, therefore, the most undoubted right to delegate just as much, or just as little, of this political power with which they are invested as they see proper, and to such agents or departments of government as they see fit to designate. To the constitution we must look for the manner and extent of this delegation; and from that instrument alone must every department of the government derive its authority to exercise any portion of political power. . . . That instrument is the letter of attorney by which alone, they are authorized to act at all, and, in all cases, they must be able to show that their acts are authorized by it. . . . The people have thus granted certain political powers, to be exercised for their benefit, until they see fit to resume them, and have retained others. On looking into the constitution, we find the granted powers assigned to three great departments of government—the legislative power to the general assembly; the executive power to the governor; and the judicial power to the courts. Unlike the Constitution of the United States, and from the necessity of the case, no attempt at a specific enumeration of the items of legislative power is made. This must, therefore, always be 'determined from the nature of the power exercised. If it is found to fall within the general terms of the grant, we can only look to the other parts of the constitution for limitations upon it; if none are there found, none exist. But, as the general assembly, like other departments of government, exercises only delegated authority, it cannot be doubted that any act passed by it, not falling fairly within the scope of legislative power, is as clearly void as though expressly prohibited.

In the case of *Burton v. U. S.*,[1] decided in 1905 by the U. S. Supreme Court, Justice Harlan said:

[1] 202 U. S. Rep., 344.

It [Congress] possesses the entire legislative authority of the United States. By the provision in the Constitution that all legislative powers herein granted shall be vested in a Congress of the United States, it is meant that Congress . . . keeping within the limits of its powers and observing the restrictions imposed by the Constitution . . . may, in its discretion enact any statute appropriate to accomplish the objects for which the National Government was established.

Statutes, Declarations of the Law.

In accordance with their constitutional powers the State legislatures and the Congress of the United States have enacted many statutes declaring new rules of law to be used by the courts in the trial of cases. For example, our State legislatures have given to married women rights denied them by the common law and the Congress has enacted social legislation, like the Pure Food and Drug Act, the White Slave Act, the Interstate Commerce Law, and the Adamson Law.

In the case of *Commonwealth v. Stearns*,[1] decided in 1841 by the Supreme Judicial Court of Massachusetts, in which the question at issue was the validity of a statute, making embezzlement a crime, Justice Bigelow said:

The questions raised in the present case require a construction of the Rev. Sts. c. 126, Sec. 29, and are of no inconsiderable importance in their consequences, in marking the distinction between those acts which are to be denominated as felonies punishable by ignominious punishment, and those defaults in the payment of money or in the discharge of contracts, for which, however unjustifiable, the law authorizes no other mode of redress than a civil action by the party aggrieved.

[1] 2 Metcalf (Mass.) Rep., 343, 345.

The principles of the common law not being found adequate to protect general owners against the fraudulent conversion of property by persons standing in certain fiduciary relations to those who were the subject of their peculations, certain statutes have been enacted, as well in England as in this Commonwealth, creating new criminal offences and annexing to them their proper punishments. The consequence is, therefore, that many acts which formerly were denominated mere breaches of trust, and subjected the party to a civil action only, have now become cognizable before our criminal courts, as offences against the Commonwealth.

The case of *Coombs v. Read*,[1] decided in 1860 by the Supreme Judicial Court of Massachusetts, hinged upon the validity of a statute that altered the rule of the common law concerning the property rights of married women. In the decision of this question, Justice Dewey said:

By the common law, marriage operates as an absolute gift to the husband of all the personal chattels which are in the possession of and owned by the wife at the time of her marriage. The husband has also the like interest in all personal chattels which come to the wife in her own right during coverture [marriage]. Clancy, *on Husband and Wife*, 2. As to choses in action [claims which might be prosecuted at law] held by her under like circumstances, a different rule of law existed, and the right of the husband was a more qualified one, requiring him to reduce the same to possession by collecting them, if he would enjoy them as absolutely his. At common law, it does not affect the absolute ownership of personal chattels acquired by the wife during coverture, that they were purchased with her money, or money received by her upon notes held by her in her own name and

[1] 16 Gray (Mass.) Rep., 271.

304 THE REASONABLENESS OF THE LAW

not reduced to possession by her husband. When she becomes the owner of personal chattels, such chattels vest absolutely in her husband, without any act of reduction to possession as his property. . . .

The horse, now the subject of controversy between the parties, was acquired by an exchange of the horse brought from Rhode Island [where the parties had lived], which exchange was made by the act of the wife, she paying ten dollars in the exchange, from money belonging to herself, and which had not been in her husband's possession or control. As this transaction was after the St. [Statute] of 1857, C. 249, had gone into effect, if the horse then purchased had been purchased wholly by her money, the question would have properly arisen, whether under the statute this horse would not have been her separate property, and exempt from attachment by her husband's creditors. . . . This horse was acquired by an exchange of a horse which was her husband's, and as such liable to an attachment. We must assume that the principal value paid in exchange to defraud creditors. The husband should, under these circumstances, be considered as having an attachable interest in the horse received in exchange.

CHAPTER XXII

ENACTMENT OF STATUTES

Rules of Legislation.

Our State and national constitutions regulate the proceedings of legislatures by provisions which promote the orderly conduct of the work of legislation, prevent hasty and improvident law-making, and give opportunity for the careful examination and consideration of proposed laws. These provisions deal with the introduction of proposed laws, usually called bills, the titles and enacting clauses, the readings to the legislatures which are to consider them, the reference to committees, the passage by each house, the submission to the executive department for approval or disapproval (veto), the passage over vetoes, and the authentication. These constitutional provisions are the rules which the people prescribe for the guidance of their representatives in legislative bodies. They are the commands of the people and must be strictly observed. A legislature cannot enact a statute in any other way or by any other procedure than is ordained by them. Consequently, if a legislature disregards any of them during the passage of a bill, the result is a nullity; their work goes for nothing; what they call a statute is not a statute at all and has no binding force. Whenever, in the course of the trial of a case, the validity of a statute is challenged on the ground that the legislature in passing it, did not follow the rules of procedure prescribed by the constitution, the judges will examine the proceedings of its enactment, and if they find that it was not adopted in conformity to those rules, will declare it a nullity.

In the case of *People ex rel. Purdy v. Marlborough,*[1] decided in 1873 by the New York Court of Appeals, the validity of a supposed statute authorizing the laying out of a highway for the town of Marlborough over lands belonging to the State was challenged on the ground that it had not been passed by the legislature by a two-thirds vote as required by a clause in the State Constitution which ordained that the assent of two-thirds of the members of each branch of the legislature should be required for the passage of any bill appropriating public property for local uses. In the decision that this supposed law was not a law at all, Judge Johnson said:

> The only remaining inquiry . . . is whether . . . the question can be raised as to the vote by which the bill was passed. . . . When it is necessary to inquire by what vote a law was passed, the judges are to determine from the printed statutes, or from the laws on file in the Secretary of State's office, whether the requisite vote was received. . . . The law in question does not appear either upon the printed statute book or upon the original act to have been passed by a two-thirds vote, and consequently it never had the effect of law.

Introduction of a Bill.

The first step in the making of a statute is its introduction as a bill into the legislature. A bill is introduced when a member hands a draft of it to the clerk

[1] 54 N. Y. Rep., 276, 279.

of the house or when a petition from a member or a communication from an executive officer or department results in an appropriate committee being authorized to draft and report a bill. This and the subsequent steps in the law-making process as prescribed in the constitution that created the legislature must be recorded in the journals of both houses. Sometimes a constitution prescribes the house into which a bill must be introduced first; for example, the Constitution of the United States provides that "all bills for raising revenue shall originate in the House of Representatives" of the United States Congress.

Title of Bill.

The constitutional requirement in some States that the subject of a proposed law shall be expressed in its title is intended to prevent the insertion of "jokers" or the enactment of statutes for other objects than those indicated by, or suggested by, the name or title given to it by those who introduce it.

In the case of *Tadlock v. Eccles*,[1] decided by the Supreme Court of Texas in 1858, Justice Wheeler said:

The intention [of a clause to this effect in the Constitution of Texas] doubtless was to prevent embracing in an act, having one ostensible object, provisions having no relevancy to that object, but really designed to effectuate other and wholly different objects, and thus to conceal and disguise the real object proposed by the provisions of an act under a false and deceptive title.

Enacting Clause.

Many State constitutions provide that every statute shall begin with an enacting clause that will show its

[1] 20 Texas Rep., 782, 793.

nature and thus prevent members of the legislature from voting for one law when they think they are voting for something very different.

In the case of *State v. Patterson*,[1] decided by the Supreme Court of North Carolina in 1887, a statute that had been passed without an enacting clause was declared a nullity. In the decision of the court, Justice Merriman said:

The Constitution [of North Carolina], in Art. II., in prescribing how statutes shall be enacted, provides as follows:
"Sec. 21. The style of the acts shall be: "'The General Assembly of North Carolina do enact.'" . . . The purpose of thus prescribing an enacting clause—"the style of the acts"—is to establish the act—to give it permanence, uniformity, and certainty—to identify the act of legislation as of the General Assembly—to afford evidence of its legislative, statutory nature, and to secure uniformity of identification, and thus prevent inadvertence, possible mistake and fraud. Such purpose is important of itself, and as it is of the Constitution, a due observance of it is essential.

Readings.

The legislative process usually calls for three readings of a bill. To save time, however, a bill ordinarily is not read on three different occasions. The general practice is that at the first and second readings the clerk reads the title and the enacting clause and then is interrupted by the presiding officer, who says that, unless objection is made, the further reading will be dispensed with. In some State legislatures, the reading of bills is made absurd by the practice of having clerks read aloud two or more bills at the same time.

In the case of *Saunders v. Board of Liquidation of City*

[1] 98 North Carolina Rep., 660.

Debt,[1] decided in 1903 by the Supreme Court of Louisiana, Chief Justice Nicholls said:

We do not understand that a constitutional requirement which simply declares in general terms that a "bill" should be "read" twice or thrice times in each house before it can be enacted into a law, would carry with it the necessity of reading over each section of the bill at each reading, though the word "bill" in its meaning covers "the proposed legislation in its entirety." . . . What is intended to be guarded against is undue haste in the consideration of matters of legislation. The purpose of the requirement is that the subject matter of the bill . . . should be brought to the attention of both houses on a certain number of occasions, rather than that the details in each section should be placed each time before the houses.

Reference to Committee.

A requirement in some States that proposed bills shall be referred to committees of each house of a legislature is intended to secure careful consideration of all measures.

In the case of *State v. Buckley*,[2] decided in 1875 by the Supreme Court of Alabama, Justice Stone said:

The foregoing clauses [that bills shall be referred to committees and returned with recommendations of legislative action] have for their main controlling aim and purpose:— First, to fasten an individual accountability on the several members of the legislature, by requiring the action or non-action of each to appear on the journal. Second, to prevent "hodge-podge" and injurious combinations by confining each law to one subject. Third, to prevent hasty and inconsiderate legislation, surprise and fraud, by requiring

[1] 110 Louisiana Rep., 313, 331.
[2] 48 Alabama Rep., 599, 612.

bills to be read on several days in each house, referred to a committee of each house, and returned therefrom.

Printing.

A constitutional provision in some States that all bills must be printed before they are considered or become laws requires the printing to be done only before the bills are debated.

In the case of *Massachusetts etc. Insurance Co. v. Colorado Loan etc. Co.*,[1] decided in 1894 by the Supreme Court of Colorado, Justice Hayt said:

The contention is that a bill cannot become a law unless it is printed before it is read. We do not think this position sound. It certainly has no foundation in the terms of the constitutional provision. This only requires the printing to be done before the bill shall be considered or become a law. The consideration here contemplated means something more than the giving of attention to the reading of a bill. Webster gives the primary meaning of the word "consider" as follows: "To fix the mind on with a view to a careful examination; to think on with care; to ponder; to study; to meditate on." It is in this sense that the word is used in the constitution, and the provision is sufficiently complied with by printing the bill before it is taken up as a subject of deliberation for debate or amendment.

Passage of a Bill.

Constitutions regularly prescribe rules to govern such matters as the presence of a quorum, the way in which the vote shall be taken and recorded, the number of votes necessary to secure the passage of a bill, and the circumstances under which the presiding officer of a house may vote. Thus, the Constitution of the United States prescribes that a majority of each house shall

[1] 20 Colorado Rep., 1.

constitute a quorum, that the *yeas* and *nays* of the members voting on any question shall at the request of one-fifth of those present be recorded in the Journal, that in certain cases a two-thirds vote instead of a majority is necessary to the passage of a bill, and that the Vice-President shall have no vote in the Senate except in case of a tie.

In the case of *Kelley v. Secretary of State*,[1] decided by the Supreme Court of Michigan in 1907, it was held that a constitutional clause providing that no bill or resolution should be adopted without the concurrence of a majority of the members elected to each house deprives the presiding officer of a casting vote in the passage of resolutions and the enactment of laws. In 1907, Patrick H. Kelley, lieutenant governor of Michigan, presented in the Supreme Court of that State a petition that a mandamus order be issued commanding George A. Prescott, the secretary of state, to submit to the electors of the State at the September election of that year the question of nomination by direct vote of each party, of candidates for United States senator, governor, and lieutenant governor as required by an alleged resolution of the State legislature of the same year. The secretary of state answered this petition by denying that any such resolution had been legally adopted by the legislature. It was shown to the court that in the senate—consisting of 32 members—16 senators had voted for the resolution, and 16 had voted against it. Thereupon the lieutenant governor, as president of the senate, had broken the tie by voting for it. The State constitution contained a provision that no bill or joint resolution should become a law without the concurrence of a majority of all the members elected to each

[1] 149 Michigan Rep., 343.

house. Inasmuch as the lieutenant governor was not a member elected to the senate, the question before the court was whether the resolution had been passed in accordance with the State constitution. In denying the application for a mandamus, Justice Carpenter said:

Can a bill or joint resolution become a law by the casting vote of the lieutenant governor without the concurrence of a majority of the members elected to each house? Those who answer this question in the affirmative must and do base their answer upon Section 14 of Article V of the Constitution which reads as follows: "The lieutenant governor shall, by virtue of his office, be president of the Senate. In committee of the whole, he may debate all questions; and when there is an equal division, he shall give the casting vote." If the above language qualifies the provision: "No bill or joint resolution shall become a law without the concurrence of a majority of all the members elected to each house": . . . We have then the task of harmonizing two provisions of the Constitution; one of which expressly states that "no bill or joint resolution shall become a law without the concurrence of a majority of all the members elected to each house," and another which is open to the contrary construction. By what principle shall we harmonize them? Obviously this—the doubtful language must receive a construction in harmony with that which is not doubtful. . . . Section 14 of Article V must therefore receive a construction in harmony with Section 19 of Article IV, but it cannot be so construed as to permit the lieutenant governor to give a casting vote for the purpose of making a law.

Presentation to the Executive.

The constitutions of the United States and of nearly all of the States[1] provide that after a bill has passed

[1] The Constitutions of Delaware, Ohio, North Carolina, and Rhode Island do not contain this provision.

both houses of the legislature, it shall be presented to the executive department for approval or disapproval. This provision of the constitution of New Hampshire was explained by the justices of the Supreme Court of that State in the following words:[1]

If a bill is presented at the usual office of the Governor by an officer of one of the Houses, and the attention of the Governor or his Secretary, or other person in charge of the room is called to the fact, this would be a good and sufficient presentation, though the Governor may not have known of it on the day it was presented.

Approval of Bills, a Legislative Act.

In approving or disapproving bills, the executive department of a government performs legislative functions.

In the case of *La Abra Mining Co. v. U. S.*,[2] Justice Harlan said:

It is said that the approval by the President of a bill passed by Congress is not strictly an executive function, but is legislative in its nature. . . . Undoubtedly the President when approving bills passed by Congress may be said to participate in the enactment of laws which the Constitution requires him to execute.

Approval or Disapproval by the President of the United States.

The U. S. Constitution allows the President ten days in which to approve or disapprove bills presented to him by Congress.

In the case of *La Abra Mining Co. v. U. S.*,[3] decided

[1] 45 N. H. Rep., 610.   [2] 175 U. S. Rep., 453.   [3] *Ibid.*

in 1899 by the U. S. Supreme Court, it was contended that a bill approved during that period, but on a day on which Congress was not in session, had not been legally enacted. The La Abra Mining Company, a New York corporation, claimed from the government of Mexico damages to the amount of $3,962,000 for losses and injuries to its property committed by the Mexican authorities in 1867 and 1868. An American and Mexican mixed commission had made an award of $4,125,-622.30 on this and other claims and had referred the claim of the La Abra Company to an umpire, who allowed it the sum of $683,041.32. Payment of this amount to the company was not made because the Mexican Government charged that the company had obtained the award by means of perjury and fraud. In 1892 Congress had directed the Attorney General of the United States, by a statute passed for that purpose, to bring suit in the Court of Claims to determine the justice of the award. The Attorney General accordingly brought an action against the company, which interposed as one of its defenses, that the act of Congress under which the suit was brought was inoperative and unconstitutional because it had never been legally approved by the President, the only alleged approval it ever received being on December 28, 1892, when Congress was not in session, both Houses having adjourned on the 22nd of December, 1892, to the 4th day of January, 1893. In the course of the decision in favor of the government on this and other points, Justice Harlan said:

The ground of this contention is that, having met in regular session at the time appointed by law, the first Monday of December, 1892, and having on the 22nd day of that month [two days after the presentation of the bill to the President] by the joint action of the two Houses taken a recess to a named day, January 4, 1893, Congress was not actually sitting when the President on the 28th day of December, 1892, by signing it formally, approved the act in question. The proposition, plainly stated, is that a bill passed by Congress and duly presented to the President does not become a law if his approval be given on a day when Congress is in recess. This implies that the constitutional power of the President to approve a bill so as to make it a law is absolutely suspended while Congress is in recess for a fixed time. . . . As the Constitution while authorizing the President to perform certain functions of a limited number that are legislative in their general nature does not restrict the exercise of those functions to the particular days on which the two Houses of Congress are actually sitting in the transaction of public business, the Court cannot impose such a restriction upon the Executive.

Veto by the Executive.

The Constitution of the United States and the constitutions of most of the States give to their respective chief executive officers the power to approve or disapprove bills presented to them by the legislature. One reason for the veto power, as it is usually called, is that it preserves the integrity of the executive branch of the government; it gives the President or a governor a voice in the making of a law that he will have to enforce. The veto power also acts as a check upon corrupt or ill-advised legislation. Some States withhold altogether the veto power from their governors; others that have initiative and referendum provisions in their constitutions, allow the governor to veto acts of their legislatures but deny him the power to veto a law passed directly by the people.

In the case of *People v. Councilmen of Buffalo*,[1] decided in the Superior Court of Buffalo, New York, in 1892, Justice Hatch reviewed the history of the veto power in the United States in the following words:

The word "veto" is of Latin extraction, and, literally translated, reads, "I forbid," or "I deny." These words have a singularly ominous sound when they are applied in a democratic government, and at once call attention to the fact and challenge the authority. There are, in constitutional governments, two fundamental theories upon which the grant of the power of veto rests: First, to preserve the integrity of that branch of the government in which the vetoing power is vested, and thus maintain an equilibrium of governmental powers; second, to act as a check upon corrupt or hasty and ill-considered legislation. These theories have entered into all debates touching the power. . . . The early colonial legislatures felt the same power both from crown and governor, for it was the practice of the latter to have money orders in his favor injected into or accompanying bills to be signed so that he might receive the former at the time or before he signed the latter, which accompaniment was much preferred; while the grievance against the Crown found expression in the declaration [of independence]; "He has refused his assent to laws the most wholesome and necessary for the public good". . . . The veto power was regarded with great distrust and disfavor by the framers of our government, both State and National, and its right of exercise is by no means universal now. Only one of the original State Constitutions—Massachusetts—gave even a qualified veto, while the Articles of Confederation withheld it entirely, reaching the other extreme of requiring the assent of nine States to important acts of legislation; thus giving to a minority of five States an absolute right of veto. The happy solution of this question

[1] 20 N. Y. Supplement, 51, 52.

by the framers of the federal Constitution had for its basis the integrity of the executive branch of the government, and very little consideration was given to the theory of a check upon ill-considered and hasty legislation. As late as 1884, and, so far as I possess information, at this date [1892], Delaware, North Carolina, Ohio, and Rhode Island still withhold the veto power from the executive; while in eight others, a majority vote of the whole number of members elected to the legislature constitutes all that is required to override a veto. . . . The people of all constitutional governments are extremely solicitous and jealous of this power, and have at all times, hedged it about by carefully expressed limitations. Consequently it follows that the right of its exercise by an executive must always be supported by plain and undoubted authority. It has of recent date been the gradual and growing belief that this power is wisely placed in the executive head of municipal authority, not as essential to preserve an equilibrium of governmental power, but for almost the sole purpose of a check upon corrupt and hasty action and ill-considered legislation.

Passage over Veto.

The Constitution of the United States and the constitutions of the States which give the veto power to governors provide for the re-enactment of vetoed bills. [1]

The procedure for the passage of a bill over the veto of an executive officer was described in the case of *City of Evansville v. State*, [2] decided by the Supreme Court of

---

[1] If a bill is presented to the President of the United States within ten days before the final adjournment of the Congress, he can, if he chooses, veto it by not returning it. This is called the "pocket veto," because the President, if he chooses, can put the bill in his pocket and keep it there. The reason is that if Congress does not by prompt action give the President the full ten day period, it is their fault, not his.

[2] 181 Indiana Rep., 426.

Indiana in 1888. The legislature of that State had passed a law establishing a metropolitan police and fire board for the City of Evansville, and the members of that board had been elected and qualified for their offices. The mayor and members of the city council refused to turn over the property and records of the two departments to these persons, who thereupon asked the Vanderburgh Circuit Court for a mandatory order requiring the city officials to recognize them as the metropolitan police and fire board of the city. In the trial in the Circuit Court, one question that arose was whether there was any evidence that the act creating the board, after being vetoed by the governor, had been again passed in accordance with the constitution of the State. The city claimed that there was no such evidence before the court because the act as passed over the governor's veto had not again been signed by the presiding officers of the two houses, transmitted to the governor and by him filed in the office of the secretary of state. The court decided on other grounds that the law was unconstitutional, but overruled the contention that it has not been properly passed over the governor's veto. Justice Berkshire said:

The act passed both branches of the General Assembly, was duly signed by the two presiding officers, and presented to the Governor. He returned it without his signature, and with objections, to the House of Representatives, the house wherein it originated; his objections were entered at large on the journals and the bill reconsidered and passed by a majority of all the members elected to that house; it was then sent to the Senate, with the Governor's objections, reconsidered, and approved by a majority of all the members elected to that house. The moment it passed the Senate, it became a law. . . . The Constitution does not require that it again be signed by the presiding officers of the two houses, transmitted to the Governor and by him filed in the office of the Secretary of State. The reconsideration of a bill which has received the Governor's condemnation, by either branch of the General Assembly, is for such branch to further consider and act upon it, and when this is done and the bill has passed both houses by the required majority, the constitutional provision has been complied with.

Records of Legislative Proceedings: Journals.

The constitutional provisions relating to the keeping of journals of legislative bodies are mandatory directions which are intended to secure publicity and to prevent legislatures from being improperly influenced in their proceedings.

In the case of *State v. Green*,[1] decided in 1895 by the Supreme Court of Florida, Chief Justice Mabry said:

It is generally held that the plain constitutional injunctions as to the mode and manner of enacting laws are mandatory, and the equally high authority that the journals of the proceedings shall be kept, strengthens the view that the evidence of a compliance with such injunctions should be found in the journals.

In the case of *Field v. Clark*,[2] decided in 1891 by the U. S. Supreme Court, Justice Harlan said:

It was assumed in argument that the object of this clause [that each house of Congress shall keep a journal of its proceedings, Art. I, Sec. 5] was to make the journal the best, if not conclusive, evidence upon the issue as to whether a bill was, in fact, passed by the two houses of Congress. But the words do not require such interpretation.

[1] 36 Florida Rep., 54, 173.   [2] 143 U. S. Rep., 649, 670.

On the contrary, as Mr. Justice Story has well said: "the object of the whole clause is to insure publicity to the proceedings of the legislature, and a correspondent responsibility of the members to their respective constituents. And it is founded in sound policy and deep political foresight. Intrigue and cabal are thus deprived of some of their main resources, by plotting and devising measures in secrecy. The public mind is enlightened by an attentive examination of the public measures; patriotism, and integrity, and wisdom obtain their due reward; and votes are ascertained, not by vague conjecture but by positive facts. . . . So long as open and known responsibility is valuable as a check or an incentive among the representatives of a free people, so long a journal of their proceedings and their votes published in the face of the world will continue to enjoy public favor and be demanded by public opinion." 1 Story, Constitution, Sec. 840, 841.

Authentication of Statutes.

The evidence which proves that a statute has been enacted by a legislature is a certificate signed by the presiding officers of each of the two houses and by the head of the executive department.

In the case of *Field v. Clark*,[1] just quoted, a number of importers, including Marshall Field & Co. of Chicago, sought to obtain refunds of customs duties upon the contention that the Tariff Act of 1883 did not have the force of law because it omitted certain clauses which the journals of both branches of Congress showed to have been regularly passed. The government defended these suits by proving that the original enrolled act in the hands of the Secretary of State was attested by the signatures of Thomas B. Reed, Speaker of the House of Representatives, and Levi P. Morton, Vice President

[1] 143 U. S. Rep., 649, 671.

of the United States and President of the Senate, and had upon it the following endorsements: "Approved October 1st, 1890, Benj. Harrison." "I certify that this act originated in the House of Representatives. Edw. McPherson, Clerk." In ruling that these attestations and certifications sufficiently authenticated the act as a statute of the United States, Justice Harlan said:

Although the Constitution does not expressly require bills that have passed Congress to be attested by the signatures of the presiding officers of the two Houses, usage, the orderly conduct of legislative proceedings and the rules under which the two houses have acted since the organization of the government, require that mode of authentication. The signing by the Speaker of the House of Representatives, and by the President of the Senate, in open session, of the enrolled bill, is an official attestation by the two houses of such bill as one that has passed Congress. It is a declaration by the two houses, through their presiding officers, to the President, that a bill, thus attested, has received, in due form, the sanction of the legislative branch of the government, and that it is delivered to him in obedience to the constitutional requirement that all bills which pass Congress shall be presented to him. And when a bill, thus attested, receives his approval, and is deposited in the public archives, its authentication as a bill that has passed Congress is complete and unimpeachable.

CHAPTER XXIII

Judicial Power over Legislation.

Constitutions are laws for the government of legislatures and courts. A State constitution confers upon a legislature the power to make State laws not inconsistent with the Constitution of the United States and with the constitution of the State. The Constitution of the United States gives to the Congress power to make national laws not inconsistent with that constitution. The constitution of a State gives to State courts the power to judge and decide cases. The Constitution of the United States confers upon the courts of the United States the power to judge and decide all cases arising under the Constitution and the laws of the United States. Under these powers, the courts of the States and of the United States decide whether or not statutes are constitutional.

In judging and deciding cases, the courts ascertain the rules of law that are to govern the questions at issue by resorting to the evidence of the law that exists in the form of the rules of the common law and of equity, of statutes, and of constitutions. In determining the law that is to govern a particular case, they take as evidence of the law the rule laid down in a statute in preference to rules of the common law and of equity, because a statute expresses the will of the people in matters of law and is binding upon the courts. But a statute is not law unless it is one that a legislature has authority to make. If a State statute is one that the legislature has power to make under the constitution of the State, the courts of the State use it as evidence of the law and enforce its provisions. If it is one that the legislature does not have power to make, they declare that it is not law and refuse to enforce it. If a State statute is inconsistent with any of the provisions of the Constitution of the United States, the courts may declare it void for unconstitutionality and refuse to enforce it. If a statute of the United States is one that the Congress does not have power to make, the courts of the United States may declare that it is not law and refuse to enforce it.

An action at law under a statute is tried by a court consisting of a judge and a jury. In such a trial, the judge determines the law that prescribes the rights of the parties from the evidence of the law in the statute, and the jury determines the real relations of the parties to one another from the oral testimony and written evidence that is offered. A proceeding in equity under a statute is tried by a court consisting of a judge who determines from the statute the rule of equity applicable to the case, and from the evidence of facts that is offered the relations of the parties to one another. In each case, whether at law or in equity, the statute furnishes the rule of law that must be followed unless it violates some command of, or is repugnant to, some provision in the constitution which created the legislature that enacted it. If the statute conflicts with the constitution, the court is in duty bound to follow the supreme law and to disregard the inferior law—to give effect to the constitution and to refuse to give effect to the statute.

After the trial of an action in which the court has refused to enforce a statute upon the ground of unconstitutionality, an appeal may be taken to higher courts, composed of judges sitting without juries, where the decision of the trial court upon the validity of the statute is reviewed and a final decision rendered.

The courts do not, and cannot, by refusing to enforce statutes on the ground of unconstitutionality, vacate or annul them. They remain on the statute books, where the legislatures caused them to be placed, unless or until the legislatures shall see fit to repeal or amend them. The courts refuse in particular cases to use them as evidence of the law. This is the extent of their action and of their power. The result of such judicial refusals to give effect to statutes is, however, much the same as if the court had really annulled them.[1]

The decisions of the Supreme Court of the United States holding statutes to be void for unconstitutionality have not been made arbitrarily or as a means of restraining the lawful powers of the other departments of the national government. In the case of *McCrary v. U. S.*,[2] decided in 1904 by the U. S. Supreme Court, Justice White said:

No instance is afforded from the foundation of the government where an act which was within a power con-

[1] An adverse decision upon the constitutionality of an Act of Congress practically nullifies it, because the U. S. Supreme Court will not reconsider its decisions unless it is made to appear either that important arguments made at the trials have been overlooked or that some controlling precedent has been misapplied. Dissenting opinion of Justice Harlan, in *Standard Oil Co. v. U. S.*, 221 U. S. Rep., 1, 92.

[2] 195 U. S. Rep., 27, 54.

ferred, was declared to be repugnant to the Constitution, because it appeared to the judicial mind that the particular exertion of constitutional power was either unwise or unjust. To announce such a principle would amount to declaring that, in our constitutional system, the Judiciary was not only charged with the duty of upholding the Constitution, but also with the responsibility of correcting every possible abuse arising from the exercise by the other departments of their conceded authority. So to hold would be to overthrow the entire distinction between the Legislative, Judicial and Executive departments of the Government, upon which our system is founded, and would be a mere act of judicial usurpation. . . . The decisions of this Court from the beginning lend no support whatever to the assumption that the Judiciary may restrain the exercise of lawful power on the assumption that a wrongful purpose or motive has caused the power to be exerted.

Chief Justice Taft in his address delivered on Memorial Day, 1923, at Cincinnati, at the unveiling of the monument to Salmon P. Chase, Chief Justice of the Supreme Court during the Reconstruction Era after the Civil War, commenting upon the power of the Supreme Court of the United States to disregard unconstitutional legislation, said:

It is convincing evidence of the sound sense of the American people in the long run and their love for civil liberty and its constitutional guarantees that, in spite of hostility frequently engendered, the court has lived with its power unabated until now.

The only court in which all stand on an equality and in which not only the Constitution and laws of the Nation but also those of the States are enforced is the Supreme Court of the United States. . . .

It is the head of the system of Federal courts established avowedly to avoid the local prejudice which non-residents may encounter in State courts, a function often likely to ruffle the sensibilities of the communities, the possibility of whose prejudice is thus recognized and avoided.

More than this, the court's duty to ignore the acts of Congress or of the State Legislatures, if out of line with the fundamental law of the Nation, inevitably throws it as an obstruction across the path of the then majority who have enacted the invalid legislation.

The stronger the majority and the more intense its partisan feeling, the less likely it is to regard constitutional limitations upon its power, and the more likely it is to enact laws of questionable validity. It is convincing evidence of the good sense of the American people that they have disregarded hostility and caused the court to live on with unimpaired jurisdiction.

State Statutes Declared Unconstitutional by State Courts.

The first decisions of the State courts declaring State statutes void for unconstitutionality caused a deal of excitement and indignation. The people of the original States during the Revolution had been governed by provincial congresses and by legislatures that had held over after the Declaration of Independence. The people apparently believed that representative government meant the making of laws by their elected representatives in their legislatures. They could not see why the adoption of the constitutions, which, in all the States except Massachusetts, Rhode Island, and Connecticut,[1] had been framed by the State legislatures, should make any difference in the powers of those bodies. In New York, a public meeting, held after the decision of the case of *Rutgers v. Waddington*,[2] resolved: "That there should be a power vested in the courts of

---

[1] See *post*, p. 328.
[2] Thayer's *Constitutional Cases*.

judicature, whereby they might control the supreme legislative power, we think is absurd in itself. Such power in courts would be destructive of liberty, and remove all security of property." The House of Assembly of the State also passed a resolution "that the judgment was in its tendency subversive of all laws and good order and leads directly to anarchy and confusion."[1] The Rhode Island judges who decided the case of *Trevitt v. Weeden*,[2] were impeached as criminals, and though they were not removed from office on account of the impeachment, were not re-elected.[3] Other similar decisions of the State courts in the first period of independence were severely criticised. The decisions of State courts holding statutes void for unconstitutionality are now seldom criticised. In such cases, those who are interested in the legislation that has been found wanting, set in motion the procedure for the amendment of the State constitution, and if they have a good case, are usually successful. For example, after the New York Workmen's Compensation Act of 1910 had been declared unconstitutional by the decision of the case of *Ives v. South Buffalo Railway Co.*,[4] the New York constitution was so amended as to enable the legislature to pass the act now in force, the validity of which was sustained by the Court of Appeals of that State in the case of *Jensen v. Southern Pacific Co.*[5] On the other hand, the attempt to amend the New York constitution so as to permit the passage of a valid soldiers' bonus act, after the first statute for that purpose had been declared void,[6] was unsuccessful.

---

[1] Thayer's *Constitutional Cases*, 63 note.   [2] *Idem.*
[3] Watson, *The Constitution of the United States*, p. 1170.
[4] 201 N. Y. Rep., 271.   [5] 215 N. Y. Rep., 514.
[6] *People v. Westchester County Nat. Bk.*, 231 N. Y. Rep., 464

In the case of *Commonwealth v. Caton*,[1] decided in
1782 by the Court of Appeals of Virginia, the court
refused to enforce a statute that deprived the governor
of the pardoning power conferred by the State constitution.

In the case of *Rutgers v. Waddington*,[2] decided in
1784 by the Mayor's Court of New York City, the court
declined to execute a statute authorizing actions for
trespass by the owners of houses against those who had
occupied them under orders of the British commander-
in-chief, while New York had been in the possession of
the British forces.

The story of the case of *Trevitt v. Weeden*,[3] decided in
1787 by the Superior Court of Rhode Island, is given
by an eminent living jurist in the following words:[4]

In 1787 the legislature of Rhode Island, having put forth
paper money of the nominal value of £100,000 made it penal
to refuse to accept the bills in payment of articles offered
for sale or to make any distinction between them and gold
or silver coin and provided further that if any one were accused of that heinous offence, he should be tried forthwith
in an inferior court by judges without a jury, on a summary
complaint, without any continuance and with no appeal.
One Weeden being charged with violating the statute ob-
jected that trial before such a special court uncontrolled by
the supreme judiciary and without a jury was repugnant to
the charter which stood as the constitution of the state, and
hence that the statute was void. The judges sustained this
objection. Thereupon, on the last Monday of September,
1787, the judges were summoned to appear before the legislature much as Coke and his colleagues had appeared before

---

[1] 4 Call (Va.) Rep., 20.   [2] Thayer's *Constitutional Cases.*
[3] Thayer's *Constitutional Cases.*
[4] Pound, *The Spirit of the Common Law*, p. 61.

James I. The judges appeared and two of them made learned and convincing arguments that they could not be compelled by statute to send a citizen to jail without trial by jury when trial by jury was guaranteed by the constitution, the supreme law of the state, under which the legislature itself was constituted. The legislature, however, voted that it was not satisfied with the reasons of the judges, and a motion to dismiss the judges from their offices followed and would doubtless have prevailed had it not appeared that the constitution unhappily required the deliberate process of impeachment.

In 1787, in the case of *Bayard v. Singleton,*[1] the Superior Court of Law and Equity of North Carolina decided that the legislature had had no power under the constitution to enact a law that deprived claimants of confiscated property of the right of trial by jury. The report of this case says:

The Court . . . after every reasonable endeavor had been used in vain for avoiding a disagreeable difference between the Legislature and the Judicial powers of the State, at length with much apparent reluctance, but with great deliberation and firmness, gave their opinion separately, but unanimously for overruling the motion for the dismission of the said suits.

In the course of which the Judges observed that the obligations of their oaths, and the duty of their office required them in that situation, to give their opinion on that important and momentous subject; and that notwithstanding the great reluctance they might feel against involving themselves in a dispute with the Legislature of the State, yet no object of concern or respect could come in competition or authorize them to dispense with the duty they owed the

[1] 1 Martin (N. C.) Rep., 42

public, in consequence of the trusts they were invested with under the solemnity of their oaths.

That they therefore were bound to declare that they considered, that whatever disabilities the persons under whom the plaintiffs were said to derive their titles, might justly have incurred against their maintaining or prosecuting any suits in the Courts of this State; yet that such disabilities in their nature were merely personal, and not by any means capable of being transferred to the present plaintiffs, either by descent or purchase; and that these plaintiffs being citizens of one of the United States, or citizens of this State, by the confederation of all the States; which is to be taken as a part of the law of the land, unrepealable by any act of the General Assembly.

That by the constitution every citizen had undoubtedly a right to a decision of his property by a trial by jury. For that if the Legislature could take away this right, and require him to stand condemned in his property without a trial, it might with as much authority require his life to be taken away without a trial by jury, and that he should stand condemned to die, without the formality of any trial at all: that if the members of the General Assembly could do this, they might with equal authority, not only render themselves the Legislators of the State for life, without any further election of the people, from thence transmit the dignity and authority of legislation down to their heirs male forever.

But that it was clear, that no act they could pass, could by any means repeal or alter the constitution, because if they could do this, they would at the same instant of time, destroy their own existence as a Legislature, and dissolve the government thereby established. Consequently the constitution (which the judicial power was bound to take notice of as much as of any other law whatever), standing in full force as the fundamental law of the land, notwithstanding the act on which the present motion was grounded, the same act must of course, in that instance, stand as abrogated and without any effect.

Unconstitutionality Curable by Amendment.

The power of the State courts to declare State statutes void for unconstitutionality has been so frequently exercised since the first formative period that any general citation of authorities is unnecessary. Nevertheless, it may be well, in order to show how unconstitutional State legislation is now dealt with by State courts, to give as examples two cases, in which a State court has declared a State law unconstitutional and the people afterward have amended the State Constitution in order to obtain the desired legislation.

In the case of *Ives v. South Buffalo Railway Company*,[1] the New York Court of Appeals declared unconstitutional a Workmen's Compensation law enacted by the New York Legislature in 1910.[2] The plaintiff in this action, a switchman on the defendant's steam railroad, claimed damages for an injury due to the necessary risk or danger of his employment. At the common law, which had been in force in New York up to the passage of the Workmen's Compensation Act, he could not have recovered damages because the risk was one which he had assumed when he had taken the job. The railroad answered by asserting that the statute was unconstitutional in that it violated the provisions of the State and Federal constitutions by abrogating the right of trial by jury and by depriving persons of their rights of life, liberty, and property without due process of law.

The New York law, modelled upon a similar law in force in England, provided for the compensation by

[1] 201 N. Y. Rep., 271, 293.
[2] The New York Constitution was so amended in 1913 as to admit of the enactment of the present Workmen's Compensation Act, which has been held valid by the New York Court of Appeals in the case of *Jensen v. Southern Pacific Co.*, 215, N. Y. Rep., 514.

employers of workmen injured while employed in dangerous trades although the danger of injury had been assumed by the workmen, and provided a simplified procedure for the prosecution of their actions for damages. The plaintiff obtained a judgment in his favor in the Supreme Court after a hearing without a jury. This judgment was affirmed by the Appellate Division of the same court, and the case was then appealed to the highest court of the State, the Court of Appeals, which held that the act was unconstitutional in that, by compelling employers to assume the risks of the work of employees, it deprived the employers of their property without due process of law. The court did not pass upon the question raised by the claim that the act violated the right of trial by jury. In the opinion of the court, Judge Werner said:

When our Constitutions were adopted it was the law of the land that no man who was without fault or negligence could be held liable in damages for injuries sustained by another. That is still the law, except as to the employers enumerated in the new statute, and as to them it provides that they shall be liable to their employees for personal injury by accident to any workman arising out of and in the course of the employment which is caused in whole or in part, or is contributed to, by a necessary risk or danger of the employment or one inherent in the nature thereof, except that there shall be no liability in any case where the injury is caused in whole or in part by the serious or willful misconduct of the injured workman. It is conceded that this is a liability unknown to the common law and we think it plainly constitutes a deprivation of liberty and property under the Federal and State Constitutions. . . .

We conclude, therefore, that in its basic and vital features the right given to the employee by this statute does not preserve to the employer the "due process" of the law guaranteed by the Constitutions, for it authorizes the taking of the employer's property without his consent and without his fault.

In the case of *People v. Westchester County National Bank*,[1] decided in 1921, the New York Court of Appeals ruled that a statute, known as the Soldiers' Bonus Act, providing for the payment of a bonus to residents of New York who had been in the military or naval service of the United States for more than two months between April 6, 1917, and November 11, 1918, was invalid because of repugnance to a provision of the State constitution that "The credit of the State shall not in any manner be given or loaned to, or in aid of, any individual."[2] The Westchester County National Bank had been the successful bidder for $25,000 of State bonds issued under the act in question and had afterward refused to accept and pay for such bonds. Thereupon the State brought an action for the amount of its bid and obtained a judgment against the bank. This judgment was affirmed by the Appellate Division of the Supreme Court, but was reversed by the Court of Appeals in a decision,[3] in the course of which Judge Andrews said:

We know that when the United States declared war, it declared it for the whole country; that the government of the State, the government of the United States were equally interested in the victory; that, while serving the United States our soldiers and sailors were also protecting New York. We were all vitally interested in the war. Defeat spelled unspeakable calamity. Yet the men who gained the victory were not in any respect servants of the State. It did

[1] 231 N. Y. Rep., 465, 479.   [2] N. Y. Const., Art. VII. Sec. 1.
[3] Judge Cardozo dissented upon the ground that the constitutional clause in question did not apply to the payment by the State of its moral obligations.

not call them from their homes or lead them to battle. It did nothing. It exercised no authority. It is said that our soldiers were taken from their homes and occupations and compelled to risk their lives for inadequate pay while others earned large wages in safety—that the statute attempts in a small way to distribute more fairly the public burden. It is all true, but again the State was not the actor. Neither it nor its servants injured anyone. It received no property for which it has not paid. Nor were services rendered to it in any sense that services were not rendered to every city in the land. That services rendered the United States incidentally benefited every State is no foundation for a claim of obligation, however great the gratitude due. Gratitude may impel an individual to aid his benefactor. One may do as he will with his own. The State of New York may not. Its Constitution forbids. It may not attempt to equalize among its citizens inequalities caused by federal legislation. . . .

The State proposes to give its credit to the soldiers and sailors, not to satisfy any obligation that it owes them, but as a gratuity. The act is, therefore, prohibited by Section 1 of Article VII of the Constitution.[1]

State Statutes Declared Unconstitutional by U. S. Courts.

Sometimes in the course of a trial in a State court, the point is made that a State statute which seems to apply to the case is repugnant to the Constitution of the United States or to some act of Congress. If, in such a case, the court decides that the point is well taken, it will refuse to enforce the statute on the ground that the Constitution and laws of the United States are the supreme law of the land by which the judges in every State are bound.[2] If, for example, the claim is

---

[1] At the election held Nov. 6, 1923, the people of New York State ratified an amendment making constitutional a soldiers' bonus act.

[2] U. S. Const., Art. VI.

made that a particular statute is contrary to a provision of the Constitution of the United States by impairing the obligation of a contract,[1] and the judge decides it does, it is his duty to rule that the statute is unconstitutional and to refuse to enforce it.

A case in a State court in which such a question arises may be taken by a party against whom a decision has been given, to the highest courts of the State and thence by means of a writ of error to the Supreme Court of the United States, where a final decision can be had that the State statute is either constitutional and enforceable or unconstitutional and unenforceable.

The power of the Supreme Court of the United States thus to control the legislation of the States was sharply challenged during the early part of the nineteenth century. In the decision in the case of *McCulloch v. Maryland*,[2] rendered March 6, 1819, the court held that a State law imposing a tax upon the operations within the State of Maryland of the Bank of the United States was repugnant to the act of Congress chartering the bank. In February, 1819, the Ohio legislature enacted a similar law imposing a tax on the operations in Ohio of the Bank of the United States, and in September of the same year passed an additional law requiring the State Auditor, if the tax were not paid, to seize by force any property of the bank which he might find within the State. In obedience to this law, the auditor took from the vault in the office of the bank at Chillicothe a large sum of money in coin and bank notes. The bank then obtained an injunction from the U. S. Circuit Court against the auditor and his agents restraining them from paying over the money that had been seized. The Ohio legislature then en-

[1] U. S. Const. Art. I., Sec. 10.   [2] 4 Wheaton (U. S.) Rep., 316.

acted a law withdrawing from the Bank of the United States the protection of the laws, forbidding jailers to receive into custody any person committed at the suit of the bank, prohibiting judicial officers to take acknowledgment of its conveyances, and preventing the courts from taking cognizance of any wrongs or crimes committed against it.[1] The U. S. Circuit Court decided the injunction proceeding in favor of the bank, and issued a decree requiring the State Auditor to pay back the money he had received. This decision was affirmed by the Supreme Court of the United States.[2]

The Supreme Court of the United States has continuously and consistently exercised the power thus challenged, especially in cases in which State laws impairing the obligation of contracts,[3] or denying to any person the rights secured by the Constitution of the United States have been challenged on the ground of unconstitutionality. Its right to exercise this power in this particular has not been seriously opposed during nearly a century, and is now firmly established. It is indeed a necessary element of the system of federal union established by the national Constitution. If any State could nullify the Constitution and laws of the United States, the national government might not be able to accomplish the objects for which it exists. Justice Holmes of the U. S. Supreme Court in a public address[4] has said:

I do not think the United States would come to an end if we [the U. S. Supreme Court] lost our power to declare an

[1] McMaster, *History of the People of the United States*, IV., 502.

[2] *Osborn v. Bank of United States*, 9 Wheaton, (U. S.) Rep., 738.

[3] Forbidden by U. S. Const. Art. I., Sec. 10.

[4] *Law and the Courts*, Collected Legal Papers of Oliver Wendell Holmes, p. 296, Harcourt, Brace & Howe, New York, 1922.

Act of Congress void. I do think the Union would be imperiled if we could not make that declaration as to the laws of the several States. For one in my place sees how often a local policy prevails with those who are not trained to national views and how often action is taken that embodies what the Commerce Clause was meant to end. But I am not aware that there is any serious desire to limit the Court's power in this regard.

Also, the historian of the Supreme Court, Charles Warren, has aptly said:[1]

It is difficult to imagine what the history of the country would have been if there had been no *Dartmouth College Case* on the security of corporate charters; no *McCulloch v. Maryland* on the right of a State to tax a national agency; no *Gibbons v. Ogden* on interstate commerce; no *Brown v. Maryland* or *Passenger Cases* on foreign commerce; no *Craig v. Missouri* on State bills of credit; no *Charles River Bridge Case* on State powers over corporations; no *Slaughterhouse Case* on the scope of the Fourteenth Amendment.

The case of *Vanhorne v. Dorrance*,[2] decided in 1795 by the U. S. Circuit Court for the District of Pennsylvania, grew out of a claim of that State to the part of the territory of Pennsylvania that would have been within the northern and southern boundaries of Connecticut, if those boundaries were extended westward to the Ohio River. On the one hand, the royal charter granted by Charles II to the Connecticut colonists gave them all the territory between those boundary lines to the Pacific Ocean. On the other hand, the royal grant made by James II to William Penn included all of what

---

[1] Warren, *The History of the Supreme Court of the United States*, p. 19, Little, Brown & Co., Boston, 1923.
[2] 2 Dallas (U. S.) Rep., 304; Federal Cases No. 16, 857.

338 THE REASONABLENESS OF THE LAW

is now the State of Pennsylvania; and Penn had purchased from the Indians the territory thus granted.
After the Revolutionary War, a number of Connecticut
people emigrated to Luzerne County, Pennsylvania,
and made settlements there on lands granted to them
by their own State, which were already owned but not
occupied by citizens of Pennsylvania. In 1788, the
Pennsylvania legislature tried to settle the dispute by a
"quieting" act, which gave to the Connecticut settlers
the lands of which they were in actual possession and
provided that by way of compensation the Pennsylvania claimants should have other lands owned by that
State. The validity of this law was challenged by the
Pennsylvanians, who claimed that it violated the provision of the Constitution of the United States (which
had been adopted before the case began) providing
that "no state shall pass any law impairing the obligation of contracts." In deciding the issue thus made,
Justice Paterson of the U. S. Supreme Court, sitting as
a Judge of the United States Circuit Court, said:

I take it to be a clear position; that if a legislative act
oppugns a constitutional principle, the former must give
way, and be rejected on the score of repugnance. I hold it
to be a position equally clear and sound, that, in such case,
it will be the duty of the Court to adhere to the constitution
and to declare the law null and void. The constitution is
the basis of legislative authority; it lies at the foundation of
all law, and is the rule and commission by which both
legislators and judges are to proceed. . . .

The intention of the legislature was to vest in Connecticut claimants of a particular description a perfect estate to
certain lands in the County of Luzerne. . . . When the
legislature undertake to give away what is not their own,
when they attempt to take the property of one man, which

he fairly acquired, and the general law of the land protects, in order to transfer it to another, even upon complete indemnification, it will naturally be considered as an extraordinary act of legislation, which ought to be viewed with jealous eyes, and scrutinized with all the severity of legal exposition. . . . This act was made after the adoption of the constitution of the United States, and the argument is that it is contrary to it; . . . because it is a law impairing the obligation of a contract. . . . It impairs the obligation of a contract and is therefore void. If the property to the lands in question had been vested in the state of Pennsylvania, then the legislature would have had the liberty and right of disposing or granting them to whom they pleased, at any time and in any manner. . . . But if the confirming act be a contract between the legislature of Pennsylvania and the Connecticut settlers, it must be regulated by the rules and principles which pervade and govern all cases of contracts; and if so, it is clearly void, because it tends, in its operation and consequences, to defraud the Pennsylvania claimants, who are third persons, of their just rights; rights ascertained, protected and secured by the constitution and known laws of the land. The plaintiff's title to the land in question is legally derived from Pennsylvania; how then, on the principles of contract, could Pennsylvania lawfully dispose of it to another? As a contract, it could convey no right, without the owner's consent; without that, it was fraudulent and void. . . . The confirming act is unconstitutional and void. It was invalid from the beginning, had no life or operation, and is precisely in the same state, as if it had not been made.

In the case of *Fletcher v. Peck*,[1] decided by the United States Supreme Court in 1809, a statute enacted by the legislature of Georgia providing for the sale of certain public lands was held unconstitutional as a viola-

[1] 6 Cranch, U. S. Rep., 87.

tion of the clause of the Constitution of the United States which provides that no State shall pass any law impairing the obligation of contracts.[1]   In 1795, the Georgia legislature had been corruptly influenced to pass a law for the sale of certain public lands.   In course of time, the lands had been bought by people who had had nothing to do with the bribery.   A succeeding State legislature, however, had passed another act annulling the original sale for fraud.   This had left the innocent holders of deeds, some of whom had not taken actual possession of their lands, nothing except title deeds to show their right of ownership.   One of the purchasers, Robert Fletcher, brought in the United States Circuit Court in Massachusetts a suit for damages against John Peck, who had made a deed in which there was a guarantee of title.   This case was carried to the Supreme Court upon the claim that the Georgia law annulling the original sale had impaired the obligation of a contract and therefore was a law which that State had no right to enact.   In his opinion, Chief Justice Marshall said:

When . . . a law is in the nature of a contract, when absolute rights have vested under that contract, a repeal of the law cannot devest those rights. . . .   Georgia cannot be viewed as a single, unconnected, sovereign power, on whose legislature no other restrictions are imposed than may be found in its own Constitution.   She is a part of a large empire; she is a member of the American Union; and that Union has a Constitution, the supremacy of which all acknowledge, and which imposes limits to the legislatures of the several States, which none claim a right to pass.   The Constitution of the United States declares that no State shall pass any bill of attainder, *ex post facto* law, or law im-

[1] U. S. Const. Art. I., Sec. 10.

pairing the obligation of contracts. Does the case now
under consideration come within this prohibitory section
of the Constitution?

In considering this very interesting question, we immediately ask ourselves what is a contract? Is a grant a
contract? A contract is a compact between two or more
parties, and is either executory or executed. An executory
contract is one in which a party binds himself to do, or not
to do, a particular thing; such was the law under which the
[original] conveyance was made by the governor. A contract executed is one in which the object of contract is performed; and this, says Blackstone, differs in nothing from
a grant. The contract between Georgia and the purchaser
was executed by the grant. A contract executed, as well as
one which is executory, contains obligations binding on the
parties. A grant, in its own nature, amounts to an extin-
guishment of the right of the grantor, and implies a contract not to reassert that right. A party is, therefore,
always estopped [prevented from trying to dispute] by his
own grant.

Since, then, in fact, a grant is a contract executed, the
obligation of which still continues, and since the Constitution used the general term contract, without distinguishing between those which are executory and those which are
executed, it must be construed to comprehend the latter as
well as the former. . . . If, under a fair construction of
the Constitution, grants are comprehended under the term
contracts, is a grant from the State excluded from the operation of the provision? Is the clause to be considered as
inhibiting the State from impairing the obligation of contracts between two individuals, but as excluding from that
inhibition contracts made with itself? . . .

It is . . . the unanimous opinion of the Court, that, in this
case, the estate having passed into the hands of a purchaser
for a valuable consideration, without notice, the State of
Georgia was restrained, either by general principles which
are common to our free institutions, or by the particular

provisions of the Constitution of the United States, from passing a law whereby the estate of the plaintiff in the premises so purchased could be constitutionally and legally impaired and rendered null and void.

In the case of *McCulloch v. Maryland*,[1] decided in 1819 by the Supreme Court of the United States, the court further asserted the power of the federal courts to declare State statutes unconstitutional. In 1816, Congress had passed a statute re-incorporating the Bank of the United States. A branch of the bank had been established at Baltimore in 1817; and in 1818, the legislature of Maryland had enacted a statute imposing a tax upon the operations within the State of all banks not chartered by its legislature. The Baltimore branch of the bank had refused to pay the tax. Suit had then been brought by the State against McCulloch, the cashier, in the State courts, which had sustained the law. The U. S. Supreme Court then, upon appeal, decided that a State law which imposed a tax upon an institution chartered by the United States and used by it as a means of executing its governmental functions was repugnant to the Constitution of the United States and the laws made in pursuance of that instrument. Chief Justice Marshall said:

In the case now to be determined, the defendant, a sovereign state, denies the obligations of a law enacted by the legislature of the Union; and the plaintiff, on his part, contests the validity of an act which has been passed by the legislature of that State. The constitution of our country, in its most interesting and vital parts, is to be considered; the conflicting powers of the government of the Union and of its members, as marked in that constitution, are to be

[1] 4 Wheaton U. S. Rep., 316, 400, 421, 425, 431, 436.

discussed; and an opinion given which may essentially influence the great operations of the government. . . . The first question made in the cause is, has Congress power to incorporate a bank? . . .

We think the sound construction of the constitution must allow to the national legislature that discretion, with respect to the means by which the powers it confers are to be carried into execution, which will enable that body to perform the high duties assigned to it, in the manner most beneficial to the people. Let the end be legitimate, let it be within the scope of the constitution, and all means which are appropriate, which are plainly adapted to that end, which are not prohibited, but which consist with the letter and spirit of the constitution, are constitutional. That a corporation must be considered as a means not less usual, not of higher dignity, not more requiring a particular specification, has been sufficiently proved. . . .

If a corporation may be employed indiscriminately with other means to carry into execution the powers of the government, no particular reason can be assigned for excluding the use of a bank, if required for its fiscal operations. To use one, must be within the discretion of congress, if it be an appropriate mode of executing the powers of goverment. . . .

It being the opinion of the court, that the act incorporating the bank is constitutional; and that the power of establishing a branch in the State of Maryland might be properly exercised by the bank itself, we proceed to inquire:

Whether the State of Maryland may, without violating the constitution, tax that branch? . . .

There is no express provision for the case, but the claim [that the bank was exempted from the power of the State to tax its operations] has been sustained on a principle which so entirely pervades the constitution, is so intermixed with the materials which compose it, so interwoven with its web, so blended with its texture, as to be incapable of being separated from it without rending it into shreds.

This great principle is, that the constitution and the laws made in pursuance thereof are supreme; that they control the constitution and laws of the respective States, and cannot be controlled by them. From this, which may be almost termed an axiom, other propositions are deduced as corollaries, on the truth or error of which, and on their application to this case, the cause has been supposed to depend. These are: 1. That a power to create implies a power to preserve. 2. That a power to destroy, if wielded by a different hand, is hostile to, and incompatible with, these powers to create and to preserve. 3. That where this repugnancy exists, that authority which is supreme must control, not yield to, that over which it is supreme. . . .

The power of congress to create, and of course to continue, the bank, was the subject of the preceding part of the opinion. . . .

That the power to tax involves the power to destroy; that the power to destroy may defeat and render useless the power to create; that there is a plain repugnance, in conferring on one government a power to control the constitutional measures of another, which other, with respect to those very measures, is declared to be supreme over that which exerts the control, are propositions not to be denied. . . .

The Court has bestowed on this subject its most deliberate consideration. The result is a conviction that the States have no power, by taxation or otherwise, to retard, impede, burden, or in any manner control, the operations of the constitutional laws enacted by congress to carry into execution the powers vested in the general government. . . .

We are unanimously of opinion, that the law passed by the legislature of Maryland, imposing a tax on the Bank of the United States, is unconstitutional and void.

In the case of *Dartmouth College v. Woodward*,[1] decided in 1819, the Supreme Court decided that a cor-

[1] 4 Wheaton's Rep., 518, 642.

poration charter is a contract, the obligation of which cannot be impaired even by the State which creates and protects it.

The Dartmouth College case originated in an attempt in 1816 by the New Hampshire legislature to amend the charter which King George the Third had granted, in 1769, to Rev. Eleazer Wheelock for an Indian mission school. Gifts of land and other property had been made by many good people, including the Earl of Dartmouth, whose name was adopted when the school became a college. Under its royal charter, the institution had been governed by a board of trustees who had power to fill all vacancies in their number. In June and December, 1816, the New Hampshire legislature had enacted laws "enlarging and improving the corporation and amending the charter" in such a way as to give the State full control over the corporation. William H. Woodward, the defendant in the case, had been secretary and treasurer of the original corporation known as the "Trustees of Dartmouth College." On August 27, 1816, he had been removed from both offices. On February 4, 1817, the college corporation had been organized according to the provisions of the new acts, and the new trustees appointed Woodward secretary and treasurer of the college. He had accepted the offices and thereby obtained custody of the books and some other property of the corporation.

The trustees under the old royal charter brought this case in order to obtain possession of the college books and other property. The case was heard first in the Court of Common Pleas of Grafton County, N. H., where the jury reported to the court that, if the New Hampshire laws changing the college charter did not impair the obligations of a contract under the provisions of the Constitution of the United States, judgment ought to be in favor of Woodward; but that, if those acts were void for unconstitutionality, the judgment should be for the old trustees. Chief Justice Marshall carried the Supreme Court with him in a far-reaching decision, in which he said:

Dr. Wheelock, acting for himself and for those who, at his solicitation, had made contributions to his school, applied for this charter, as the instrument which should enable him and them to perpetuate their beneficent intention. It was granted. An artificial, immortal being was created by the crown, capable of receiving and distributing forever, according to the will of the donors, the donations which should be made to it. On this being, the contributions which had been collected were immediately bestowed. These gifts were made, not indeed to make a profit for the donors or their posterity, but for something in their opinion of inestimable value; for something which they deemed a full equivalent for the money with which it was purchased. The consideration for which they stipulated, is the perpetual application of the fund to its object, in the mode prescribed by themselves. Their descendants may take no interest in the preservation of this consideration. But in this respect their descendants are not their representatives. They are represented by the corporation. The corporation is the assignee of their rights, stands in their place, and distributes their bounty as they would themselves have distributed it, had they been immortal. So with respect to the students who are to derive learning from this source. The corporation is a trustee for them also. Their potential rights, which, taken distributively, are imperceptible, amount, collectively, to a most important interest. These are in the aggregate, to be exercised, asserted, and protected, by the corporation. . . .

Had parliament, immediately after the emanation of

this charter, and the execution of those conveyances which followed it, annulled the instrument, so that the living donors would have witnessed the disappointment of their hopes, the perfidy of the transaction would have been universally acknowledged. Yet, then, as now, the donors would have had no interest in the property; then, as now, those who might be students would have had no rights to be violated; then, as now, it might be said, that the trustees, in whom the rights of all were combined, possessed no private, individual, beneficial interest in the property confided to their protection. Yet the contract would at that time have been deemed sacred by all. What has since occurred to strip it of its inviolability? Circumstances have not changed it. In reason, in justice, and in law, it is now what it was in 1769.

This is plainly a contract to which the donors, the trustees, and the crown (to whose rights and obligations New Hampshire succeeds), were the original parties. It is a contract made on a valuable consideration. It is a contract for the security and disposition of property. It is a contract on the faith of which, real and personal estate has been conveyed to the corporation. It is a contract within the letter of the Constitution, and within its spirit also, unless the fact that the property is invested by the donors in trustees, for the promotion of religion and education, for the benefit of persons who are perpetually changing, though the objects remain the same, shall create a particular exception, taking this case out of the prohibition contained in the Constitution.

It is more than possible that the preservation of rights of this description was not particularly in the view of the framers of the Constitution, when the clause under consideration was introduced into that instrument. It is probable that interferences of more frequent recurrence, to which the temptation was stronger, and of which the mischief was more extensive, constituted the great motive for imposing this restriction on the State legislatures. But although a particular and a rare case may not, in itself, be of sufficient magnitude to induce a rule, yet it must be governed by the rule, when established, unless some plain and strong reason for excluding it can be given. It is not enough to say, that this particular case was not in the mind of the convention, when the article was framed, nor of the American people when it was adopted. . . . The case being within the words of the rule, must be within its operation likewise, unless there be something in the literal construction so obviously absurd or mischievous, or repugnant to the general spirit of the instrument, as to justify those who expound the Constitution in making it an exception.

The founders of the college contracted, not merely for the perpetual application of the funds which they gave, to the objects for which those funds were given; they contracted also, to secure that application by the constitution of the corporation. They contracted for a system, which should, as far as human foresight can provide, retain forever the government of the literary institution they had formed, in the hands of persons approved by themselves. This system is totally changed. The charter of 1769 exists no longer. It is reorganized; and reorganized in such a manner as to convert a literary institution, moulded according to the will of its founders, and placed under the control of private literary men, into a machine entirely subservient to this will of government. This may be for the advantage of the college in particular, and may be to the advantage of literature in general; but it is not according to the will of the donors, and is subversive of that contract, on the faith of which the property was given. . . .

It results from this opinion, that the acts of the legislature of New Hampshire . . . are repugnant to the Constitution of the United States.

In the case of *Lochner v. New York*,[1] decided in 1905 by the U. S. Supreme Court, the question was upon the

[1] 198 U. S. Rep., 45, 56.

constitutionality of a New York statute that no employee shall be required or permitted to work in a bakery or confectionery establishment more than sixty hours in any one week or more than ten hours in any one day except for the purpose of making a shorter Saturday work day. Lochner, who had been tried and convicted in the State courts under this law, in a case in which all the employees were men, took the question from the New York Court of Appeals, which had held the statute valid, to the U. S. Supreme Court, which ruled that as to male employees in such establishments it was an unconstitutional interference with the right of individuals to make such contracts for labor as they might wish. In the opinion of the Court,[1] Justice Peckham said:[2]

In every case that comes before this Court, . . . where legislation of this character is concerned and where the protection of the Federal Constitution is sought, the question necessarily arises: Is this a fair, reasonable and appropriate exercise of the police power of the State, or is it an unreasonable, unnecessary and arbitrary interference with the right of the individual to his personal liberty or to enter into those contracts in relation to labor which may seem to him appropriate or necessary for the support of himself and his family? Of course the liberty of contract relating to labor includes both parties to it. The one has as much right to purchase as the other to sell labor. . . .

The question whether this act is valid as a labor law, pure and simple, may be dismissed in a few words. There is no reasonable ground for interfering with the liberty of person, or the right of free contract, by determining the hours of labor, in the occupation of a baker. There is no

---

[1] Three justices dissented in this case.
[2] This decision no longer holds. See *ante*, p. 87.

contention that bakers as a class are not equal in intelligence and capacity to men in other trades or manual occupations, or that they are not able to assert their rights and care for themselves without the protecting arm of the State, interfering with their independence of judgment and of action. They are in no sense wards of the State. . . . The law must be upheld, if at all, as a law pertaining to the health of the individual engaged in the occupation of a baker. . . .

We think the limit of the police power has been reached and passed in this case. There is, in our judgment, no reasonable foundation for holding this to be necessary or appropriate as a health law to safeguard the public health or the health of individuals who are following the trade of a baker. . . .

We think that there can be no fair doubt that the trade of a baker, in and of itself, is not an unhealthy one to that degree which would authorize the legislature to interfere with the right to labor, and with the right of free contract on the part of the individual. . . . In looking through statistics regarding all trades and occupations, it may be true that the trade of a baker does not appear to be as healthy as some other trades, and is also vastly more healthy than still some others. To the common understanding the trade of a baker has never been regarded as an unhealthy one. . . .

It is also urged . . . that it is to the interest of the State that its population should be strong and robust, and therefore any legislation which may be said to tend to make people healthy must be valid as health laws, enacted under the police power. If this be a valid argument and justification for this kind of legislation, it follows that the protection of the Federal Constitution from undue interference with liberty of person and freedom of contract is visionary, wherever the law is sought to be justified as a valid exercise of the police power. . . . Not only the hours of employes, but the hours of employers, could be regulated,

STATUTE LAW 351

and doctors, lawyers, scientists, all professional men, as
well as athletes and artisans, could be forbidden to fatigue
their brains and bodies by prolonged hours of exercise, lest
the fighting strength of the State be impaired. . . . We
do not believe in the soundness of the views which uphold
this law. On the contrary, we think that such a law as this,
although passed in the assumed exercise of the police power,
and as relating to the public health, or the health of the
employes named, is not within that power and is invalid.
. . . It seems to us that the real object and purpose
[of the law] were simply to regulate the hours of labor between the master and his employes (all being men, *sui juris*),
in a private business, not dangerous in any degree to morals
or in any real and substantial degree, to the health of the
employes. Under such circumstances the freedom of master and employe to contract with one another in relation to
their employment, and in defining the same, cannot be prohibited or interfered with, without violating the Federal
Constitution.

CHAPTER XXIV

U. S. Statutes Declared Unconstitutional by U. S. Courts.

Justice Holmes, in saying he did not think the United States would come to an end if its Supreme Court lost its power to declare an act of Congress void,[1] may have had in mind that the acts of each co-ordinate department of the national government in relation to national matters create political issues which in one way or another may finally be determined by the people. The case of *Marbury v. Madison*[2] did little more than hint to the Congress that it ought not to try to give the courts of the United States any powers not conferred by the Constitution. The *Dred Scott Case*[3] was little more than an incident in the "irrepressible" conflict, which ended in the abolition of slavery. The first *Employers Liability Case* suggested to Congress the particulars in which a labor law was invalid and the corrections which ought to be made and were made. The decisions in the *Child Labor Cases*,[4] and in the recent *Minimum Wage Case*[5] declare that if the People of the United States wish to have laws to prevent the employment of children in factories and to regulate the wages of women and children, they should so amend

[1] See *ante* p. 336. [2] See *post* p. 356. [3] See *ante* p. 96.
[4] See *post* p. 354. [5] See *post* pp. 362-364.

their Constitution as to give Congress power to enact them. An excellent authority[1] has said:

During the first eighty years, only four Federal statutes were held unconstitutional, of which but two were of any importance, and even if the courts had possessed no power to determine the validity of these two, the Mandamus Act in *Marbury v. Madison* and the Missouri Compromise Act in the *Dred Scott Case*, it cannot be said that the course of events would have been fundamentally affected. So with regard to the thirty-two Acts of Congress held unconstitutional between 1869 and 1917, with the possible exception of the decision in the *Civil Rights Cases*, the integral history of the country would have been little altered had the Court not possessed or exercised its power.

The indisputable fact remains that the Supreme Court of the United States under its power to judge cases arising under the Constitution and laws of the United States,[2] can refuse to enforce statutes made by the People of the United States through their duly elected representatives and senators in the Congress and approved by their duly elected President. A number of resolutions proposing constitutional amendments either concerning the number of justices that must concur in decisions of this nature or giving the Congress power to review the action of the Court were offered in the Congress which ended March 3, 1923. None of these resolutions received the two-thirds vote required by the amending clause.[3] Hence, the question remains unsettled. The problem, if it be a problem, is not easy of solution. Any withdrawal from the Su-

[1] Warren, *The History of the Supreme Court of the United States*, p. 16, Harcourt, Brace and Howe, New York, 1922.
[2] U. S. Const., Art. VI.   [3] U. S. Const., Art. V.

354 THE REASONABLENESS OF THE LAW

preme Court of the power as now exercised to declare
Acts of Congress unconstitutional and void would
operate to deprive litigants of rights which a majority
of the members of the highest tribunal in the United
States—all of them famous lawyers and jurists—believe
they ought to have.

In 1803, the U. S. Supreme Court in the case of *Marbury v. Madison*,[1] ruled for the first time that an Act of
Congress, not authorized by the Constitution of the
United States, must be disregarded by the courts.
President John Adams, during the last hours of his administration, had appointed one William Marbury a
justice of the peace of the District of Columbia, and
had signed but had not delivered the commission to the
appointee. Madison, as Jefferson's Secretary of State,
refused to deliver the commission; and Marbury petitioned the Supreme Court for a writ of *mandamus*, or
court order commanding him to do so. This petition
was based upon a provision of the Judiciary Act passed
by Congress in 1789 that authorized the Supreme Court
"to issue writs of *mandamus*, in cases warranted by the
principles and usages of law, to any courts appointed,
or persons holding office, under the authority of the
United States." Chief Justice Marshall, giving the
decision of the court, declared that it was the duty of
Secretary Madison to deliver the commission to Marbury, but refused to issue the writ of *mandamus*, upon
the ground that the provision of the Judiciary Act was
not authorized by the national Constitution, thus de-
clining to enforce a law enacted by Congress. He said:

The act to establish the judicial courts of the United
States authorizes the Supreme Court "to issue writs of

[1] I Cranch (U. S.) Rep., 137, 173.

mandamus, in cases warranted by the principles and usages of law, to any courts, appointed, or persons holding office, under the authority of the United States." . . . The constitution vests the whole judicial power of the United States in one supreme court, and such inferior courts as congress shall, from time to time, ordain and establish. This power is expressly extended to all cases arising under the laws of the United States. . . . In the distribution of this power it is declared that "the supreme court shall have original jurisdiction in all cases affecting ambassadors, other public ministers and consuls, and those in which a State shall be a party. In all other cases, the supreme court shall have appellate jurisdiction." . . . If it had been intended to leave it in the discretion of the legislature to apportion the judicial power between the supreme and inferior courts according to the will of that body, it would certainly have been useless to have proceeded further than to have defined the judicial power, and the tribunals in which it should be vested. The subsequent part of the section is mere surplusage, is entirely without meaning, if such is to be the construction. If Congress remains at liberty to give this Court appellate jurisdiction, where the constitution has declared their jurisdiction shall be original; and original jurisdiction where the constitution has declared it shall be appellate; the distribution of jurisdiction, made in the constitution, is form without substance. . . .

It cannot be presumed that any clause in the constitution is intended to be without effect; and, therefore, such a construction is inadmissible, unless the words require it. . . .

When an instrument organizing fundamentally a judicial system, divides it into one supreme and so many inferior courts as the legislature may ordain and establish; then enumerates its powers, and proceeds so far to distribute them, as to define the jurisdiction of the supreme court by declaring the cases in which it shall take original jurisdiction, and that in others it shall take appellate jurisdiction;

the plain import of the words seems to be, that in one class of cases its jurisdiction is original and not appellate; in the other it is appellate, and not original. . . .

The authority, therefore, given to the supreme court, by the act establishing the judicial courts of the United States, to issue writs of *mandamus* to public officers, appears not to be warranted by the constitution. . . .

If a law be in opposition to the constitution; if both the law and the constitution apply to a particular case, so that the court must either decide that case conformably to the law, disregarding the constitution, or conformably to the constitution, disregarding the law, the court must determine which of these conflicting rules governs the case. . . .

It is apparent that the framers of the constitution contemplated that instrument as a rule for the government of the courts, as well as of the legislature. . . .

The particular phraseology of the constitution of the United States confirms and strengthens the principle, supposed to be essential to all written constitutions, that a law repugnant to the constitution is void; and that courts, as well as other departments, are bound by that instrument.

In the case of *Dred Scott v. Sandford*,[1] decided in 1856 by the Supreme Court of the United States, the court declared unconstitutional the Missouri Compromise Act, passed by Congress in 1820, which provided that slavery should not exist in any part of the great territorial area west of the Mississippi River and north of the parallel of 36° 30'. In 1836, Dred Scott, a negro slave, had been taken by his master, an army surgeon, to Fort Snelling, now St. Paul, Minn., where he lived for some years, going afterward to Missouri, where he brought this action, as a means of securing his freedom. In order to have his case heard in the courts of the United States, he alleged in his complaint that he

[1] 19 Howard (U. S.) Rep., 393, 451.

was a citizen of the State of Missouri and that the defendant was a citizen of the State of New York,[1] claiming that his residence in a part of the territory of the United States in which slavery was forbidden had made him a free man and a citizen of the United States. Upon the issue raised by this allegation, the Court, by a vote of six justices to three, decided that the Missouri Compromise Act was void because it prohibited a citizen from owning in any part of the United States a kind of property that was recognized and protected by the Constitution of the United States. Chief Justice Taney said:

The powers of the government, and the rights of the citizen under it, are positive and practical regulations plainly written down. The people of the United States have delegated to it certain enumerated powers, and have forbidden it to exercise others. It has no power over the person or property of a citizen but what the citizens of the United States have granted. . . . And if the constitution recognizes the right of property of the master in a slave, and makes no distinction between that description of property and other property owned by a citizen, no tribunal, acting under the authority of the United States, whether it be legislative, executive, or judicial, has a right to draw such a distinction, or deny to it the benefit of the provisions and guarantees which have been provided for the protection of private property against the encroachments of the government.

Now, as we have already said, . . . the right of property in a slave is distinctly and expressly affirmed in the constitution. The right to traffic in it, like an ordinary article of merchandise and property, was guaranteed to the citi-

[1] U. S. Const., Art. III., Sec. 2, provides that the judicial power of the United States shall extend to controversies between citizens of different States.

zens of the United States, in every State that might desire
it, for twenty years. And the government in express terms
is pledged to protect it in all future time, if the slave escapes from his owner. This is done in plain words—too
plain to be misunderstood. And no word can be found in
the constitution which gives congress a greater power over
slave property, or which entitles property of that kind to
less protection than property of any other description. The
only power conferred is the power coupled with the duty of
guarding and protecting the owner in his rights. Upon
these considerations, it is the opinion of the court that the
act of congress which prohibited a citizen from holding and
owning property of this kind [negro slaves] in the territory
of the United States north of the line therein mentioned, is
not warranted by the constitution, and is therefore void.

In the case of *Pollock v. The Farmers' Loan and Trust
Co.*,[1] decided by the United States Supreme Court in
1894, an act of Congress providing for the taxation of
incomes was held to be unconstitutional in so far as it
affected rents or incomes derived from real estate. The
ground of the decision was that such taxes were direct
taxes which were not valid unless apportioned to the
States in proportion to their populations, as required
by Article I, Section 9, Sub. 4, of the Constitution of
the United States. Chief Justice Fuller said:

Thus was accomplished one of the great compromises of
the Constitution, resting on the doctrine that the right of
representation ought to be conceded to every community
on which a tax is to be imposed but crystallizing it in such
form as to allay jealousies in respect of the future balance
of power; to reconcile conflicting views in respect of the
enumeration of slaves; and to remove the objection that, in

[1] 157 U. S. Rep., 429.

adjusting a system of representation between the States, regard should be had to their relative wealth, since those who were to be most heavily taxed ought to have a proportionate influence in the government. The compromise, in embracing the power of direct taxation, consisted not simply in including part of the slaves in the enumeration of population, but in providing that as between State and State, such taxation should be proportioned to representation . . .

It is apparent: 1. That the distinction between direct and indirect taxation was well understood by the framers of the Constitution and those who adopted it. 2. That under the State systems of taxation all taxes on real estate or personal property or the rents or income thereof were regarded as direct taxes. 3. That the rules of apportionment and of uniformity were adopted in view of that distinction and those systems. . . . 5. That the original expectation was that the power of direct taxation would be exercised only in extraordinary exigencies, and down to August 15, 1894 [the date of the income tax law under consideration], this expectation has been realized. The act of that date was passed in a time of profound peace, and if we assume that no special exigency called for unusual legislation, and that resort to this mode of taxation is to become an ordinary and usual means of supply, that fact furnishes an additional reason for circumspection and care in disposing of this case. . . .

The requirement of the Constitution is that no direct tax shall be laid otherwise than by apportionment—the prohibition is not against direct taxes on land, from which the implication is sought to be drawn that indirect taxes on land would be constitutional, but it is against all direct taxes—and it is admitted that a tax on real estate is a direct tax. . . . An annual tax upon the annual value or annual user of real estate appears to us the same in substance as an annual tax on the real estate, which would be paid out of the rent or income. . . .

We are of opinion that the law in question, so far as it

levies a tax on the rents or income of real estate, is in violation of the Constitution, and is invalid.[1]

The question in *The Employers Liability Cases*,[2] decided in 1907 by the U. S. Supreme Court, was upon the constitutionality of an act of Congress, passed in 1906, which made common carriers, such as railroads or steamship companies, engaged in interstate commerce, liable for damages suffered by their employees through the negligence or carelessness either of the carriers or of fellow employees. Up to that time, actions for damages for personal injuries could be heard in the U. S. courts only when brought by citizens of one State against persons who resided in another, and were decided according to the laws of the State in which the accident happened. Such actions could not, up to that time, be brought in a Federal court by a citizen of a State against a carrier belonging in the same State. This statute was an attempt to extend the jurisdiction or judicial power of the Federal courts so as to include actions which would naturally be brought in the State courts, and the ground on which the statute was based was that a carrier engaged in interstate commerce was subject to any laws which Congress might see fit to pass under its power "to regulate commerce among the several States." In the opinion of the Court the statute was repugnant to the Constitution[3] because it made carriers engaged in interstate commerce liable

[1] The Sixteenth Amendment to the U. S. Constitution, adopted in 1913, gives Congress power to levy taxes on incomes from any source without an apportionment among the States and without regard to any census.

[2] 207 U. S. Rep., 463, 498, 504.

[3] In 1908 Congress passed another Employers Liability Act, which was declared constitutional in the *Second Employers Liability Cases*, 223 U. S. Rep., 1.

for all injuries suffered by their employees, whether such carriers were or were not engaged in such commerce when the injuries were suffered.[1] For example, under the act, a railroad, whose line ran from New York to Chicago, might be called upon to defend an action for damages caused by an accident to a local train that did not run outside of the State of New York. Justice White, who afterward was Chief Justice of the United States, said:

This act . . . being addressed to all common carriers engaged in interstate commerce, and imposing a liability upon them in favor of any of their employes, without qualification or restriction as to the business in which the carriers or their employes may be engaged at the time of the injury, of necessity includes subjects wholly outside of the power of Congress to regulate commerce. . . . A few illustrations showing the operation of the statute as to matters wholly independent of interstate commerce will serve to make clear the extent of the power which is exerted by the statute. Take a railroad engaged in interstate commerce, having a purely local branch operated wholly within a State. Take again the same road having shops for repairs, and it may be for construction work, as well as a large accounting and clerical force, and having, it may be, storage elevators and warehouses, not to suggest besides the possibility of its being engaged in other independent enterprises. Take a telegraph company engaged in the transmission of interstate and local messages. Take an express company engaged in local as well as in interstate business. Take a trolley line moving wholly within a State as to a large part of its business and yet as to the remainder crossing the State line.

As the act thus includes many subjects wholly beyond the power to regulate commerce and depends for its sanc-

[1] Justices Moody, Holmes, Harlan, and McKenna dissented.

tion upon that authority, it results that the act is repugnant to the Constitution, and cannot be enforced. . . .

Concluding, as we do, that the statute, whilst it embraces subjects within the authority of Congress to regulate commerce, also includes subjects not within its constitutional power, and that the two are so interblended in the statute that they are incapable of separation, we are of the opinion that the courts below rightly held the statute to be repugnant to the Constitution and non-enforceable.

The Congress has made two attempts to enact laws prohibiting, or rather preventing, the employment of children in industry.

In the case of *Hammer v. Degenhart*,[1] decided in 1918, the U. S. Supreme Court declared unconstitutional an act of Congress, passed in 1916, which prohibited the transportation in interstate commerce of goods made in factories in which within thirty days prior to their removal, children under the age of fourteen had been employed or permitted to work or in which children between the ages of fourteen and sixteen had been employed or permitted to work more than eight hours in any day, or more than six days in any week, or after seven P.M. or before six A.M. In stating the opinion of the Court,[2] Justice Day said:

The thing intended to be accomplished by this statute is the denial of the facilities of interstate commerce to those manufacturers in the States who employ children within the prohibited ages. The act in its effect does not regulate transportation among the States, but aims to standardize the ages at which children may be employed in mining and manufacturing within the States. . . .

[1] 247 U. S. Rep., 251.
[2] Justices Holmes, Brandeis, McKenna, and Clarke refused to concur in this decision.

There is no power vested in Congress to require the States to exercise their police power so as to prevent possible unfair competition. Many causes may co-operate to give one State, by reason of local laws or conditions, an economic advantage over others. The Commerce Clause was not intended to give Congress a general power to equalize such conditions. In some of the States, laws have been passed fixing minimum wages for women, in others the local law regulates the hours of labor of women in various employments. Business done in such States may be at an economic disadvantage when compared with States which have no such regulations; surely, this fact does not give Congress the power to deny transportation in interstate commerce to those who carry on business where the hours of labor and the rate of compensation for women has not been fixed by a standard in use in other States and approved by Congress.

The grant of power to Congress over the subject of interstate commerce was to enable it to regulate such commerce, and not to give it authority to control the States in the exercise of the police power over local trade and manufacture. The grant of authority over a purely federal matter was not intended to destroy the local power always existing and carefully reserved to the States in the Tenth Amendment to the Constitution. . . .

That there should be limitations upon the right to employ children in mines and factories in the interest of their own and the public welfare, all will admit. That such employment is generally deemed to require regulation is shown by the fact that . . . every State in the Union has a law upon the subject, limiting the right to thus employ children. . . .

In our view the necessary effect of this act is, by means of a prohibition against the movement in interstate commerce of ordinary commercial commodities, to regulate the hours of labor of children in factories and mines within the State, a purely state authority. Thus the act in a twofold sense is repugnant to the Constitution. It not only transcends the authority delegated to Congress over commerce, but also exerts a power as to a purely local matter to which the federal authority does not extend. The far-reaching effect of upholding the act cannot be more plainly indicated than by pointing out that if Congress can thus regulate matters entrusted to local authority by prohibition of the movements of commodities in interstate commerce, all freedom of commerce will be at an end, and the power of the States over local matters may be eliminated, and thus our system of government be practically destroyed.

For these reasons, we hold that this law exceeds the constitutional authority of Congress.

In 1918, Congress enacted the Child Labor Tax Law, which provided that every person operating any mine or quarry in which children under 16 have been employed or permitted to work during any part of the taxable year; or any mill, cannery, workship, factory, or manufacturing establishment in the United States in which children under the age of 14 have been employed or permitted to work or children between 14 and 16 have been employed or allowed to work more than eight hours in any day or more than six days in any week or before six A.M. or after seven P.M., shall pay for each taxable year, in addition to all other taxes, an excise tax equivalent to ten per cent of their entire net profits of the year.

The validity of this law was challenged by the Drexel Furniture Co., which brought a suit against the collector of internal revenue of North Carolina, to recover an assessment of $6,312.79, which it had paid under protest. In passing upon the issues of the case, *Bailey v. Drexel Furniture Co.*,[1] decided by U. S. Supreme Court, May 15, 1922, Chief Justice Taft said:

[1] 259 U. S. Rep., 20.

Does this law impose a tax with only that incidental restraint and regulation which a tax must inevitably involve? Or does it regulate by the use of the so-called tax as a penalty? If a tax, it is clearly an excise. If it were an excise upon a commodity or other thing of value we might not be permitted, under previous decisions of this court, to infer, solely from its heavy burden, that the act intends a prohibition instead of a tax. But this act is more. It provides a heavy exaction for a departure from a detailed and specified course of conduct in business. That course of business is that employers shall employ in mines and quarries, children of an age greater than sixteen years; in mills and factories children of an age greater than fourteen years; and shall prevent children of an age less than sixteen years from working more than eight hours a day or six days in the week. If an employer departs from this prescribed course of business, he is to pay to the government one-tenth of his entire net income in the business for a full year. The amount is not to be proportioned in any degree to the extent or frequency of the departures, but is to be paid by the employer in full measure whether he employs five hundred children for a year, or employs only one for a day. Moreover, if he does not know that the child is within the named age limit, he is not to pay; that is to say, it is only where he knowingly departs from the prescribed course that payment is to be exacted. *Scienters* [allegations of knowledge] are associated with penalties, not with taxes. The employer's factory is to be subject to inspection at any time not only by the taxing officers of the Treasury, the Department normally charged with the collection of taxes, but also by the Secretary of Labor and his subordinates, whose normal function is the advancement and protection of the welfare of the workers. In the light of these features of the act, a court must be blind not to see that the so-called tax is imposed to stop the employment of children within the age limits prescribed. Its prohibiting and regulatory effect and purpose are palpable. . . .

It is the high duty and function of this Court in cases regularly brought to its bar to decline to recognize or enforce seeming laws of Congress, dealing with subjects not entrusted to Congress, but left or committed by the supreme law of the land [Constitution of U. S.] to the control of the States. We cannot avoid the duty even though it require us to refuse to give effect to legislation designed to promote the highest good. The good sought in unconstitutional legislation is an insidious feature because it leads citizens and legislators of good purpose to promote it without thought of the serious breach it will make in the ark of our covenant, or the harm which will come from breaking down recognized standards. In the maintenance of local self-government, on the one hand, and the national power on the other, our country has been able to endure and prosper for near a century and a half.

Out of a proper respect for the acts of a co-ordinate branch of the government, this court has gone far to sustain taxing acts as such, even though there has been ground for suspecting from the weight of the tax it was intended to destroy its subject. But in the act before us, the presumption of validity cannot prevail, because the proof of the contrary is found in the very face of its provisions. Grant the validity of this law, and all that Congress would need to do hereafter, in seeking to take over to its control any one of the great number of subjects of public interest, jurisdiction of which the States have never parted with, and which are reserved to them by the 10th Amendment, would be to enact a detailed measure of complete regulation of the subject, and enforce it by a so-called tax upon departures from it. To give such magic to the word "tax" would be to break down all constitutional limitation of the powers of Congress and completely wipe out the sovereignty of the States.

The difference between a tax and a penalty is sometimes difficult to define, and yet the consequences of the distinction in the required method of their collection often are important. When the sovereign enacting the law has power to impose both tax and penalty, the difference between revenue production and mere regulation may be immaterial; but not so when one sovereign can impose a tax only, and the power of regulation rests in another. Taxes are occasionally imposed in the discretion of the legislature on proper subjects with the primary motive of obtaining revenue from them, and with the incidental motive of discouraging them by making their continuance impossible. They do not lose their character as taxes because of the incidental motive. But there comes a time in the extension of the penalizing features of the so-called tax when it loses its character as such and becomes a mere penalty, with the characteristics of regulation and punishment. Such is the case in the law before us. Although Congress does not invalidate the contract of employment, or expressly declare that the employment within the mentioned ages is illegal, it does exhibit its intent practically to achieve the latter result by adopting the criteria of wrongdoing, and imposing its principal consequence on those who transgress its standard.

CHAPTER XXV

CONSTRUCTION AND INTERPRETATION OF STATUTES

Application of Statutes.

The courts in giving effect to the will of legislatures ascertain the objects and purposes for which statutes have been made from the history of the times when they were enacted and ascertain the meaning of statutes from the words in which they are expressed. They do not take into account the views expressed by individual members in the course of the debates or the motives which influenced their votes, because the statutes speak the will of the majorities that passed them.[1] Thus the rules for the construction and interpretation of statutes are much the same as the rules for the construction and interpretation of constitutions.[2]

Construction of Statutes.

In the case of *Holy Trinity Church v. U. S.,*[3] decided in 1892, the U. S. Supreme Court construed the act of congress passed in 1885 making unlawful the importation and migration of aliens under contract or agreement to perform labor in the United States, its Territories, and the District of Columbia. This statute

[1] *Aldridge v. Williams*, 3 Howard (U. S.) Rep., 22, 24; *U. S. v. Union Pacific R. R. Co.*, 91 U. S. Rep., 71, 79.

[2] See Chapter IX.

[3] 143 U. S. Rep., 457.

had been enacted during a period of industrial depression at the instance of the Federation of Labor Unions of the District of Columbia, the Window Glass Workers of Pittsburgh, the Knights of Labor, and other labor organizations, in order to prevent the lowering of the standards of living of American workingmen. It exempts from its provisions secretaries, servants, and domestics imported by foreigners residing temporarily in this country; skilled workmen to perform labor in new industries not already established in the United States; professional actors, artists, lecturers, and singers. In 1887, the Church of the Holy Trinity of New York City, commonly called Trinity Church, made an agreement with Rev. E. Walpole Warren, an English clergyman, by which he was to come to New York City to be its rector at a stipulated salary. An action to recover the penalty prescribed by the statute was brought against the church in the U. S. Circuit Court at New York, which ruled that since clergymen were not within the exempted classes, they could not be brought to this country under contracts to serve as religious leaders. The case was then taken by writ of error to the U. S. Supreme Court, which decided that the statute was not intended to include such persons. Justice Brewer construed the act as follows:

Plaintiff in error is a corporation, duly organized and incorporated as a religious society under the laws of the State of New York. E. Walpole Warren was, prior to September, 1887, an alien residing in England. In that month the plaintiff in error made a contract with him, by which he was to remove to the City of New York and enter into its service as rector and pastor; and in pursuance of such contract, Warren did so remove and enter upon such service. It is claimed by the United States that this con-

tract on the part of the plaintiff in error was forbidden by
the act of February 26, 1885, . . . and an action was
commenced to recover the penalty prescribed by that act.
The Circuit Court held that the contract was within the
prohibition of the statute, and rendered judgment accordingly, . . . and the single question presented for our
determination is whether it erred in that conclusion. . . .

It must be conceded that the act of the corporation is
within the letter of this section [Sect. 1, making unlawful
prepayment of transportation or other encouragement of
the importation of any alien under contract previously
made to perform labor or services], for the relation of rector
to his church is one of service, and implies labor on the one
side with compensation on the other. . . . We cannot
think Congress intended to denounce with penalties a
transaction like that in the present case. It is a familiar
rule that a thing may be within the letter of the statute and
yet not within the statute, because not within its spirit, nor
within the intention of its makers. . . . This is not the
substitution of the will of the judge for that of the legislator,
for frequently words of general meaning are used in a
statute, words broad enough to include an act in question,
and yet a consideration of the whole legislation, or of the
circumstances surrounding its enactment, or of the absurd
results which follow from giving such a broad meaning to
the words, makes it unreasonable to believe that the legislator intended to include the particular act. . . .

The situation which called for this statute was briefly
but fully stated by Mr. Justice Brown when, as District
Judge, he decided the case of *United States v. Craig*, 28 Fed.
Rep., 795, 798: "The motives and history of the act are
matters of common knowledge. It had become the practice for large capitalists in this country to contract with their
agents abroad for the shipment of great numbers of an
ignorant and servile class of foreign laborers, under contracts, by which the employer agreed, upon the one hand, to
prepay their passage, while, upon the other hand, the

laborers agreed to work after their arrival for a certain time at a low rate of wages. The effect of this was to break down the labor market, and to reduce other laborers engaged in like occupations to the level of the assisted immigrant. The evil finally became so flagrant that an appeal was made to Congress for relief by the passage of the act in question, the design of which was to raise the standard of foreign immigrants, and to discountenance the migration .of those who had not sufficient means in their own hands, or those of their friends, to pay their passage."

We find . . . that the title of the act, the evil which was intended to be remedied, the circumstances surrounding the appeal to Congress, the reports of the committee of each house, all concur in affirming that the intent of Congress was simply to stay the influx of . . . cheap, unskilled labor.

It appears, also, from the petitions, and in the testimony presented before the committees of Congress, that it was this cheap unskilled labor which was making the trouble, and the influx of which Congress sought to prevent. It was never suggested that we had in this country a surplus of brain toilers. . . . And referring back to the report of the Committee of the House, there appears this language: "It seeks to restrain and prohibit the immigration or importation of laborers who would have never seen our shores but for the inducements and allurements of men whose only object is to obtain labor at the lowest possible rate, regardless of the social and material well-being of our own citizens and regardless of the evil consequences which result to American laborers from such immigration. This class of immigrants care nothing about our institutions, and in many instances never even heard of them; they are men whose passage is paid by the importers; they come here under contract to labor for a certain number of years; they are ignorant of our social condition, and they may remain so, they are isolated and prevented from coming into contact with Americans. They are generally from the lowest social stratum, and live upon the coarsest food and in hovels of a character before unknown to American workmen. They, as a rule, do not become citizens, and are certainly not a desirable acquisition to the body politic. The inevitable tendency of their presence among us is to degrade American labor, and to reduce it to the level of the imported pauper labor." Page 5359, Congressional Record, 48th Congress.

The construction invoked [that the act applied to clergymen coming here under [contract] cannot be accepted as correct. It is a case where there was presented a definite evil, in view of which the legislature used general terms with the purpose of reaching all phases of that evil, and therefore, unexpectedly, it is developed that the general language thus employed is broad enough to reach cases and acts which the whole history and life of the country affirms could not have been intentionally legislated against. It is the duty of the courts, under those circumstances, to say that, however broad the language of the statutes may be, the act, although within the letter, is not within the intention of the legislature, and therefore cannot be within the statute.

Interpretation of Statutes.

In the case of *Counselman v. Hitchcock*,[1] decided in 1892, the U. S. Supreme Court interpreted the federal statute which provided that the evidence obtained from a witness in a judicial proceeding shall not be used against him in a subsequent criminal proceeding. The statute is intended to prevent witnesses who rely on the provision of the U. S. Constitution that no person "shall be compelled in any criminal case to be a witness against himself,"[2] from refusing to testify on the ground that their testimony

[1] 142 U. S. Rep., 547.   [2] U. S. Const., Amendment V.

may incriminate them. Charles Counselman, a Chicago commission merchant who had been called as a witness before a grand jury that was investigating violations of the Interstate Commerce Act, had refused to testify whether or not he had received on grain shipments lower rates than those prescribed by the schedules on file with the Interstate Commerce Commission. His ground for so refusing to testify was that any evidence he might give might enable the government to obtain other evidence to use against him in a criminal proceeding. He had then been fined $500 and sentenced to imprisonment during the pleasure of the Court on the ground that his refusal to testify was a contempt of court. He had thereupon petitioned for release by writ of habeas corpus and had taken the case to the U. S. Supreme Court by appeal from the order of the circuit court dismissing the writ. In the decision interpreting the act relating to the immunity of witnesses in federal courts, Justice Blatchford said:

The relations of Counselman to the subject of inquiry before the grand jury, as shown by the questions put to him, in connection with the provisions of the Interstate Commerce Act, entitled him to invoke the protection of the Constitution. . . . It remains to be considered whether Sec. 860 of the Revised Statutes removes the protection of the constitutional privilege of Counselman. That section must be construed as declaring that no evidence obtained from a witness by means of a judicial proceeding shall be given in evidence, or in any manner used against him or his property or estate, in any court of the United States in any criminal proceeding or for the enforcement of any penalty or forfeiture. It follows, that any evidence which might have been obtained from Counselman by means of his examination before the grand jury could not be given in evidence or used against him or his property in any court of the United States, in any criminal proceeding, or for the enforcement of any penalty or forfeiture. This, of course, protected him against the use of his testimony against him or his property, in any criminal proceeding, in a court of the United States. But it had only that effect. It could not, and would not, prevent the use of his testimony to search out other testimony to be used in evidence against him or his property, in a criminal proceeding in such court. It could not prevent the obtaining and the use of witnesses and evidence which should be attributable directly to the testimony he might give under compulsion, and on which he might be convicted, when otherwise and if he had refused to answer, he could not possibly have been convicted.

The constitutional provision distinctly declares that a person shall not be "compelled in any criminal case to be a witness against himself"; and the protection of Sec. 860 is not coextensive with the constitutional provision. Legislation cannot detract from the privilege afforded by the Constitution. It would be quite another thing if the Constitution had provided that no person shall be compelled in any criminal case to be a witness against himself, unless it should be provided by statute that criminating evidence extracted from a witness against his will should not be used against him. But a mere act of Congress cannot amend the Constitution, even if it should engraft thereon such a proviso.

Effect of Judicial Construction and Interpretation.

The effect of a judicial decision construing or interpreting a statute is exactly the same as the effect of an act of the legislature amending its provisions. The statute as originally enacted was evidence of the law until the courts determined its meaning and application. After such determination, the statute as modified by the decision becomes evidence of the law. In the

case of *Douglass v. County of Pike,*[1] decided in 1879 by
the U. S. Supreme Court, Chief Justice Waite said:

We are . . . to consider, whether . . . we must follow
the later decisions [of the Courts of Missouri upon the
constitutionality of an act] to the extent of destroying rights
which have become vested under those given before. As
a rule, we treat the construction which the highest court
of a State has given to a statute of the State as part of the
statute, and govern ourselves accordingly; but where
different constructions have been given to the same statute
at different times, we have never felt ourselves bound to
follow the latest decisions, if thereby contract rights which
have accrued under earlier rulings will be injuriously
affected. . . . The true rule is to give a change of judicial
construction in respect to a statute the same effect in its
operation on contracts and existing contract rights that
would be given to a legislative amendment; that is to say,
make it prospective, but not retroactive. After a statute
has been settled by judicial construction, the construction
becomes, so far as contract rights acquired under it are
concerned, as much a part of the statute as the text itself,
and a change of decision is to all intents and purposes the
same in its effect on contracts as an amendment of the
law by means of legislative enactment.

[1] 101 U. S. Rep., 677, 686.

CONSTITUTION OF THE UNITED STATES

WE THE PEOPLE of the United States, in order to form a more perfect union, establish justice, insure domestic tranquility, provide for the common defence, promote the general welfare, and secure the blessings of liberty to ourselves and our posterity, do ordain and establish this CONSTITUTION for the United States of America.

ARTICLE I

SECTION 1. All legislative powers herein granted shall be vested in a Congress of the United States, which shall consist of a Senate and House of Representatives.

SECTION 2. The House of Representatives shall be composed of members chosen every second year by the people of the several States, and the electors in each State shall have the qualifications requisite for electors of the most numerous branch of the State Legislature.[1]

No person shall be a Representative who shall not have attained to the age of twenty-five years, and been seven years a citizen of the United States, and who shall not, when elected, be an inhabitant of that State in which he shall be chosen.

Representatives and direct taxes shall be apportioned among the several States which may be included within this Union, according to their respective numbers, which shall be determined by adding to the whole number of free persons, including those bound to service for a term of years, and excluding Indians not taxed, three fifths of all other persons. The actual enumeration shall be made within three years after the first meeting of the Congress of the United States, and within every subsequent term of ten years, in such manner as they shall by law direct. The number of Representatives shall not exceed one for every thirty thousand, but each State shall have at least one Representative; and until such enumeration shall be made, the State of New Hampshire shall be entitled to chuse three, Massachusetts eight, Rhode-Island and Providence plantations one, Connecticut five, New-York six, New Jer-

---

[1] Amendment XIV., Section 1, first sentence.

377

sey four, Pennsylvania eight, Delaware one, Maryland six, Virginia ten, North Carolina five, South Carolina five, and Georgia three.[1]

When vacancies happen in the representation from any State, the executive authority thereof shall issue writs of election to fill such vacancies.

The House of Representatives shall chuse their speaker and other officers; and shall have the sole power of impeachment.

SECTION 3. The Senate of the United States shall be composed of two Senators from each State, chosen by the Legislature thereof, for six years; and each Senator shall have one vote.[2]

Immediately after they shall be assembled in consequence of the first election, they shall be divided as equally as may be into three classes. The seats of the Senators of the first class shall be vacated at the expiration of the second year, of the second class at the expiration of the fourth year, and of the third class at the expiration of the sixth year, so that one-third may be chosen every second year; and if vacancies happen by resignation, or otherwise, during the recess of the Legislature of any State, the executive thereof may make temporary appointments until the next meeting of the Legislature, which shall then fill such vacancies.[3]

No person shall be a Senator who shall not have attained to the age of thirty years, and been nine years a citizen of the United States, and who shall not, when elected, be an inhabitant of that State for which he shall be chosen.

The Vice President of the United States shall be President of the Senate, but shall have no vote, unless they be equally divided.

The Senate shall chuse their other officers, and also a President pro tempore, in the absence of the Vice President, or when he shall exercise the office of President of the United States.

The Senate shall have the sole power to try all impeachments. When sitting for that purpose, they shall be on oath or affirmation. When the President of the United States is tried, the chief justice shall preside: And no person shall be convicted without the concurrence of two thirds of the members present.

Judgment in cases of impeachment shall not extend further than to removal from office, and disqualification to hold and enjoy any office of honor, trust or profit under the United States: but the party convicted shall nevertheless be liable and subject to indictment, trial, judgment and punishment, according to law.

SECTION 4. The times, places and manner of holding elections for

---

[1] Amendment XIV., Section 2.
[2] Amendment XVII., first paragraph.
[3] Amendment XVII., paragraphs two and three.

Senators and Representatives, shall be prescribed in each State by the Legislature thereof; but the Congress may at any time by law make or alter such regulations, except as to the places of chusing Senators.

The Congress shall assemble at least once in every year, and such meeting shall be on the first Monday in December, unless they shall by law appoint a different day.

SECTION 5. Each House shall be the judge of the elections, returns and qualifications of its own members, and a majority of each [House] shall constitute a quorum to do business; but a smaller number may adjourn from day to day, and may be authorized to compel the attendance of absent members, in such manner, and under such penalties as each House may provide.

Each House may determine the rules of its proceedings, punish its members for disorderly behaviour, and, with the concurrence of two thirds, expel a member.

Each House shall keep a journal of its proceedings, and from time to time publish the same, excepting such parts as may in their judgment require secrecy; and the yeas and nays of the members of either House on any question shall, at the desire of one fifth of those present, be entered on the journal.

Neither House, during the session of Congress, shall, without the consent of the other, adjourn for more than three days, nor to any other place than that in which the two Houses shall be sitting.

SECTION 6. The Senators and Representatives shall receive a compensation for their services, to be ascertained by law, and paid out of the treasury of the United ;States. They shall in all cases, except treason, felony, and breach of the peace, be privileged from arrest during their attendance at the session of their respective Houses, and in going to and returning from the same; and for any speech or debate in either House, they shall not be questioned in any other place.

No Senator or Representative shall, during the time for which he was elected, be appointed to any civil office under the authority of the United States, which shall have been created, or the emoluments whereof shall have been encreased during such time; and no person holding any office under the United States, shall be a member of either House during his continuance in office.

SECTION 7. All bills for raising revenue shall originate in the House of Representatives; but the Senate may propose or concur with amendments as on other bills.

Every bill which shall have passed the House of Representatives and the Senate, shall, before it become a law, be presented to the President of the United States; if he approve he shall sign it, but if not he shall return it, with his objections to that House in which it shall have originated, who shall enter the objections at large on their journal, and proceed to reconsider it. If after such reconsideration two thirds of that House shall agree to pass the bill, it shall be sent, together with the objections, to the other House, by which it shall likewise be reconsidered, and if approved by two thirds of that House, it shall become a law. But in all such cases the votes of both Houses shall be determined by yeas and nays, and the names of the persons voting for and against the bill shall be entered on the journal of each House respectively. If any bill shall not be returned by the President within ten days (Sundays excepted) after it shall have been presented to him, the same shall be a law, in like manner as if he had signed it, unless the Congress by their adjournment prevent its return, in which case it shall not be a law.

Every order, resolution, or vote to which the concurrence of the Senate and House of Representatives may be necessary (except on a question of adjournment) shall be presented to the President of the United States; and before the same shall take effect, shall be approved by him, or being disapproved by him, shall be repassed by two thirds of the Senate and House of Representatives, according to the rules and limitations prescribed in the case of a bill.

SECTION 8. The Congress shall have power to lay and collect taxes, duties, imposts and excises, to pay the debts and provide for the common defence and general welfare of the United States; but all duties, imposts, and excises shall be uniform throughout the United States;

To borrow money on the credit of the United States;

To regulate commerce with foreign nations, and among the several States, and with the Indian tribes;

To establish an uniform rule of naturalization, and uniform laws on the subject of bankruptcies throughout the United States;

To coin money, regulate the value thereof, and of foreign coin, and fix the standard of weights and measures;

To provide for the punishment of counterfeiting the securities and current coin of the United States;

To establish post offices and post roads;

To promote the progress of science and useful arts, by securing for limited times to authors and inventors the exclusive right to their respective writings and discoveries;

To constitute tribunals inferior to the Supreme Court;

To define and punish piracies and felonies committed on the high seas, and offences against the law of nations;

To declare war, grant letters of marque and reprisal, and make rules concerning captures on land and water;

To raise and support armies, but no appropriation of money to that use shall be for a longer term than two years;

To provide and maintain a navy;

To make rules for the government and regulation of the land and naval forces;

To provide for calling forth the militia to execute the laws of the Union, suppress insurrections and repel invasions;

To provide for organizing, arming, and disciplining, the militia, and for governing such part of them as may be employed in the service of the United States, reserving to the States respectively, the appointment of the officers, and the authority of training the militia according to the discipline prescribed by Congress;

To exercise exclusive legislation in all cases whatsoever, over such district (not exceeding ten miles square) as may, by cession of particular States, and the acceptance of Congress, become the seat of the Government of the United States, and to exercise like authority over all places purchased by the consent of the Legislature of the State in which the same shall be, for the erection of forts, magazines, and arsenals, dock-yards, and other needful buildings;—And

To make all laws which shall be necessary and proper for carrying into execution the foregoing powers, and all other powers vested by this Constitution in the Government of the United States, or in any department or officer thereof.[1]

SECTION 9. The migration or importation of such persons as any of the States now existing shall think proper to admit, shall not be prohibited by the Congress prior to the year one thousand eight hundred and eight, but a tax or duty may be imposed on such importation, not exceeding ten dollars for each person.

The privilege of the writ of habeas corpus shall not be suspended, unless when in cases of rebellion or invasion the public safety may require it.

No bill of attainder or ex post facto law shall be passed.

No capitation, or other direct, tax shall be laid, unless in proportion to the census or enumeration herein before directed to be taken.[2]

No tax or duty shall be laid on articles exported from any State.

No preference shall be given by any regulation of commerce or revenue to the ports of one State over those of another: nor shall vessels bound to, or from, one State, be obliged to enter, clear, or pay duties in another.

No money shall be drawn from the treasury, but in consequence of appropriations made by law; and a regular statement and account of the receipts and expenditures of all public money shall be published from time to time.

[1] Amendment XIII., Section 2; Amendment XIV., Section 5; Amendment XV., Section 2.
[2] Amendment XVI.

No title of nobility shall be granted by the United States: And no person holding any office of profit or trust under them, shall without the consent of the Congress, accept of any present, emolument, office, or title, of any kind whatever, from any king, prince, or foreign state.

SECTION 10. No State shall enter into any treaty, alliance, or confederation; grant letters of marque and reprisal; coin money; emit bills of credit; make any thing but gold and silver coin a tender in payment of debts; pass any bill of attainder, ex post facto law, or law impairing the obligation of contracts, or grant any title of nobility.[1]

No State shall, without the consent of the Congress, lay any impost or duties on imports or exports, except what may be absolutely necessary for executing it's inspection laws: and the net produce of all duties and imposts, laid by any State on imports or exports, shall be for the use of the treasury of the United States; and all such laws shall be subject to the revision and controul of the Congress.

No State shall, without the consent of Congress, lay any duty of tonnage, keep troops, or ships of war in time of peace, enter into an agreement or compact with another State, or with a foreign power, or engage in war, unless actually invaded, or in such imminent danger as will not admit of delay.[2]

ARTICLE II

SECTION 1. The executive power shall be vested in a President of the United States of America. He shall hold his office during the term of four years, and together with the Vice President, chosen for the same term, be elected, as follows:

Each State shall appoint, in such manner as the Legislature thereof may direct, a number of electors, equal to the whole number of Senators and Representatives to which the State may be entitled in the Congress; but no Senator or Representative, or person holding an office of trust or profit under the United States, shall be appointed an elector.

The electors shall meet in their respective States, and vote by ballot for two persons, of whom one at least shall not be an inhabitant of the same State with themselves. And they shall make a list of all the persons voted for, and of the number of votes for each; which list they shall sign and certify, and transmit sealed to the seat of the Government of the United States, directed to the President of the Senate. The President of the Senate shall, in the presence of the Senate and

---

[1] Amendment XIV., Section 1, second sentence.

[2] Amendments I.; II.; III.; IV.; V., last four clauses; VI., in part; VII.; VIII.; IX.; X.; XIII., Section 1; XIV., Section 4, second sentence; XV., Section 1.

House of Representatives, open all the certificates, and the votes shall then be counted. The person having the greatest number of votes shall be the President, if such number be a majority of the whole number of electors appointed; and if there be more than one who have such majority, and have an equal number of votes, then the House of Representatives shall immediately chuse by ballot one of them for President; and if no person have a majority, then from the five highest on the list the said House shall in like manner chuse the President. But in chusing the President, the votes shall be taken by States, the representation from each State having one vote; a quorum for this purpose shall consist of a member or members from two-thirds of the States, and a majority of all the States shall be necessary to a choice. In every case, after the choice of the President, the person having the greatest number of votes of the electors shall be the Vice President. But if there should remain two or more who have equal votes, the Senate shall chuse from them by ballot the Vice-President.[1]

The Congress may determine the time of chusing the electors, and the day on which they shall give their votes; which day shall be the same throughout the United States.

No person except a natural born citizen, or a citizen of the United States, at the time of the adoption of this Constitution, shall be eligible to the office of President; neither shall any person be eligible to that office who shall not have attained to the age of thirty-five years, and been fourteen years a resident within the United States.

In case of the removal of the President from office, or of his death, resignation, or inability to discharge the powers and duties of the said office, the same shall devolve on the Vice President, and the Congress may by law provide for the case of removal, death, resignation or inability, both of the President and Vice President, declaring what officer shall then act as President, and such officer shall act accordingly, until the disability be removed, or a President shall be elected.

The President shall, at stated times, receive for his services, a compensation, which shall neither be encreased nor diminished during the period for which he shall have been elected, and he shall not receive within that period any other emolument from the United States, or any of them.

Before he enter on the execution of his office, he shall take the following oath or affirmation:—"I do solemnly swear (or affirm) that I will faithfully execute the Office of President of the United States, and will to the best of my ability, preserve, protect and defend the Constitution of the United States. "

SECTION 2. The President shall be commander-in-chief of the

---

[1] Amendment XII.

384 THE REASONABLENESS OF THE LAW

army and navy of the United States, and of the militia of the several States, when called into the actual service of the United States; he may require the opinion, in writing, of the principal officer in each of the executive departments, upon any subject relating to the duties of their respective offices, and he shall have power to grant reprieves and pardons for offences against the United States, except in cases of impeachment.

He shall have power, by and with the advice and consent of the Senate, to make treaties, provided two-thirds of the Senators present concur; and he shall nominate, and by and with the advice and consent of the Senate, shall appoint ambassadors, other public ministers and consuls, judges of the Supreme Court, and all other officers of the United States, whose appointments are not herein otherwise provided for, and which shall be established by law; but the Congress may by law vest the appointment of such inferior officers, as they think proper, in the President alone, in the courts of law, or in the heads of departments.

The President shall have power to fill up all vacancies that may happen during the recess of the Senate, by granting commissions which shall expire at the end of their next session.

SECTION 3. He shall from time to time give to the Congress information of the state of the Union, and recommend to their consideration such measures as he shall judge necessary and expedient; he may, on extraordinary occasions, convene both Houses, or either of them, and in case of disagreement between them, with respect to the time of adjournment, he may adjourn them to such time as he shall think proper; he shall receive ambassadors and other public ministers; he shall take care that the laws be faithfully executed, and shall commission all the officers of the United States.

SECTION 4. The President, Vice President, and all civil officers of the United States, shall be removed from office on impeachment for, and conviction of, treason, bribery, or other high crimes and misdemeanors.

ARTICLE III

SECTION 1. The judicial power of the United States shall be vested in one Supreme Court, and in such inferior courts as the Congress may from time to time ordain and establish. The judges, both of the supreme and inferior courts, shall hold their offices during good behaviour, and shall, at stated times, receive for their services, a compensation, which shall not be diminished during their continuance in office.

SECTION 2. The judicial power shall extend to all cases, in law and equity, arising under this Constitution, the laws of the United States, and treaties made, or which shall be made, under their authority;—to all cases affecting ambassadors, other public ministers and consuls;—

to all cases of admiralty and maritime jurisdiction;—to controversies to which the United States shall be a party;—to controversies between two or more States;—between a State and citizens of another State[1];—between citizens of different States;—between citizens of the same State claiming lands under grants of different States, and between a State, or the citizens thereof, and foreign States, citizens or subjects.

In all cases affecting ambassadors, other public ministers and consuls, and those in which a State shall be a party, the Supreme Court shall have original jurisdiction. In all the other cases before mentioned, the Supreme Court shall have appellate jurisdiction, both as to law and fact, with such exceptions, and under such regulations as the Congress shall make.

The trial of all crimes, except in cases of impeachment, shall be by jury; and such trial shall be held in the State where the said crimes shall have been committed; but when not committed within any State, the trial shall be at such place or places as the Congress may by law have directed.[2]

SECTION 3. Treason against the United States, shall consist only in levying war against them, or in adhering to their enemies, giving them aid and comfort. No person shall be convicted of treason unless on the testimony of two witnesses to the same overt act, or on confession in open court.

The Congress shall have power to declare the punishment of treason, but no attainder of treason shall work corruption of blood, or forfeiture except during the life of the person attainted.[3]

ARTICLE IV

SECTION 1. Full faith and credit shall be given in each State to the public acts, records, and judicial proceedings of every other State. And the Congress may by general laws prescribe the manner in which such acts, records and proceedings shall be proved, and the effect thereof.

SECTION 2. The citizens of each State shall be entitled to all privileges and immunities of citizens in the several States.

A person charged in any State with treason, felony, or other crime, who shall flee from justice, and be found in another State, shall on demand of the executive authority of the State from which he fled, be delivered up, to be removed to the State having jurisdiction of the crime.

---

[1] Amendment XI.

[2] Amendments V., first half; VI., in part.

[3] Amendment XIV., Section 3.

No person held to service or labour in one State, under the laws thereof, escaping into another, shall in consequence of any law or regulation therein, be discharged from such service or labour, but shall be delivered up on claim of the party to whom such service or labour may be due.

SECTION 3. New States may be admitted by the Congress into this Union; but no new State shall be formed or erected within the jurisdiction of any other State; nor any State be formed by the junction of two or more States, or parts of States, without the consent of the Legislatures of the States concerned as well as of the Congress.

The Congress shall have power to dispose of and make all needful rules and regulations respecting the territory or other property belonging to the United States; and nothing in this Constitution shall be so construed as to prejudice any claims of the United States, or of any particular State.

SECTION 4. The United States shall guarantee to every State in this Union a republican form of Government, and shall protect each of them against invasion; and on application of the Legislature, or of the Executive (when the Legislature cannot be convened) against domestic violence.

ARTICLE V

The Congress, whenever two-thirds of both Houses shall deem it necessary, shall propose amendments to this Constitution, or, on the application of the Legislatures of two-thirds of the several States, shall call a convention for proposing amendments, which, in either case, shall be valid to all intents and purposes, as part of this Constitution, when ratified by the Legislatures of three-fourths of the several States, or by conventions in three-fourths thereof, as the one or the other mode of ratification may be proposed by the Congress; provided that no amendment which may be made prior to the year one thousand eight hundred and eight shall in any manner affect the first and fourth clauses in the ninth section of the first article; and that no State, without its consent, shall be deprived of its equal suffrage in the Senate.

ARTICLE VI

All debts contracted and engagements entered into, before the adoption of this Constitution, shall be as valid against the United States under this Constitution, as under the Confederation.[1]

This Constitution, and the laws of the United States which shall be

---

[1] Amendment XIV., Section 4, first sentence.

made in pursuance thereof; and all treaties made, or which shall be made, under the authority of the United States, shall be the supreme law of the land; and the judges in every State shall be bound thereby, any thing in the constitution or laws of any State to the contrary notwithstanding.

The Senators and Representatives before mentioned, and the members of the several State Legislatures, and all executive and judicial officers, both of the United States and of the several States, shall be bound by oath or affirmation, to support this Constitution; but no religious test shall ever be required as a qualification to any office or public trust under the United States.

ARTICLE VII

The ratification of the conventions of nine States shall be sufficient for the establishment of this Constitution between the States so ratifying the same.

Done in convention by the unanimous consent of the States present the seventeenth day of September in the year of our Lord one thousand seven hundred and eighty-seven and of the independence of the United States of America the twelfth. In witness whereof we have hereunto subscribed our names,

Gº. WASHINGTON—
Presidt. and Deputy from Virginia.
[Signed also by the deputies of twelve States.]

ARTICLES IN ADDITION TO, AND AMENDMENT OF, THE CONSTITUTION OF THE UNITED STATES OF AMERICA, PROPOSED BY CONGRESS, AND RATIFIED BY THE LEGISLATURES OF THE SEVERAL STATES PURSUANT TO THE FIFTH ARTICLE OF THE ORIGINAL CONSTITUTION.

ARTICLE I. Congress shall make no law respecting an establishment of religion, or prohibiting the free exercise thereof; or abridging the freedom of speech, or of the press; or the right of the people peaceably to assemble, and to petition the Government for a redress of grievances.

ARTICLE II. A well regulated militia, being necessary to the security of a free State, the right of the people to keep and bear arms, shall not be infringed.

ARTICLE III. No soldier shall, in time of peace be quartered in any house, without the consent of the owner, nor in time of war, but in a manner to be prescribed by law.

ARTICLE IV. The right of the people to be secure in their persons, houses, papers, and effects, against unreasonable searches and seizures, shall not be violated, and no warrants shall issue, but upon probable cause, supported by oath or affirmation, and particularly describing the place to be searched, and the persons or things to be seized.

ARTICLE V. No person shall be held to answer for a capital, or otherwise infamous crime, unless on a presentment or indictment of a grand jury, except in cases arising in the land or naval forces, or in the militia, when in actual service in time of war or public danger; nor shall any person be subject for the same offence to be twice put in jeopardy of life or limb; nor shall be compelled in any criminal case to be a witness against himself; nor be deprived of life, liberty, or property, without due process of law; nor shall private property be taken for public use, without just compensation.

ARTICLE VI. In all criminal prosecutions, the accused shall enjoy the right to a speedy and public trial, by an impartial jury of the State and district wherein the crime shall have been committed, which district shall have been previously ascertained by law, and to be informed of the nature and cause of the accusation; to be confronted with the witnesses against him; to have compulsory process for obtaining witnesses in his favor, and to have the assistance of counsel for his defence.

ARTICLE VII. In suits at common law, where the value in controversy shall exceed twenty dollars, the right of trial by jury shall be preserved, and no fact tried by a jury shall be otherwise re-examined in any court of the United States, than according to the rules of the common law.

ARTICLE VIII. Excessive bail shall not be required, nor excessive fines imposed, nor cruel and unusual punishments inflicted.

ARTICLE IX. The enumeration in the Constitution, of certain rights, shall not be construed to deny or disparage others retained by the people.

ARTICLE X. The powers not delegated to the United States by the Constitution, nor prohibited by it to the States, are reserved to the States respectively, or to the people.

ARTICLE XI. The judicial power of the United States shall not be construed to extend to any suit in law or equity, commenced or prosecuted against one of the United States by citizens of another State, or by citizens or subjects of any foreign State.

ARTICLE XII. The electors shall meet in their respective States, and vote by ballot for President and Vice-President, one of whom, at least, shall not be an inhabitant of the same State with themselves; they shall name in their ballots the person voted for as President, and in distinct ballots the person voted for as Vice-President, and they shall make distinct lists of all persons voted for as President, and of all persons voted for as Vice-President, and of the number of votes for each, which lists they shall sign and certify, and transmit sealed to the seat of the Government of the United States, directed to the President of the

Senate;—The President of the Senate shall, in presence of the Senate and House of Representatives, open all the certificates, and the votes shall then be counted;—The person having the greatest number of votes for President, shall be the President, if such number be a majority of the whole number of electors appointed; and if no person have such majority, then from the persons having the highest numbers not exceeding three on the list of those voted for as President, the House of Representatives shall choose immediately, by ballot, the President. But in choosing the President, the votes shall be taken by States, the representation from each State having one vote; a quorum for this purpose shall consist of a member or members from two-thirds of the States, and a majority of all the States shall be necessary to a choice. And if the House of Representatives shall not choose a President whenever the right of choice shall devolve upon them, before the fourth day of March next following, then the Vice-President shall act as President, as in the case of the death or other constitutional disability of the President. The person having the greatest number of votes as Vice-President, shall be the Vice-President, if such number be a majority of the whole number of electors appointed, and if no person have a majority, then from the two highest numbers on the list, the Senate shall choose the Vice-President; a quorum for the purpose shall consist of two-thirds of the whole number of Senators, and a majority of the whole number shall be necessary to a choice. But no person constitutionally ineligible to the office of President shall be eligible to that of Vice-President of the United States.

ARTICLE XIII., SECTION 1. Neither slavery nor involuntary servitude, except as a punishment for crime whereof the party shall have been duly convicted, shall exist within the United States, or any place subject to their jurisdiction.

SECTION 2. Congress shall have power to enforce this article by appropriate legislation.

ARTICLE XIV., SECTION 1. All persons born or naturalized in the United States, and subject to the jurisdiction thereof, are citizens of the United States and of the State wherein they reside. No State shall make or enforce any law which shall abridge the privileges or immunities of citizens of the United States; nor shall any State deprive any person of life, liberty, or property, without due process of law; nor deny to any person within its jurisdiction the equal protection of the laws.

SECTION 2. Representatives shall be apportioned among the several States according to their respective numbers, counting the whole number of persons in each State, excluding Indians not taxed. But when the right to vote at any election for the choice of electors for President and Vice-President of the United States, Representatives in Congress, the Executive and Judicial officers of a State, or the members of the Legislature thereof, is denied to any of the male inhabitants of such State, being twenty-one years of age, and citizens of the United States, or in any way abridged, except for participation in rebellion, or other crime, the basis of representation therein shall be reduced in the proportion which the number of such male citizens shall bear to the whole number of male citizens twenty-one years of age in such State.

SECTION 3. No person shall be a Senator or Representative in Congress, or elector of President and Vice-President, or hold any office, civil or military, under the United States, or under any State, who, having previously taken an oath, as a member of Congress, or as an officer of the United States, or as a member of any State Legislature, or as an executive or judicial officer of any State, to support the Constitution of the United States, shall have engaged in insurrection or rebellion against the same, or given aid or comfort to the enemies thereof. But Congress may, by a vote of two-thirds of each House, remove such disability.

SECTION 4. The validity of the public debt of the United States, authorized by law, including debts incurred for payment of pensions and bounties for services in suppressing insurrection or rebellion, shall not be questioned. But neither the United States nor any State shall assume or pay any debt or obligation incurred in aid of insurrection or rebellion against the United States, or any claim for the loss or emancipation of any slave; but all such debts, obligations, and claims shall be held illegal and void.

SECTION 5. The Congress shall have power to enforce, by appropriate legislation, the provisions of this article.

ARTICLE XV., SECTION 1. The right of citizens of the United States to vote shall not be denied or abridged by the United States or by any State on account of race, color, or previous condition of servitude.

SECTION 2. The Congress shall have power to enforce this article by appropriate legislation.

ARTICLE XVI. The Congress shall have power to lay and collect taxes on incomes, from whatever source derived, without apportionment among the several States, and without regard to any census or enumeration.

ARTICLE XVII. The Senate of the United States shall be composed of two Senators from each State, elected by the people thereof, for six years; and each Senator shall have one vote. The electors in each State shall have the qualifications requisite for electors of the most numerous branch of the State Legislatures.

When vacancies happen in the representation of any State in the Senate, the executive authority of such State shall issue writs of election to fill such vacancies: *Provided*, that the Legislature of any State may empower the executive thereof to make temporary appointment until the people fill the vacancies by election as the Legislature may direct.

This amendment shall not be so construed as to affect the election or term of any Senator chosen before it becomes valid as part of the Constitution.

ARTICLE XVIII., SECTION 1. After one year from the ratification of this article, the manufacture, sale or transportation of intoxicating liquors within, the importation thereof into or exportation thereof from the United States and all territory subject to the jurisdiction thereof for beverage purposes, is hereby prohibited.

SECTION 2. The Congress and the several States shall have concurrent power to enforce this article by appropriate legislation.

ARTICLE XIX., SECTION 1. The right of citizens of the United States to vote shall not be denied or abridged by the United States, or by any State on account of sex.

SECTION 2. The Congress shall have power to enforce this article by appropriate legislation.

INDEX

D

www.ingramcontent.com/pod-product-compliance
Lightning Source LLC
Chambersburg PA
CBHW021547210326
41599CB00010B/338